A CALL TO THE INFINITE

A CALL TO THE INFINITE

by

Rabbi Aryeh Kaplan

MAZNAIM PUBLISHING CORPORATION
NEW YORK / JERUSALEM

Copyright © 1986

by Maznaim Publishing Corporation

All rights reserved. This book, or parts thereof, may not be reproduced in any form without the written permission of the publisher.

For information write:

Maznaim Publishing Corporation
4304 12th Avenue
Brooklyn, New York 11219

Printed in the United States of America

Table of Contents

Introduction 1

Chapter One
- A Call to the Infinite 5
- God Desires Prayer 5
- God's Desire 6
- How Near is God 8
- Greater Than Deeds 9
- Tefillah 11
- The Way of Our Fathers 13
- Hearing 16

Chapter Two
- Why Do We Pray 17
- Why Does Prayer Help 22
- Greater Than Sacrifice 33

Chapter Three
- Formal Worship 39
- Biblical Forms 39
- The Order of Prayer 41
- Three Daily Prayers 43

Chapter Four
- Eighteen Blessings 51
- Biblical Forms 51
- Why Eighteen 54
- Rules 60

Chapter Five
- The Daily Service 65
- Blessings of the Sh'ma 68
- The Order of Prayer 72

v

Alenu	75
Kaddish	76
Amen	79
Traditional Forms	82
Different Rites	85

Chapter Six
Congregation and Synagogue	89
Ten Men	93
A Special Place	95
The Synagogue	99

Chapter Seven
Alone With God	101
In Time of Trouble	106

Chapter Eight
Service of the Heart	109
Passion	113
Before Whom You Stand	115
Heart	116
Self Motivation	117
Extraneous Thoughts	119
Joy and Reverence	120
Mysteries	122

Chapter Nine
Addressing God	125
Long and Short	129
Extravagent Praise	132
Including Everyone	136
Recalling Patriarchs	139

Chapter Ten
Body and Soul	141
Melody and Song	141
Tears	143
Motions	145
Uplifted Hands	148
Kneeling	149

Chapter Eleven

How to Pray	151
Two Thoughts at Once	152
Before Troubles Come	153
Vain Prayers	153
Generalities and Particulars	156
All Needs	157
Formal Petition	160
Godly Things First	160
Praying For God	163
No Reproach	166
God Knows the Heart	167

Chapter Twelve

Helping Others	169
Saints	172
For the Sick	174
Sinners	175
The Dead	178

Chapter Thirteen

Opening Doors	181
Merit	183
Noblemen and Servants	185
The Poor	186
Barriers	187
Aids	189
Fluency	191
God's name	191
Before We Pray	195
Anticipating Answers	196
Never Give Up	198

Chapter Fourteen

Effectiveness	201
The Wicked	202
Confidence	203

Chapter Fifteen

Intercession	207

    A Principle of Faith   208
    Angles   210
    The Dead   214
    Attributes   216
    God's Prayer   221

Chapter Sixteen
    Biblical Foundations   225

Notes   235

Index
    Biblical Verses   239
    Index of Sources   247
    Index of Names   249
    Subject Index   251

INTRODUCTION

Classical Jewish literature is a fabric consisting of many threads, interwoven in numerous variegated patterns. Although threads sometimes escape the woof, they are almost always rewoven into the weave in the end.

The warp of the fabric is the Bible itself—the Torah, Prophets and Writings—and it is rare that a discussion is not backed up with some Biblical quotation. Where these are obvious, they have been included in the text; where the evidence requires knowledge of Hebrew, it has been omitted. The Talmud and Midrash, compiled between the first and sixth centuries c.e., contain the major body of Jewish thought of that period, and have been virtually canonized as infallible spokesmen of Jewish religious ideology.

Among the threads that we shall encounter, one of the most important is the vast Halakhic literature, which includes the discussion and codification of Jewish Law. Based primarily on the Talmud, together with considerable philosophical and theological reasoning, this body of literature sets the norms of Jewish life as expressed in actual practice. Like most common law, it is based largely on precedent, with each later authority citing the works of others wherever applicable.

Another thread is that of commentary, both Biblical, and more extensively, Talmudic. Since many of the early commentaries have become classics in their own right, they have become the subjects of supercommentaries and extensive discussion. A simple Talmudic statement might be found to contradict some important theological principle, or two passages may conflict, and it is the task of the commentaries to resolve the difficulty. In these commentaries one also finds explanations of statements that may otherwise be startling, obscure, or otherwise unintelligible.

An important ingredient of this body of literature is Jewish philosophy. It has often been necessary to interpret the entire body of Jewish thought in terms of contemporary thought and to systematize the results. This has been the task of the great Jewish philosophers—some of whom can be ranked among the world's greatest thinkers. This school reached its zenith between the eleventh and fourteenth centuries, until it was overshadowed by another important thread of Jewish thought—the Kabbalah.

Although people often think of Kabbalah as mere mysticism or a kind of white magic, it also embodies a most profound self-contained philosophical system—more lavish and detailed than that of the classical philosophers, and with a depth of thought that pales their best efforts. A natural outgrowth of this is the extensive body of Hassidic literature, where one encounters passions of beatitude, as well as new depth of thought.

All of these threads converge in the subject of prayer. It is the realm of the Talmudist and legalist, as well as that of the philosopher and Kabbalist. In prayer, the soul can soar in Hasidic ecstasy; while at the same time, the wealth of ritual in Jewish worship has begotten a vast body of Halakhic literature and commentary. Prayer is our most direct means of communicating with the Ultimate, and hence, it is intimately related to every religious experience.

The modern reader might be surprised at the pietism and innocent faith of even the most sophisticated classical Jewish writers, but this too is part of the traditional Jewish ethos. Although they do not write in the modern idiom, their thought has an appeal that has survived through the ages. Many discussions found in this literature are highly relevant today, and much of the material presents novel ideas that contemporary Jewish thought might well explore more thoroughly.

All the material in this book has been freshly translated by the compiler especially for this work. Even where previous translations are available, a new translation has been made, first, to present the material in uniform style, and secondly, to provide a clarity often missing in older translations. The "modern" style of translation, which stresses readability and intelligibility, has been used, even at the expense of slavish literalness.

Besides giving the reader a unique insight into prayer, this book should also give him new insight into Judaism as a whole. Tell me how a person prays, and I will see into his soul. I will know very much about his entire system of beliefs and values. One prays for what he considers to have ultimate value, and the manner in which he worships reveals his view of the ultimates of existence. Prayer, in its deepest sense, is one of the most sublime of all experiences, communion with the Infinite, with the very Root of all creation. Much of this has been lost to modern man, and it is hoped that this will help him regain it.

Aryeh Kaplan
14 Tammuz, 5735

Chapter 1

A CALL TO THE INFINITE

God Desires Prayer

Rabbi Yitzchak said: Why were our forefathers barren? Because God desires the prayers of the righteous.

Talmud, Yevamoth 64a.

Rabbi Assi discussed an apparent contradiction in scripture. One verse states, "The earth brought forth plants" (Genesis 1:12), on the third day of creation; while another verse says, "All the bushes of the field had not yet grown" (Genesis 2:5), just before the Sabbath.

This indicates that plants sprouted, but they did not emerge from the ground until Adam was created and he prayed for them. Rain then fell, and the plants grew.

The lesson is that God desires the prayer of the righteous.

Rabbi Nachman bar Pappa had a garden. He planted seeds, but they did not grow. Finally, he prayed for mercy, whereupon it rained and they grew. He said, "This is Rabbi Assi's teaching."

Talmud, Hullin 60b

When Israel saw that they were surrounded on three sides, the sea was closing and the enemy and wild beasts were pursuing them, they turned to their father in Heaven and cried out to God as it is written,

"The children of Israel cried out to God" (Exodus 14:10). Why did God cause this? Because He desired to hear their prayers.

Rabbi Joshua ben Levi said: What is this like? A king was traveling and he heard a princess crying, "Save me from these robbers!" He heard her cry and saved her.

Several days passed, and the king decided that he wanted to marry the princess. He wanted to speak to her, but she did not wish to see him. What did the king do then? He hired robbers to attack her again, so that she would cry out and he should hear. As soon as the robbers attacked, she began to cry out to the king. The king later explained, "I desired to hear your voice."

The same is true of God and Israel. When Israel was subjugated in Egypt, they placed all their hope in God, and cried out to Him. It is thus written, "In the course of those many days . . . they cried out" (Exodus 2:23). Immediately after this it is written, "God saw the children of Israel" (Exodus 2:25). He then began to rescue them with a strong hand and an outstretched arm.

God then wished to hear their voice again, but they did not want to call Him. What did He do? He sent Pharaoh to pursue them again. It is thus written, "Pharaoh drew close" (Exodus 14:10), and immediately afterward, "the children of Israel cried out" (Exodus 14:10).

God said, "I desired to hear your voice." It is thus written, "O My dove, in the clefts of the rock, in the covert of the cliff, let Me hear your voice" (Song of Songs 2:14)—the same voice that He heard in Egypt.

Midrash, Sh'moth Rabbah 21:5

God's Desire

A Hasidic View

When God wishes to bestow good, man must be able to accept it. It is God's nature constantly to bestow His love upon us. Our sages thus teach us, "More than the calf wants to suckle, the cow wants to provide it with milk."[1] Therefore, when man puts himself in a state where he can accept God's good, this is His delight.

Rabbi Levi Yitzhak of Berdichov,
Kedushath Levi, Likutim (p. 289).

The Greatest Praise

All things sing before God: the sun, the moon, the stars, and the angels. It is thus written, "Praise God from the heavens, praise Him in the heights; praise Him all His angels, praise Him all His hosts; praise Him sun and moon, praise Him stars of light" (Psalms 148:1–3).

But even though all things sing before Him, the song of the righteous and the upright is the most pleasant before Him. It is thus written, "Rejoice in God, O you righteous, the praise of the upright is pleasant" (Psalms 33:1).

Midrash Tehillim 33:1

Israel is more beloved before God than the ministering angels.

Israel sings out to God each hour, while the angels only sing out once each day....

Israel mentions God's name after only two words, as it is written, "Listen Israel, God is our Lord..." (Deuteronomy 6:4). The angels can only mention God's name after three words: "Holy, Holy, Holy, God of Hosts..." (Isaiah 6:3).

The ministering angels cannot sing before God on high, until after Israel sings down below.

Talmud, Hullin 91b

There is nothing sought by God except to hear the prayers of Israel.

Midrash Tehillim 116:1

God Hears All

It is written, "You hear prayer, all flesh comes to You" (Psalms 65:3).

A flesh and blood king can't listen to even two or three people at once, and he surely cannot hear all mankind. This is not true of God. Everyone prays, and He hears all their prayers at once.

Midrash Tehillim 65:2

No Bother

Rabbi Zeira said: When a person has a friend, the more he asks him for things and borrows from him, the more the latter detests him and repulses him. But this is not true of God. The more a person seeks his needs and petitions Him, the more He loves him. It is thus written, "Call Me, and I will answer you" (Jeremiah 33:3).

When a person has a visitor, the first time he comes, he is offered a couch. The second time he comes, he is offered a chair, and on the third time, a stool. The fourth time he comes, he is told, "How much you bother me and crowd me."

This is not true of God. The more we press and come to His place of prayer, the more joy exists before Him.

Midrash Tehillim 4:3

It is written, "Cast your burden upon God, and He will sustain you" (Psalms 55:23).

If a human being has a patron and goes to him once, he is received. The second time he is also received, but the third time, he is refused an audience. By the fourth time, no attention is paid to him at all.

This is not true of God. No matter how many times you bother Him, He receives you.

Midrash Tehillim 55:6

How Near is God

Rabbi Pinchas said in the name of Rav Yehudah bar Simon:

Idols seem near, but they are really far off. It is thus written, "[You hire a goldsmith that he may make you a god, to bow down to, to worship.] It is born on the shoulder, it is carried, and set in its place it stands. [From its place it does not move, and though you cry out to it, it cannot answer nor save you from your trouble]" (Isaiah 46:6,7). This person's god is with him in his house, but he can scream until he dies and it does not hear him nor save him from trouble.

God appears far, but no one is closer than Him. He is high above His universe, but a person can enter the synagogue, stand near the pulpit, and pray in a whisper—and God hears his prayer.

Talmud Yerushalmi, Berakhoth 9:1

Far Yet Close

God is both far and near. How is this?

Rabbi Yehudah bar Simon said: From here to the heavens is a journey of five hundred years. We thus see that God is far.

How do we know that He is close? A person can stand in prayer, meditating in his heart, and God is close enough to hear his prayer. It is thus written, "You hear prayer, all flesh comes to You" (Psalms 65:3).

Midrash, Devarim Rabbah 2:6

Serving God

Rabbi Yochanan said: How do we serve God? With prayer.

Midrash Tehillim 66:1

Greater than Deeds

Rabbi Eleazar said: Prayer is greater than good deeds. No one had done more good deeds than Moses, but still, he was only answered after he prayed.

Talmud, Berakhoth 32b

The Path to Greatness

What caused Mordecai to attain all this greatness? It is taught that it was because he prayed at all times. It is thus written, "Mordecai knew all that had happened . . . [and he cried a great and bitter cry]" (Esther 4:1).

Midrash, Sh'moth Rabbah 38:4

Service of the Spirit

Human prayer is the service of the spirit. Although people do not realize it, in involves the highest mysteries. For prayers split through the atmosphere, through all firmaments, open all doors, and ascend on high.

Zohar, VaYakhel 201a.

The Best Request

I heard the following parable from my master, [the Baal Shem Tov]:

A great king once announced that any request presented to him would be granted. Many people came with petitions, some asking for silver, some for gold, some for high positions.

But there was one wise man who made a very different request. He asked the king if he could have permission to speak to him three times each day.

The king was very pleased with this unusual request, seeing that this wise man valued conversation with the king even more than gold and riches. He therefore decreed that when this wise man would have access to the king, he would pass through and have access to all the king's treasuries, taking whatever he desired without restraint.

Rabbi Yaakov Yosef of Polonoye,
Toledoth Yaakov Yosef, VaEthchanan (Warsaw 1881, p. 356a).

The parallel is obvious.

The Main Purification

In these times in particular, the main purification of the soul is through prayer. Through prayer, one can serve God and approach knowing His Essence.

Since the time of the Baal Shem Tov, the light of prayer's great holiness has shone in the world, illuminating the way for anyone who wants to approach God and serve Him.

Rabbi Kelonemos Kalman of Cracow,
Maor VaShamesh, on Genesis 49:22,24.

"You"

We are bits of dust, full of sin and transgression. Still, we are worthy of speaking and praying before the King of Glory, the Creator of all, of whom it is said, "No thought can grasp Him at all."[2]

We can even call God "You," as we speak to someone standing before us.

This is certainly a very great expression of God's love. It is nothing less than the miracle of God's love and mercy toward all creatures.

*Rabbi Yisrael of Koznitz,
Avodath Yisrael, Lekh Lekha (New York, 1972 p. 6a).*

Tefillah

Judgment

It is written, "Pinchas stood up and prayed" (Psalms 106:30). [Rabbi Eleazar said: It is not written that he prayed *vayithpalel*, but *vayphalel*] that he entered into judgment. He entered into judgment with his Maker.

Talmud, Sanhedrin 44a.

[The word for prayer, *hith-palel*, comes from the root *palel*, meaning "to judge."] This is because one who prays asks that God judge him with mercy, not paying attention to his many wrongdoings. Pure justice would demand that this person be ignored because of his sins, but [in His mercy,] God does not recall them at all. The prophet thus said, "O God, correct me, but with judgment, and not with Your wrath, lest You diminish me" (Jeremiah 10:24).

*Rabbi David Kimchi (Radak),
Sefer HaShorashim, s.v. Palal (582).*

The Hebrew word hith-palel [meaning prayer] is actually the reflexive (hith-pael) form of a verb meaning "to judge." Therefore, it denotes judging oneself, or coming to a correct opinion of oneself, or at least, an inner attempt to accomplish this. In other words, [prayer] is an attempt to gain true judgment of oneself.

Therefore, prayer denotes a step out of active life, so as to gain a true judgment about oneself. It is an attempt to gain true knowledge about one's ego, about his relationship to God and the world, and of the relationship that God and the world have to himself. It strives to infuse the mind and heart with the power of such judgment, in such a manner to direct the mind and heart to an active life that is purified, strengthened and made more sublime.

The process of arousing such self-judgment is called *tefillah*. In the vernacular, we speak of this as prayer, but the vernacular word is an incomplete expression of the concept. "Prayer" denotes asking for something, but this is only a minor aspect of *tefillah*.

Rabbi Shimshon Raphael Hirsch,
Horeb 618

The word *hit-palel* comes from the root *palal* (פָּלַל), which in turn is related to the root *balal* (בָּלַל). . . . The root *balal*, . . . denotes bringing a fresh element into a mass, incorporating this element into all parts of the mass, and thus forming a new material out of the mass.

This is the Jewish concept of a judge's task, [and it is for this reason that the verb *palal* means "to judge"]. The judge must bring justice and fairness, which are elements of Divine Truth, into the case. This must penetrate all elements of the dispute. Therefore, by bringing true justice into what was angry dissension, the judge transforms it into harmonious unity.

When one does this to himself, he is said to *hith-palel*, that is, "to judge himself." Hith-palel means to take the element of God's truth and make it penetrate all phases and conditions of our being and our lives. This allows our entire being to gain a degree of harmony in God.

Jewish *tefillah* is hence very different from what is usually conceived of as prayer. It is not an expression from within, or an expression of that with which the heart is already filled. Rather, it is a renewal and penetration of truth which comes from the outside.

If our prayers were not *tefillah* . . . working on our inner selves to bring them to the heights of recognition of the truth and to resolutions for serving God, then there would be no sense in having fixed times and prescribed forms for them. But our prescribed prayers are not facts and truths of which we are already conscious; they are concepts which we wish to awaken and renew in ourselves. The less one may feel inclined to recite a prayer, the more necessary it may be to say it.

Rabbi Shimshon Raphael Hirsch,
Commentary on Genesis 20:7.

Untying the Knot

It is written, "Abraham prayed (*hith-palel*) to God" (Genesis 20:17). Rabbi Chama ben Chanina said: This is the first time in the Torah that this word occurs. When Abraham prayed (*hith-palel*), the knot was untied.

Midrash, Bereshith Rabbah 52:13.

The meaning of this Midrash is that no person prayed to annul a decree until Abraham came and opened this door. It is for this reason that we begin the Amidah with the blessing, "the Shield of Abraham."

Rabbi David Luria (Radal),
Commentary ad loc.

In my opinion, when the Midrash says that the "knot was untied," it is assuming that the word *tefilla* (prayer) comes from the same root as the expression, "God has disentangled me (*niftalti*)" (Genesis 30:8), according to Rashi's explanation. The Targum, however, renders [the word *niftalti*] to mean prayer and petition. In my humble opinion, both interpretations are correct.

When God created man and the world, all things were straight. But when man sinned, he entangled the world and made it crooked. The purpose of prayer, then, is to straighten that which is crooked, and disentangle that which is knotted. . . .

Prayer [therefore comes from a root meaning "to disentangle,"] since it removes this entanglement.

Rabbi Zev Volf of Gorodna,
Commentary ad loc. (Maharzav).

Seeking God

In my opinion, "seeking God" always refers to prayer. It is thus written, "I sought God and He answered me" (Psalms 34:5), and, "Seek Me and live" (Amos 5:4).

Rabbi Moshe ben Nachman (Ramban),
Commentary on Genesis 25:22.

The Way of Our Fathers

God said: Cry out to Me with prayer, and I will accept it.
When your fathers were enslaved in Egypt, did I then not redeem

them through prayer? It is thus written, "And the children of Israel groaned because of their bondage, and they cried out" (Exodus 2:23).

In the days of Joshua, did I not do miracles for them through prayer? It is thus written, "And Joshua tore his clothing [and fell to the earth upon his face, before the ark of God]" (Joshua 7:6). I then said to him, "Stretch out the javelin [that is in your hand towards Ai, for I will give it into your hand]" (Joshua 8:18).

In the days of the Judges, they cried out and I heard their call. It is thus written, "It came to pass when the children of Israel cried out to God . . ." (Judges 6:7).

In the days of Samuel, did I not listen to them through prayer? It is thus written, "Samuel cried out to God for the sake of Israel, and God answered him" (1 Samuel 7:9).

And even though the men of Jerusalem angered Me, I had mercy on them because they cried out to Me. It is thus written, "Thus says God: Sing with gladness for Jacob . . ." (Jeremiah 31:6).

I require from you neither sacrifice nor offering, but only words of prayer.

Midrash, Sh'moth Rabbah 38:4.

Our Ancestors' Weapon

[When Israel saw Pharaoh approaching,] it is written, "The children of Israel lifted their eyes . . . and they were very much afraid, and they cried out to God" (Exodus 14:10).

They made use of their ancestors' weapon.

Regarding Abraham, it is written, "He called in the name of God" (Genesis 12:8). Regarding Isaac, it is written, "Isaac went to pray in the field" (Genesis 24:63). In the case of Jacob, it is written, "He communed in that place" (Genesis 28:11). . . .

It is written, "Fear not, O worm Jacob" (Isaiah 41:14). Why is Israel likened to a worm? A worm can fell the mightiest cedars, but only with its mouth. It is a soft creature, but it can fell the hardest tree. Israel likewise can make use of prayer. . . .

It is also written [that Jacob said to Joseph], "Behold, I will give you a portion above your brothers, which I took from the hand of the Amorite with my sword and my bow" (Genesis 48:22). Did he then actually conquer it with sword and bow? It is not written, "I will not

Chapter 2

WHY DO WE PRAY?

A Saint's Prayer

It is told that one of the saints would include the following prayer after his worship:

O my God: I would not presume to stand before You, realizing my lowly state and lack of understanding of Your greatness and loftiness, for You are high and exalted, while I am lowly and despised.

I am too small to ask anything from You, to call to You with praise and adulation, or to sanctify Your Name that is praised by the highest holy angels.

But I can presume to do so, because You have elevated me with Your commandment to call upon You. You have given me authority to praise Your highest Name, according to my understanding of You, and my knowledge of Your glory.

When I express my worship to You, and my lowly state before You, You know what is best for me and how to provide for me.

I do not express my needs to You to make You aware of them, but so that I be made to realize my dependence upon You, reinforcing my trust in You.

If in my foolishness, I ask for something not good for me, petitioning You for that which will not improve me, then Your lofty decision is better than mine.

I therefore leave all my concerns to Your abiding decree and highest providence.

> Bachya ibn Pakudah (12th Century),
> Chovoth HaLevavoth, Shaar Cheshbon
> HaNefesh 3:18.

Reinforcing Faith

There is a category of commandments whose reason is clearly evident. They aim at the glorification of God, and prescribe actions that reinforce belief in God's greatness.

Belonging to this category is the commandment to cry to God in time of trouble: "You shall sound the alarm with the trumpet" (Numbers 10:9).

We are also commanded to offer prayer to God. This firmly reinforces the true principle that He takes notice of our ways. He can make them successful if we worship Him, and disastrous if we disobey Him.

We must believe that things are not the result of chance or accident. This is the idea conveyed in the verse, "If you walk with Me with chance" (Leviticus 26:21). This means that, when I bring troubles upon you as punishment, you dismiss them as the result of mere chance. If you do this, I will again send you some of these things that you consider "chance," but of a more serious and severe nature. This is the meaning of the later verse, "If you walk with Me with chance—then I will also walk with you in the fury of 'chance'" (Leviticus 26:27,28).

This is because when people believe that their troubles are the result of mere chance, they continue their evil traits and immoral actions, and do not abandon their wickedness. It is thus written, "You have stricken them, but they have not grieved" (Jeremiah 5:3).

This is why God commanded us to pray to Him, to entreat Him, and to cry out to Him in time of trouble.

> Maimonides (Rambam),
> Moreh Nevukhim 3:36.

To All Who Call

The concept of prayer implies belief that God lets Himself be moved by the request of one who prays and genuinely places all his trust in

Him. It is thus written, "God is close to all who call Him, to all who call Him in truth" (Psalms 145:18).

Calling "in truth" means that one cannot call God with his lips alone, without belief and faith. Regarding this, the prophet said [to God], "You are near in their mouths, but far from their thoughts" (Jeremiah 12:2).

It is written, "to *all* who call Him," indicating that this is true even though one would not otherwise be worthy of attaining his request. Besides the reward for the act of prayer itself, it is now fitting that he receive what he asked for, since he has genuinely placed his trust in God....

This basic concept is alluded to in Solomon's prayer, where he said, "and also the stranger..." (1 Kings 8:41).[1] This indicates that even though one is not worthy of attaining his request in his own merit, he can become worthy through the means of prayer.

Chasdai Crescas (1340–1410),
Or HaShem 3b:1:1 (82b).

Confirming Providence

Even though prayer is not a fundamental concept of the Torah, it is closely related to the concept of Divine Providence. The fact that God accepts prayer clearly indicates this providence....

If a person believes in providence, it is both fitting and obligatory that he believe that prayer is effective in helping him avoid evil. If one does not pray in time of trouble, this must mean that he does not believe in providence, or, if he does believe, he doubts that God has the ability to save him. Both of these amount to disbelief.

But even if a person believes in providence, and does not doubt God's omnipotence and ability to save him, he may still have doubts as to whether he is worthy of having his prayers accepted. Even though one should not be righteous in his own eyes, one should not use this as an excuse to refrain from praying to God for his needs.

One who refrains for this reason does so because he believes that good is only granted by God as a reward for one's deeds, and never as an act of love and mercy on the part of God. This opinion is not correct. It is explicitly written, "[We do not present our supplications before You] because of our righteousness, but because of Your great compassion" (Daniel 9:18).

Yosef Albo (1380–1435),
Sefer HaIkkarim 4:16.

The Tree of Faith

If a person needs something and wants to pray for it, it is obvious that he should pray only to God. But if he does not want to pray, there should be nothing wrong in refraining from doing so.

It is taught that whenever any trouble comes upon the community, there is a commandment to pray and to decree fasts . . . but what is the reason for this commandment? If there is trouble or need, we can certainly pray if we desire, but why does God command us to do so?

It is necessary to realize . . . that the reason for prayer is not only to achieve its intended result; there are other important things bound to it. The concept of prayer involves strong faith, without which true prayer cannot exist. In this sense, prayer is a great tree, with many important roots. . . . These roots included three basic concepts, upon which is built our faith in God.

One who petitions God with strong faith must first admit that God exists, that He has the ability to fulfill the request, and that He oversees those who petition Him and desires their good. These are concepts that must be assumed before one even begins to pray for his needs. If [these three things] were not true, why would we pray?

Moses himself made use of such an introduction when he prayed. It is thus written, "I beseeched God at that time, saying: O God, You have begun to show Your servant Your greatness and Your strong hand, for what god is there [in heaven or on earth that can do according to Your works and mighty acts]. Let me go over, I pray, and see [the good land that is over the Jordan]" (Deuteronomy 3:23–25).

From these roots emanate a number of wondrous branches, perfecting and elevating man, each one according to its concept.

The first root is the fact of God's existence. From this comes the branch of intellectual perception of Him and His deeds. The second root involves His ability, and from it emanate the branches of reverence and worship. The third root involves God's providence, and from it come the branches of love of God and humility.

Rabbi Yitzchak Arama (1420–1494),
Akedath Yitzchak, Tzav 58 (3:13a,b).

The Crucial Initiation

One of the things ordained by the Highest Wisdom was that in order for a person to receive any sustenance from God, he must first motivate himself and bring himself to God, requesting the things that he needs. The amount of sustenance that he receives will then depend on the degree to which he is so motivated. If a person is not aroused at all, then no Divine sustenance will come to him.

[This is the significance of prayer.]

Since God constantly desires to benefit mankind, He has arranged this as a kind of daily service for them. Through this, they can receive God's sustenance, all the success and blessing needed according to their condition in the physical world.

In order to understand this on a deeper level, we must realize that God gave man an intellect so that he could function in the physical world. Along with this, He gave man the responsibility of caring for all his own needs.

This in turn involves two principles.

The first is the significance and importance of man himself. Man alone was given the intellect and knowledge to be able to conduct himself properly.

The second principle is based on the fact that man must be involved with the physical world, and is therefore bound to its various concepts. This stems from the fact that man must maintain himself in his physical human state. . . . Although this is a worldly, rather than a holy, path, it is required by man during the period of his physical existence, according to the general Divine plan.

In one respect, this lowers man and his essence. It is a lowering, however, that is necessary for his ultimate elevation.

Although it is necessary that to some degree man be lowered in this manner, it is also imperative that he not be lowered too much. The more he becomes entangled in worldly concepts, the more he darkens himself spiritually and divorces himself from the highest Light.

God therefore established a remedy for this. Man must initiate all worldly endeavor by first bringing himself close to God, petitioning Him for all his worldly needs. He thus "casts his burden upon God."[2]

This initiation is crucial for all human effort. When one subsequently engages in various forms of human activity, he is no longer considered to be entangled and immersed in the physical and the worldly. He is supported by this remedy, having initiated all this effort by making it depend on God. He is therefore not lowered by the worldly to nearly as great a degree.

Among God's acts of love was the fact that He gave man the opportunity to approach Him, even in this physical world. Even though man is immersed in darkness and is far from the Light in his natural physical state, he is still permitted to stand before God and call upon His name. Man is thus able temporarily to elevate himself from his lowly natural state to exist in a state of closeness to God, casting his burden on Him, as discussed earlier.

Rabbi Moshe Chaim Luzzatto (1707–1746),
(A Kabbalist Philosopher)
Derekh HaShem 4:5:1–3.

Why Does Prayer Help?

Some people question the concept of prayer . . . saying that it cannot escape a basic paradox. For either a certain good is decreed by God for a particular person, or it is not decreed. If it is decreed, then prayer should not be necessary. If it is not decreed, how can prayer help to change God's will and cause Him to grant good to this individual? God cannot be changed from willing something to not willing it, or vice versa.

Using this argument, they claim that proper conduct does not help man receive any good from God. They also say that prayer does not help one attain any good, nor can it save a person from any evil that may be decreed against him.

We find that Job asked this very question in the name of the wicked. He raised the question, that if God indeed oversees the deeds of man, why are the wicked not punished for this false belief. He said, "Why do the wicked live, become old, and wax mighty in power . . .? Yet they say to God, 'Depart from us, for we desire not the knowledge of Your ways. What is the Almighty that we should serve Him, and what good does it do if we pray to Him?'" (Job 21:7,14).

In their opinion, proper conduct is of no avail, and they say, "What is the Almighty that we should serve Him?" They also hold that prayer does not help, saying, "What good does it do if we pray to Him?" They thought that once a certain evil was decreed against an individual, it was impossible to annul it in any way. . . .

This, however, is not correct. Influence from on High is granted to a recipient when he is on a given level, and when he has a certain degree of readiness to receive it. If a person does not prepare himself to receive that bounty, he is the one preventing himself from receiving it.

Thus, for example, it may be decreed that an individual's harvest be successful in a given year. But still, if he does not plow or sow, even if God grants his lands the most abundant rain, his harvest will not be successful. Since the individual did not plant or sow, he is preventing himself from receiving that good, by not having made the necessary preparations.

In a similar manner, when we say that a certain good is decreed for an individual, this decree assumes that he will be on a certain level of proper conduct. This is the general rule regarding all reward mentioned in the Torah. Similarly, when a certain evil is decreed, it is decreed when the individual is on a certain level of wickedness.

Everything therefore depends on the individual's level of preparation. If his level of preparedness is changed, then the degree must also be changed, whether for the better or for the worse.

This is very much like a king who decrees that anyone in his land who remains uncircumcised will be killed, and that all who circumcise themselves will receive gold and silver. When a person circumcises himself, he is not changing or annulling the decree. The decree is conditional, depending on the individual's action. . . .

Prayer and proper conduct therefore help to annul a decree at all times. Our sages similarly taught, "A cry is beneficial, whether before a decree, or afterward."[3]

There is therefore no question regarding God's will being changed as the result of our prayers. From the very beginning it is God's will that His decree be contingent on a person's level and readiness. If the degree of readiness changes, the decree is accordingly also changed.

Yosef Albo (1380–1435),
Sefer HaIkkarim 4:18

Human Status

Some people ask the following questions regarding prayer. If it is fitting that God give a person the thing for which he is praying, why can He not give it to him without prayer? and if the person is not worthy of it, this should remain true even though he prays for it. Just because one prays for something, why should it be given to him?

Another question often asked is, Why must one pray with the spoken word? Since God knows the thoughts of man, why is a thought alone not enough? . . .

The intent of prayer is that God should listen to one's petition and grant what this human being is lacking. It is as a human being that he is lacking something that needs fulfillment. One is only considered human, however, because of his ability to speak, and without the power of speech, one does not have human status.[4] If one does not make use of speech to petition God, then there is no recipient, since every recipient must seek to receive what he lacks. One must therefore petition with speech, since he is then doing so with his full status as a human being. . . . This is not true when one prays in his heart alone.

If a person is absolutely righteous, that is he is completely spiritual, however, then God listens even if he calls out in his heart.[5]

Rabbi Judah Loew (the Maharal)
of Prague (1525–1609),
Netivoth Olam, Avodah 2.

The Language of Man

One may ask the following question: God does not change in any way, and He does not love one person and hate another, but all depends on the purification of the soul. Therefore, what is the use of prayer and petition? If we are ashes, how can we pray that we be made into gold? All depends on the corruption and purification of the soul. How does it help when we say, "Forgive us, our Father?" We know that we are unclean, and that justice demands that we should be destroyed and punished—this is a result of our deeds, and "everything depends on deed."[6]

If we say that things change as a result of prayer, then there is the greatest possible change in God.

But actually, we do not pray to God and cry out to Him in order that He change His mind. When a person asks God for food and livelihood, he bears witness that the world has a Creator who supports all, sustains all, and rules over all. One does not ask for food or livelihood other than from the Master who rules over his servants.

One also admits that God is aware of all deeds, both good and otherwise.

Then, when the soul involves itself with praising God and testifying that all is in His hand, it is constantly purified and sanctified. With each prayer that we offer, we remove a barrier separating ourselves from God. In this manner, we purify the soul and remove its corruption.

If we did not say "forgive us" and "pardon us," never mentioning these concepts, we would not feel that we had done something wrong. But when we express shame for our sins and ask forgiveness, we are less likely to return and repeat them.

Similarly, if we did not pray to God and ask him for food, then we would forget God's love, with which He sustains us . . . But when we constantly ask for food and livelihood, we continuously bring our souls close to Him, thereby purifying them. Then, when the barrier is removed, He oversees us and grants us good.

God does not change. When we say "forgive us," we are actually effecting a change in ourselves.

Still, we have a rule that, "The Torah speaks in the language of man."[7] When a person wrongs his neighbor, he must ask forgiveness. In order to satisfy the minds of the masses, we say these things in a language that they can understand. Otherwise people would be confused and the gates of prayer would be closed.

If we did not pray in the "language of man," with what words could we pray?

This is true of all types of prayer. Even though God does not change, when the soul is involved in praise and thanksgiving, it constantly draws closer to God and yearns to perceive Him. The prayer is then accepted, the sins forgiven, and the food provided. This is because the soul has been drawn closer through prayer and repentance, and if defiled, it is cleansed.

From all this, it is evident that prayer is the pillar of the universe. When a person prays and petitions God with truth and feeling, he attaches his intellect to his Benefactor, and becomes one with Him, thus bringing about the desired effect. God says, "I will magnify Myself and sanctify Myself," (Ezekiel 38:23), and the individual likewise says, "May His Name be magnified and sanctified," then He takes pride in him.

If we did not pray, we would cease to be aware of the Creator of all, and would cease to realize that there is a Master ruling over all, granting all things their fitting portion. But whenever we pray and repent our sins, we listen to our own words.

This basic concept is alluded to in a Talmudic teaching: "If one confesses a sin but does not stop doing it, [even if he prays all day and all night, he is not forgiven]." This is likened to one who immerses in a Mikvah while holding an unclean reptile. "As long as he holds the reptile in his hand, even if he immerses in all the waters in the world, his immersion does not help."[8]

This alludes to the fact that the entire concept of prayer is not meant to change God's will. Prayer is a door for the soul . . . elevating a person from defilement to purity, bringing him closer to God. God, however, does not change in any manner. . . .

Rabbi Abraham Ibn Ezra, of blessed memory, thus writes, "We know that the Blessed Creator is One and is not changed by His creatures, for they are all made in wisdom. But all change involves the recipient."

Rabbi Meir Aldabi (14th Century),
Shevilei Emunah 1 (Warsaw 1874, 6a–b).

A Chasidic View

The early masters asked why prayer was ordained, since God knows everything that man will request. . . .

We find in the *Zohar* that the Infinite Being does not have any representation whatsoever, even through the simplest point.[9] The question immediately rises. How can we call Him by so many names, and speak of Him with so many descriptions? How can we make use of so many representations when praying to God?

The *Zohar* also provides us with an answer, stating that, "He is called loving and merciful, in order that He might make Himself known."[10] When we want God to have mercy on us, then, as it were, He constricts His essence into the word "Merciful," into the lights and vessels of the letters making up the word. . . .

The men of the Great Assembly knew the transmission of Godly lifeforce that is necessary at all times. . . . They therefore composed an order of worship, containing all the words and letters necessary to transmit this lifeforce. God granted them the wisdom to do this . . . and everything in the worship service is thus calculated with great accuracy. . . .

One question still remains. How does the transmission of lifeforce depend on our speech and prayer?

It is written, "From my flesh, I shall see God" (Job 19:26). [By understanding the human body, we can also understand God's ways.]

Man is filled with lifeforce and breath, but it is diffused inside him. When he wishes to speak, he must constrict this breath through his larynx, modulating it with his throat, palate, lips, tongue and teeth. Only then can he express his desires. Only then can his speech, voice and wisdom be communicated. He can do so because his lifeforce, wisdom and voice are constricted in his speech.

When a righteous person stands in prayer, he certainly attaches his thoughts and lifeforce to the Infinite Essence, which is absolute formless Unity. When he begins to speak, he transmits the Creator's lifeforce into his words and speech. As these leave his lips, they are very strongly bound to his breath and lifeforce, constricted into the sounds that he expresses.

Then it is as if, as it were, the Infinite Essence is bound to this person's breath and lifeforce, and so is modulated and constricted in his expression of words.

Rabbi Dov Baer (1704–1772),
The Maggid of Mezrich,
Maggid Devarav LeYaakov 269 (Jerusalem 1971, p. 100a–b).

Service of the Heart

It is written, "Love the Lord your God, and serve Him with all your heart" (Deuteronomy 11:13).

What is the service of the heart? We say that it is prayer.

Talmud, Taanith 2a.

Must we say that it is prayer? Perhaps the reference is to the sacrificial service? The Torah therefore says "with all your heart." What kind of service is performed with a person's heart? We must say that it is prayer.

It is thus written, "Let my prayer be set forth as incense before You, the lifting of my hands as the evening sacrifice" (Psalms 141:2).

It is written, "When Daniel knew that the writ was signed, he went into his house. His windows were open in his upper chamber toward Jerusalem, and he kneeled on his knees three times a day, praying and giving thanks to God, as he had done previously" (Daniel 6:11).

It is also written, "And when [the king] came into the den to Daniel, he cried with a pained voice. The king spoke to Daniel, 'O Daniel, servant of the living God, was your God, whom you continually serve, able to deliver you from the lions?'" (Daniel 6:21). Did the sacrificial service exist in Babylon? We must therefore say that "serving God" also refers to prayer. Just like the sacrificial system is called a "service," so is prayer.

Sifrei, Ekev 41 (3rd Century).

A Commandment

It is a commandment of the Torah to pray each day, as it is written, "You shall serve God your Lord" (Exodus 23:25).

By tradition we know that this service is prayer. It is thus written, "Serve Him with all your heart" (Deuteronomy 11:13, and our sages state that service of the heart is prayer.

The Torah, however, does not specify the number of daily prayers, their form, nor their time.

Maimonides (1135–1204),
Yad Chazakah, Tefillah 1:1.

God commanded us to serve Him, and this commandment is repeated twice in the Torah. It is thus written, "You shall serve God your Lord" (Exodus 23:25), and, "Him shall you serve" (Deuteronomy 13:5).

Even though this is a general commandment to serve God in all ways ... it also has a particular meaning, referring specifically to prayer....

In the teachings of Rabbi Eliezer, son of Rabbi Yose of Galilee, we find: "Where is the main commandment of prayer? In the verse, 'You shall fear God your Lord and Him shall you serve'" (Deuteronomy 6:13).

It is also taught, "Serve Him with His Torah; serve Him in His sanctuary." This indicates that one should pray concentrating on the sanctuary, as specified in King Solomon's prayer [... when they shall pray toward this place (I Kings 8:30)].

Sefer HaMitzvoth, Commandment #5.

An Opposing View

We must dispute Maimonides' contention that prayer is a commandment of the Torah, since the Talmud clearly states that it was ordained by the Rabbis....[11]

Maimonides himself states that even though the time and text of prayer is not ordained by the Torah, the basic obligation is. This also does not seem to be correct.... For if it is not a daily obligation, then when does the Torah require prayer? Is it enough that one pray once a year, or even once during his entire lifetime?....

It is therefore certain that the concept of prayer is not an obligation at all. It is merely a feature of God's love, that He listens and answers whenever we call Him.

When the Torah says, "Serve Him with all your heart," the main intent is to command that all our service of God be with all our hearts. The complete intent should be for His name, without any ulterior motive. One should not observe the commandments without feeling, or in order to obtain some personal benefit.

Nachmanides—Ramban (1194–1270),
Commentary on Sefer HaMitzvoth.

Each Day

The question remains, how do we know that one must pray every day?

The reason is that the commandment to pray is derived from the verse, "You shall serve God your Lord, and He will bless your bread and your water" (Exodus 23:25). Just as bread and water are daily necessities, so is prayer a daily obligation, for it is through prayer that we ask for what we need.

Rabbi Moshe of Trani (Mabit: 1505–1585),
Kiryath Sefer.[12]

It is written, "You shall serve God your Lord"—this is prayer and the recitation of the *Sh'ma*—"and He will bless your bread and your water"—this is bread in salt and a dipper of water.

Talmud, Bava Kama 92b.

The disciples of Rabbi Shimon bar Yochai asked him: Why could the Manna not have fallen just once a year?

He replied: I will give you an example. If a mortal king has a son, and gives him his needs once a year, the son then only sees his father that one time. But if he gives him his needs each day, then he sees his father every day.

The same is true of the Israelites. He has four or five children, and worries, "Maybe the Manna will not descend tomorrow, and they will all die of starvation." He therefore directs his heart to his Father in heaven each day.

Talmud, Yoma 76a.

With Devotion

Even though the main order of prayer was ordained by the rabbis, there is still a concept of prayer that is decreed by the Torah itself. It is thus written, "From there you shall seek God your Lord, and you will find Him, if you seek Him with all your heart and with all your soul" (Deuteronomy 4:29).

From this we learn that one must have devotion in all the prayers that the sages later ordained.

What is the meaning of such devotion? One must concentrate on the meaning of each word, and be most careful not to skip a single word—just as if one were counting money.

Rabbi Isaac of Corbeil (1214–1280),
Sefer Mitzvoth Katan 11.

Roots of the Commandment

Among the roots of this commandment is the concept . . . that all blessing and good comes to man according to his deeds, the goodness of his heart, and the uprightness of his thoughts. God, who created man, wants him to have good. He therefore guides him, and through His commandments, helps him be worthy and successful.

God also opens a door, teaching men how they can attain all their desires. This is that they should ask Him, Whom it is in His hand to fill all needs. From heaven He answers all who call Him in truth.

Besides teaching them this concept, He also commanded man to make use of it, and to constantly petition Him for all his needs and desires.

Besides helping us to attain what we desire, prayer provides us with additional merit. It arouses our spirit, and makes us realize that God is a good and beneficent Master, whose "eyes are open to all our ways." He hears our cries at every instant and at all times, for "the guardian of Israel does not slumber nor sleep." We therefore believe in His authority and omnipotence without any question or doubt, for there is nothing that can prevent Him from doing whatever He desires.

Sefer HaChinuch 433.
attr. to Aaron HaLevi of Barcelona (d. 1293),

The Universal Remedy

Prayer involves a commandment of the Torah. It is therefore fitting that it be rewarded like every other commandment. Each commandment has its own particular, reward as, for example, we find in the case of charity, "That God your Lord bless you in all your endeavors, and in all the work of your hands" (Deuteronomy 15:10). In the case of the commandment to send the mother bird away from its nest before taking eggs, we find, "That it may be good with you, and that your days be increased" (Deuteronomy 22:7).

The commandment of prayer, however, is a remedy which, in its own right, helps for all things.

We thus find that it helps heal the sick. It accordingly helped King Hezekiah, to whom God said, "I have heard your prayer. . . . Behold I will heal you, and on the third day you shall ascend to the house of God" (2 Kings 20:5).

Prayer also helps to save one from death. When Israel sinned with the Golden Calf, God said to Moses, "Let Me alone that I may destroy them" (Deuteronomy 9:14), but they were nevertheless saved through Moses' prayer. Jonah was likewise saved from the belly of the fish through prayer.

Prayer also helps make the barren conceive, as we find, "Isaac entreated God [for the sake of his wife, because she was barren,] and God let Himself be entreated, [and Rebecca his wife conceived]" (Genesis 25:21). Hannah similarly was able to conceive as the result of her prayer.

It also helps in the case of famine: "There was a famine for three years in the days of David, and David entreated God. . ." (2 Samuel 21:1). It also helps in time of war, as in the war against Sennacherib: "Hezekiah the king, and Isaiah son of Amoz the prophet prayed for this, and they cried out to heaven. And God sent an angel, and he cut off all the mighty men of valor and the leaders and the captains, in the camp of the king of Assyria" (2 Chronicles 32:20,21).

Prayer is therefore like a universal remedy, which helps for all diseases and toxins, whether they involve fever or chills. It is not like some medicines that help only for specific sicknesses, some for fever and others for chills. But other than the great universal remedy, we do not find any other drug that can cure both fever and chills, as well as other sicknesses having varied symptoms.

Prayer likewise helps for all things, even opposites. In his prayer, Moses said, "Remember Abraham," (Exodus 32:13), while Asaph said, "Do not remember the sins of our forefathers" (Psalms 79:8). We therefore see that prayer helps both to make God remember, and to make Him forget. There is no precept that helps for all things other than prayer.

The Torah states, "You shall serve God your Lord" (Exodus 23:25). Our sages explain that the Torah is not speaking of sacrifice, which can only be offered in a specific place, but of a service that can be offered in any place, namely prayer.

Since God does not need anyone to serve Him, it cannot be said that this is the same service that a slave does for his master. Therefore, this service must certainly mean that one should speak of God's praise in every place, realizing that all comes from Him, and asking Him for all one's needs. When a person petitions God and admits that he has no help or support other than Him, this is considered His service.

The very next passage mentions four things that can be obtained through this service, and we do not find any other commandment that helps for these things. They therefore said that this "service" must be prayer, which is the service of the heart.

[The Torah thus says, "You shall serve God your Lord, and He will bless your bread and your water. He will remove sickness from your midst, none shall miscarry or be barren in your land, and He will fulfill the number of your days. He will send His terror before you, and will discomfit all the people to whom you shall come, and He will make your enemies turn their backs to you" (Exodus 23:25-27).]

The verse specifies, "He will bless your bread and your water." This indicates that prayer helps in time of famine, as in the days of King David, mentioned above. Similarly, "He will remove sickness from your midst"—as in the case of Hezekiah. "None shall miscarry or be barren in your land"—as in the case of Hannah. "He will fulfill the number of your days"—as in the case of Hezekiah, and when the Israelites sinned with the Golden Calf. "He will send His terror before you"—as in the case of Hezekiah and Sennacherib, king of Assyria, and his camp.

We thus see that prayer helps for all troubles. Solomon accordingly prayed, "If in the land there be famine, or plague, blight or mildew, . . . any epidemic or sickness . . ." (1 Kings 8:37).

Prayer also helps in order to save one from trouble and exile. When Israel was in Egypt, it is written, "And they cried out, and their cries went up to God . . . and God heard their groaning . . ." (Exodus 2:23,24). Through their prayers, Daniel and Ezra were similarly able to bring Israel out of the Babylonian exile.

We therefore see that prayer is the universal remedy, healing all sickness, and helping all people.

It is something that can be used by all mankind, Jew and non-Jew alike. King Solomon thus said, "There may also be strangers, not from Your people Israel . . ." (1 Kings 8:41). It even helps for the most wicked . . . as in the case of Menasseh's prayer.

Yosef Albo (1380–1435)
Sefer HaIkkarim 4:16.

Greater Than Sacrifice

Rabbi Eleazar said: Prayer is better than all sacrifice.

Talmud, Berakhoth 32b.

A prayer on the tongue is better than any sacrifice. It is thus written, "I will praise the name of God with a song, I will exalt Him with thanksgiving and it shall please God better than a bullock" (Psalms 69:31,32).

Midrash Tehillim 39:3.

God Only Requires Words

The people of Israel say, "We are poor. We have no sacrifices to bring as an offering."

God replies, "I need only words, as it is written, 'Take with you words' (Hosea 14:2). This refers to words of Torah."

The people say, "But we do not know words of Torah."

God replies, "Weep and pray, and I will receive you."

Midrash, Sh'moth Rabbah 38:4.

God said:
Let he who has a bullock bring a bullock.
Let he who has a ram bring a ram.
Let he who has a sheep bring a sheep.
Let he who has a dove bring a dove.
Let he who has none of these bring a flour offering.
And let he who has no flour bring words.

Midrash Tanchuma B, Tzav 5 (9a).

We have Nothing but Prayer

It is written, "You are not a God who has pleasure in wickedness" (Psalms 5:4).

You have no pleasure when people remain guilty. It is thus written, "God has no pleasure in the death of the wicked, but that he should turn from his way and live" (Ezekiel 33:11).

God desires that his creatures pray before Him, and He then accepts them.

Rabbi Yitzchak said: We now have neither prophet nor priest, sacrifice nor temple, nor any altar upon which to make atonement. From the day that the Temple was destroyed, nothing was left for us but prayer. Therefore, O God, hearken and forgive.

Midrash Tehillim 5:7.

Moses foresaw that the Temple would be destroyed . . . he therefore ordained that Israel should pray three times each day. He understood that prayer is more desirable to God than all good deeds and sacrifices. It is thus written, "May my prayer be like incense before You, the spreading of my hands like the evening offering" (Psalms 141:2).

Tanchuma, Ki Thavo 1.

The Meaning of Service

When a person brings a sacrifice to God, this is called service (*Avodah*), and there is no service greater than this.

When a person serves another and does what he needs, this is called service, since it indicates that he is the other's servant. All the more so when a person devotes himself to God, since this itself indicates that he is God's servant. It is for this reason that sacrifice is called service.

Rabbi Judah Loew (1525–1609),
The Maharal of Prague,
Netivoth Olam, Avodah 1.

The one service that Israel has in all places in their exile is prayer. . . .

Prayer is also called a service. The reason for this is . . . because when a person prays to God, this indicates that he depends on God and needs Him, and can in no way exist without Him. This is the concept of Godliness, where all that exists need Him, depend on Him, and must seek their needs from Him. . . .

Reverence alone is not considered service, since it does not indicate that man depends on God. Prayer indicates that we depend on Him, that He is all, and that His name is blessed over all.

The entire concept of prayer, therefore, is that one needs God, one depends on Him, and one cannot endure by himself, but only through God. It is for this reason that one prays to God for all his needs.

When a person depends on God, he is also drawn close to Him. For whenever a person depends on another, he is drawn close and given over to him. Prayer is therefore a complete service to God.

Netivoth Olam, Avodah 3.

Soul

It is written, "Serve Him with all your heart and with all your soul" (Deuteronomy 11:13). Perfect prayer is a service that also includes the soul. This is an important concept for those who know and understand it to some degree. . . .

In many places we find that prayer is called "soul" (*nefesh*). Thus, in Hannah's prayer, from which we learn many important laws, we find, "I poured out my soul before God" (1 Samuel 1:15). It is likewise written, "Let my soul bless God" (Psalms 103:1), and, "Let my soul praise God" (Psalms 146:1). . . .

Rashi expliticly states, ". . .Soul is prayer, as it is written, 'I poured out my soul before God.'"[13]

The service of prayer is meant to emulate that of sacrifice.

The purpose of sacrifice was to elevate the animal's soul on high. The main atonement thus consisted of the sprinkling of the animal's blood on the altar, and, "The blood is the soul" (Deuteronomy 12:23). Similarly, when the animal's innards were burned on the altar, the main intent was to elevate the soul.

The main concept of prayer is to elevate one's soul and bring it on high. The human power of speech is called "soul." It is thus written, "And man became a living soul" (Genesis 2:7), and the Targum renders it, "And man became a speaking spirit." . . . Speech is the main expression of the human soul, since this is the primary advantage that man has over the beasts. Each word that one utters therefore is the power and a portion of his soul.

Rabbi Chaim of Volozhin (1749–1821),
(Talmudist and Kabbalist)
Nefesh HaChaim 2:14.

Mysteries

With these mysteries, you can attach yourself to your Master, perceiving the perfection of wisdom in the highest mystery when you serve your Master with prayer. With desire and concentration of the heart, you can bind yourself to His will, like fire to the coal . . .

When your mouth and lips move, your heart should concentrate, and your will can then ascend higher and higher, unifying all in the mystery of mysteries. It is there that all desire and thought is embedded, existing in the mystery of the Infinite.

Meditate on this in every prayer, each and every day. You will then, by your worship of God, crown all your days with the mystery of the supernal days.

Zohar 2:213b.

Food of the Universes

When a person prays before God at the proper time, he provides nourishment both to the supernal universes and to his own soul.

The Zohar thus says, "His food is prayer, which is the counterpart of sacrifice."[14] . . .

"With regard to the prohibition of eating before the morning service, Rabbi Shimon thus said that the reason is because one may not eat before his Master. And what is His food? It is prayer."[15]

This nourishment is the transmission of additional holiness, blessing, and light to all worlds.

*Rabbi Chaim of Volozhin,
Nefesh HaChaim 2:9.*

Partners in Creation

Every word of prayer ascends higher and higher through the Masters of the Voices and the Masters of Wings who carry it. These words then have an effect on the highest Root to which they pertain. Through this, one becomes a partner with the Creator, building and creating many universes.

We find this in the Tikkunei Zohar:[16]

"When a person emits breath and words in prayer, many birds spread their wings and open their mouths to accept them. This is the meaning of the verse, 'A bird of heaven takes the voice, and the Master of Wings speaks a word' (Ecclesiastes 10:20).

"The Blessed Holy One takes these words, and with them, He builds universes, regarding which it is written, 'The new heavens and the new earth' (Isaiah 66:22).

"This is the mystery of the verse, 'I will place My word in your mouth . . . to spread out the heaven and found the earth, and say to Zion, you are My people' (Isaiah 51:16). Do not read *Ami*—'My people'—but *Imi*—'with Me.' You are with Me, as My partners in creation."

Nefesh HaChaim 2:10.

Chapter 3

FORMAL WORSHIP

Biblical Forms

The Priestly Blessing

God spoke to Moses saying: Speak to Aaron and his sons, saying: So shall you bless the children of Israel, say to them:

"God bless you and keep you.
God make His face shine toward you and be gracious to you.
God lift up His face toward you and grant you peace."

They shall place My name upon the children of Israel, and I will bless them.

Numbers 6:22–27.

The Unsolved Murder

All the elders of the city nearest to the murder victim shall wash their hands over the heifer . . . and they shall speak up and say:
"Our hands have not shed this blood, and our eyes have not seen it. O God, forgive Your people Israel, whom You redeemed, and do not allow innocent blood to remain in the midst of Your people Israel."

Deuteronomy 21:6–8.

Confession after Tithing

When you have finished tithing all your crops in the third year, which is the year of tithing, and when you have given it to the Levite, the stranger, the orphan and the widow, that they may eat within your gates and be satisfied, then you shall say before God your Lord:

"I have put away the holy things out of my house, and have given them to the Levite, the stranger, the orphan and the widow, as Your entire commandment that You have bidden me—I have not transgressed any of Your commandments, and I have not forgotten. . . . I have hearkened to the voice of God my Lord, and I have done all that You have commanded me.

"Look down from Your holy abode, from heaven, and bless Your people Israel, and the land that You have given us, a land flowing with milk and honey, as You swore to our fathers."

Deuteronomy 26:12-15.

The Sh'ma

> (According to most authorities, the Sh'ma is also a prayer ordained by the Torah.)

Hear O Israel, God is our Lord, God is One.

And you shall love God your Lord with all your heart, with all your soul, and with all your might.

And these words which I command you this day shall be on your heart. You shall teach them to your children, and you shall recite them, when you sit at home and when you go on the way, when you lie down and when you rise up.

And you shall bind them as a sign on your hand, and they shall be Tefillin between your eyes.

And you shall write them on the doorposts (*Mezuzoth*) of your houses and gates.

Deuteronomy 6:4-9.

The Basic Service

The House of Shammai said: In the evening, each person should recline and recite the Sh'ma, and in the morning he should stand, as it is written, "When you lie down and when you rise up."

The House of Hillel said: Every person should recite it in his own way, as it is written, "When you go on the way."

If so, what is the meaning of the verse, "When you lie down and when you rise up?" At the time when people lie down [at night], and when people rise up [in the morning. These, then, are the times when the Sh'ma must be said.]

Mishnah, Berakhoth 1:3.

The Order of Prayer

One may think that a person should petition God for his needs, pray, and then finish. King Solomon therefore said, "Hearken to the song and to the prayer" (1 Kings 8:28). Song is praise, while prayer is petitioning for one's needs.

Tosefta, Berakhoth 3:9.

Rabbi Simlai taught: A person should always offer praise to God, and only then should he pray.

We learn this from Moses. It is written [that Moses said], "I pleaded to God at that time" (Deuteronomy 3:23). The scripture then continues, "O Lord, God, You have begun to show Your servant Your greatness and Your mighty hand—where in heaven or earth is there a power that can emulate Your deeds and Your strength?" (3:24) Only then did Moses pray, "Please let me cross that I may see the good land..." (3:25).

Talmud, Berakhoth 32a.

Codification

The obligation of the commandment to pray implies that one must petition and pray every day. He should first utter God's praise, and only then should he ask for his needs with prayer and supplication. Finally, he should give praise and thanksgiving to God for the good that He has granted him. Each individual should do this according to his ability.

Maimonides (1135–1204),
Yad Chazakah, Tefillah 1:2.

Reasons

At first thought, it would not appear correct to offer special praise to God before asking for one's needs. When a person praises his neighbor and then asks for a favor, it is evident that the only reason for this praise was so that the request would be granted.

When one looks into the concept of prayer more deeply, however, it becomes apparent why such praise is necessary before prayer is accepted.

No human being is perfect, and therefore any praise of a mortal man must contain some overstatement.... When one asks a favor and praises his neighbor, it is impossible that his praise not contain some overstatement, speaking of qualities that he does not have. This is mere flattery, its only purpose being that the request be granted.

When a person prays to God, on the other hand, he must realize that no one can fulfill his request and petition other than God, since He is the Creator of all and the Prime Mover. We must therefore begin by uttering His praise, stating that we know and recognize His greatness.... It is fitting to pray to Him, since He is the one who makes poor and rich, lifts up and casts down, who "says, does, decrees and fulfills."... It is for this reason that we "cast our burden upon Him, and He sustains us."

Just as it is necessary to praise God before praying, it is also necessay to conclude by giving thanks for one's portion. One is then like a servant who receives his portion from his master, who praises him and then departs, as taught by our sages.[1]

It is somewhat difficult to understand what is meant when they say that he is like a slave who had received a portion from his master. This would seem to indicate that his prayer has already been answered.

Here, however, we are taught a major point regarding prayer. When a person prays, his aim should not necessarily be that his prayer be answered. Our sages thus teach that one who anticipates an answer to his prayer will end up with pain in his heart, as it is written, "Hope deferred makes the heart ache" (Proverbs 13:12).[2] We also have Rabbi Chama bar Chanina's teaching that one who prays and is not answered should pray again, as it is written, "Hope in God ... hope in God" (Psalms 27:14).[3]

When our sages say that such a person is like a servant who has received a portion from his master, the intention is that he should consider it as if he has already been answered.

The main goal of prayer is not that his request be fulfilled, but to reinforce the concept that in all creation, there is none to whom it is fitting to pray other than God. One must be aware of his needs and lacks, and must realize that no one can fulfill them other than God. When a person expresses his needs before God, he is expressing this concept, and the reward will ultimately also come.

We therefore see that the main purpose of prayer is not to receive that which one requests. For then, if he knew that he would not be answered in a particular prayer, he would not say it at all.

This also answers another difficulty regarding prayer. At first thought it would appear improper to make the same request numerous times. If one asked an earthly king for the same thing two or three times, the king would become angry at him. If the king had wanted to fulfill the request, he would have done so the first time or the second. If a person keeps on urging the king, his request becomes superfluous, and can actually injure his position.

It is therefore difficult to understand why we pray to God each day, morning, noon and night, saying the same prayer. . . . For the most part, our prayers are not answered, but still, we do not desist from saying these daily prayers.

The main intent of prayer is that we should recognize and express the fact that there is nothing in the universe to whom it is fitting to pray other than God. He is the Master of the universe, and we mention our many needs in our prayers in order that we should recognize that there is none who can grant our needs, and save us from all our troubles, other than God. Upon Him we cast our burden.

It is with this intent that we fulfill our obligation to pray. God will do what is good in His eyes, whether He accepts our prayers or not.

Rabbi Moshe of Trani (1505–1585),
Beth Elokim, Tefillah 2.

Three Daily Prayers

I will call upon God,
    And God will save me.
Evening, morning and afternoon,
    I pray and call out,
    And He hears my voice.

Psalms 55:17,18.

Daniel ... went to his house. The windows of his upstairs room were open toward Jerusalem, and he kneeled upon his knees three times a day and prayed, and he gave thanks before his God, as he had done before.

Daniel 6:11

The morning prayer can be said until noon. Rabbi Yehudah says, until [the end of] the fourth hour.

The afternoon prayer can be said until evening. Rabbi Yehudah says, until the mid-afternoon.

The evening prayer does not have any set time.

The additional prayer [said on the Sabbath and holidays] can be said all day. Rabbi Yehudah says, until the [the end of] seventh hour.

Mishnah, Berakhoth 4:1.

Parallels

Just as the Torah set a time for reciting the Sh'ma, so the sages set a time for the prayer.

Why did they say that the morning prayer should be until noon? Because the daily morning sacrifice could be offered until noon. . . .

Why did they say that the afternoon prayer should be until evening? Because the daily afternoon sacrifice could be offered until evening. . . .

Why did they say that the evening prayer had no set time? Because the limbs and fats were burned all night long.

Why did they say that the additional service could be all day? Because the additional sacrifice could be offered all day long. . . .

Tosefta, Berakhoth 3:1 (3rd Century).

Lessons

We may think that one can pray as often as he wants during the day. We therefore learn a lesson from Daniel, ". . . And he kneeled upon his knees three times a day and prayed" (Daniel 6:11).

We may think that one may pray in any direction that one wishes. It is therefore written, "The windows of his upstairs room were open toward Jerusalem" (Daniel 6:11).

We may think that he had only begun after he went into exile. It is therefore written, "as he had done before" (Daniel 6:11).

We may think that one should make his voice heard in prayer. It is therefore written, "Hannah spoke in her heart, [only her lips moved, but her voice could not be heard]" (1 Samuel 1:13).

One may think that they should all be included in a single service. David therefore states, "Evening, morning and noon, [I pray and call out]" (Psalms 55:18). "Evening" is the *ma'ariv* service, "morning" is the *shacharith* service, and "afternoon" is the *minchah* service.

Tosefta, Berakhoth 3:8,9.

Changes in the Day

From where do we derive the three daily services?

Rabbi Shmuel bar Nachmani said: They parallel the three times that the day changes for man.

In the morning one must say, "I give thanks to You, O Lord my God and God of my fathers, for bringing me from darkness to light."

In the afternoon one must say, "I give thanks to You, O Lord my God and God of my fathers, for just as I was worthy of seeing the sun in the east, so was I worthy of seeing it in the west."

In the evening one must say, "May it be Your will, O Lord my God and God of my fathers, that just as I was in darkness and You brought me to light, so may You once again bring me from darkness to light."

Talmud Yerushalmi, Berakhoth 4:1.

Patriarchs and Sacrifice

Rabbi Yose, the son of Rabbi Chanina, said, "The daily services were ordained by the patriarchs."

Rabbi Yehoshua ben Levi said, "The services were ordained to parallel the daily sacrifices."

Earlier teachings support both Rabbi Yose and Rabbi Yehoshua ben Levi.

The following earlier teaching supports Rabbi Yosi, son of Rabbi Chanina:

Abraham ordained the morning service, as it is written, "Abraham awoke early in the morning, in the place where he had stood" (Genesis

19:27). "Standing" is nothing other than prayer, as it is written, "Pinchas stood up and prayed" (Psalms 106:30).

Isaac ordained the afternoon prayer, as it is written, "Isaac went out to commune in the field toward evening" (Genesis 24:63). "Communing" is nothing other than prayer. . . .

Jacob ordained the evening prayer, as it is written, "He approached the place and rested there, [for the sun had set]" (Genesis 28:11).

There is also an earlier teaching that agrees with Rabbi Yehoshua ben Levi. [Tosefta 3:9, quoted above in "Lessons"] . . . Do we then say that this contradicts Rabbi Yose, son of Rabbi Chanina?

Rabbi Yose, the son of Rabbi Chanina, can answer that the Patriarchs originally ordained the services, but the rabbis later based them on the daily sacrifices.

If we do not accept this, then what is the origin of the Additional *Musaf* service according to Rabbi Yose, son of Rabbi Chanina? But the services were ordained by the Patriarchs, and the sages based them on the sacrifices.

Talmud, Berakhoth 26b.

Three Songs

It is written, "Sing to God a new song; sing to God all the earth; sing to God, bless His name" (Psalms 96:1,2).

Rabbi Abahu said: These three songs parallel the three services with which Israel praises God each day.

"Sing to God a new song" speaks of the morning service, for God renews the act of creation each day.

"Sing to God all the earth" speaks of the afternoon prayer. Everyone then sees the sun as it illuminates all the earth.

"Sing to God, bless His name," speaks of the evening prayer. Everyone then blesses God, who brings the twilight.

Midrash Tehillim 96:1.

Three Exiles

The exiles of their children are alluded to in the prayers of the Patriarchs.

Abraham ordained the morning prayer, and this parallels the Egyptian exile. This was the first exile, and it was revealed to Abraham, as it is written, "Know that your children [will be strangers in a land that is not theirs . . .]" (Genesis 15:13). Abraham passed ten tests, and therefore, ten miracles were done for his descendants.[4]

Isaac ordained the afternoon prayer, and this parallels the Babylonian exile, which was in the middle. They were only tested there in a few instances, just like Isaac.

Jacob ordained the evening prayer, and its time is all night until dawn. This parallels the long, dark, bitter exile [in which we are now,] which will last until the coming of the great light of redemption. . . .

Menorath HaMaor 3:3:1:2 (92).

Codification

It was ordained that the number of daily services should equal the number of daily sacrifices.

The two daily services parallel the two daily sacrifices. On every day when a special additional (*Musaf*) sacrifice was offered, a third service was ordained, paralleling this additional sacrifice.

The prayer that parallels the morning sacrifice is called *Shacharith*. That which parallels the afternoon sacrifice is called *Minchah*. The service that parallels the additional sacrifice [on the Sabbath and festivals] is called *Musaf.*

It was also ordained that each person should offer a prayer at night. This is because the afternoon sacrifice would be allowed to burn on all night on the altar. It is thus written, "This is the burnt offering [on the embers all night long until morning, and the fire of the altar shall be kindled with it]" (Leviticus 6:2). . . .

This evening prayer is not an obligation like the morning and afternoon services. Nevertheless, all Israel, wherever they live, have accepted the custom of reciting the evening prayer. It was therefore accepted just like an obligation.

Maimonides,
Yad Chazakah, Tefillah 1:5,6.

Self-Subjugation

It might be asked why services were ordained especially at these times. This can be explained simply.

A person must subjugate himself to God in worship with his body, with his soul, and with his financial resources. It is thus written, "You shall love God your Lord with all your heart, with all your soul, and with all your might" (Deuteronomy 6:5).

"With all your heart" refers to the body. Our sages thus interpret this to mean that one must serve God with his two urges, the Good Urge and the Evil Urge.[5] It is known that the Evil Urge is in man's body.

"With all your soul" is interpreted to mean, "even at the expense of your soul." "With all your might" means "even at the expense of your financial resources."[6]

Morning sleep is very pleasant . . . When a person wants to remain asleep in the morning, he is in a highly physical state. No state is more physical than sleep, since only the body functions, and not the soul. But one must force himself to wake up for the morning service. When a person overcomes his body in this way, he subjugates his body to God.

The afternoon service comes during the main part of the day when one is engaged in his business affairs. When one turns aside from these affairs to pray, he subjugates his financial resources to God.

In the evening, one is tired from his business and concerns, and his soul wishes to rest. It is the soul that motivates him all through the day, and in the evening it seeks rest and relaxation, so that it can be rejuvenated through sleep. . . Our sages teach that one should not take a nap in the evening or eat before the evening service.[7] He should first pray, indicating that he is subjugating his soul to God. The soul is tired from its activities, and wants to rest, but one subjugates it and first prays.

Rabbi Judah Loew (1525–1609),
Netivoth Olam, Avodah 3.

Rectifications

Day is divided into morning and afternoon, and night is also divided into two parts. In each of these four divisions, God's illumination and influence must be transmitted to all universes, according to the aspect of that particular time of day.

It is for this reason that a fixed number of daily services was ordained. For the morning and afternoon, there are the morning and afternoon services. Since the morning is the time when God's sustenance is renewed each day according to that day's particular aspect, it requires a longer and more inclusive prayer service. In the afternoon, it is only necessary to continue drawing the divine sustenance that began flowing in the morning, and a lesser effort is therefore required. [It is for this reason that the afternoon prayer is the shortest of the three daily services.]

The difference between night and day is greater than that between morning and afternoon, and nightfall involves a greater conceptual change. It is for this reason that the Evening Service is longer than the Afternoon Service. The Evening Service contains the Sh'ma and its blessings, but since the sustenance from the morning service is still flowing, it is shorter than the Morning Service.

No universal service was ordained for the second part of the night, since this would unduly burden the community. A midnight service (*Tikkun Chatzoth*) was left for the especially devout, who rise and cry out to God, each one according to his own understanding.

Rabbi Moshe Chaim Luzzatto (1707–1746),
Derekh HaShem 4:6:16.

Importance

Rabbi Chelbo said in the name of Rav Hunah: One should always be careful in reciting the Afternoon Service, for Elijah was answered only during the time of this service. It is thus written, "It was when the afternoon sacrifice was offered, and Elijah approached and said. . . , 'Answer me, O God, answer me'" (1 Kings 18:37). . . .

Rabbi Yochanan said: This is also true of the Evening Service. It is thus written, "May my prayer be like incense before You, the spreading of my hands like the evening offering" (Psalms 141:2).

Rabbi Nachman bar Yitzchak said: This is also true of the Morning Service. It is thus written, "O God, hear my voice in the morning, in the morning I will arrange my prayer to You, and will anticipate" (Psalms 5:4).

Talmud, Berakhoth 6b.

The First Prayer

The reason why one must be especially careful during the Afternoon Service is because the very first prayer in the world was offered at this time. Adam was created in the afternoon, just before the Sabbath, and it was at this time that he uttered the world's first prayer.

Rabbi Chaim Yosef David Azulai,
The Chida (1724–1806),
Midbar Kedemoth, Tav 4.

Chapter 4

EIGHTEEN BLESSINGS

Biblical Forms

Noah's Blessings

Blessed be God, the Lord of Shem...

Genesis 9:26.

Melchizedek to Abraham

Blessed be God, the Most High, who has delivered your enemies into your hand....

Genesis 14:20.

Eliezer, Servant of Abraham

Blessed be God, Lord of my master Abraham, who has not forsaken His mercy and truth toward my master....

Genesis 24:27.

Jethro to Moses

Blessed be God, who has delivered you out of the hand of Egypt and out of the hand of Pharaoh, who has delivered the people from under the hand of the Egyptians.

Exodus 18:10.

David to Abigail

Blessed be God, Lord of Israel, who has sent you this day to meet me.

1 Samuel 25:32.

Blessings

Blessed are You O God, teach me Your decrees.

Psalms 119:12.

Then the Levites . . . said: "Stand up and Bless God your Lord, from eternity to eternity," and let them respond, "Blessed be Your glorious Name, that is exalted above all blessing and praise."

Nehemiah 9:5.

David blessed God before all the congregation, and David said, "Blessed are You O God, Lord of Israel our father, from eternity to eternity."

1 Chronicles 29:10.

Beginnings

Rabban Gamaliel said, "Each day a person should pray eighteen [blessings]."

Mishnah, Berakhoth 4:3.

The Great Assembly

Rabbi Chiyah bar Abba said in the name of Rabbi Yochanan, "The men of the Great Assembly ordained for Israel blessings, prayers, Kiddush and Havdalah. . .

Talmud, Berakhoth 33a.

Yavneh

Shimon the cotton broker arranged Eighteen Blessings in order before Rabban Gamaliel in Yavneh.

Rabbi Yochanan said, "One hundred and twenty elders, and among them many prophets, composed the Eighteen Blessings in a set order." This is also found in an earlier teaching....

If this prayer was composed and arranged by one hundred and twenty elders and numerous prophets, what was the accomplishment of Shimon the cotton broker? It was forgotten, and he arranged it over again.

Talmud Megillah 17b, 18a.

Maimonides' History

If a person could, he would recite many supplications and petitions. If it was difficult for him to speak, he would pray as much as he could, at any time he desired.

The same was true of the number of prayers. Each individual would pray according to his ability, some once each day, and others many times.

Everyone who prayed would face the Temple, no matter where they were.

This is the situation that existed continuously, from the time of Moses until Ezra.

When Israel was exiled in the days of Nebuchadnezzar, they became assimilated in Persia, Greece and other nations. Children were born in these foreign lands, and their language was completely confused. They spoke a mixture of languages, and could not express themselves adequately in any single language, just with a confused jargon. It is thus written, "Their children spoke half in the language of Ashdod. They could not speak the language of the Jews, without the language of foreigners" (Nehemiah 13:24).

Their language was therefore not suitable for prayer. They could not ask for their needs or praise God in pure Hebrew, without mixing in other languages.

When Ezra and his legislature saw this, they composed Eighteen Blessings in a given order. The first three blessings were in praise of God, while the last three were thanksgiving. The middle blessings contain petitions for all things which, in general, are the needs of the individual and the community as a whole.

Their motive was to provide a service that would be familiar to all. Nonexpressive individuals could then recite as perfect a prayer as a master of expressive language.

It was because of this that they ordained all the blessings and prayers that are familiar to all Israel. The substance of each blessing is thus familiar even to one who is not expressive.

Maimonides,
Yad Chazakah, Tefillah 1:3,4.

Why Eighteen?

Rabbi Yehoshua ben Levi said: The Eighteen Blessings parallel the eighteen psalms from the beginning of the book until, "God will answer you in the day of trouble" (Psalm 20). If you are told that there are nineteen psalms there, reply that "Why are the nations in an uproar" (Psalm 2) is not counted. . . .

Rabbi Simon said: They parallel the eighteen vertebrae in the human backbone—since one must bow with them all. The reason for this is because it is written, "All my bones shall say, 'O God, who is like You?'" (Psalms 35:10).

Rabbi Levi said: They parallel the eighteen times that God's name is mentioned in, "Ascribe to God you sons of the mighty" (Psalm 29). Rav Huna said: If you are told that there are nineteen, reply that a blessing for the heretics was ordained in Yavneh. . . .

Rabbi Chanina said in the name of Rabbi Pinchas: They parallel the eighteen times that the Patriarchs, Abraham, Isaac and Jacob, are mentioned together in the Torah. . . .

Rabbi Shmuel bar Nachmani said in the name of Rabbi Yochanan: They parallel the eighteen commandments in the second portion regarding the Tabernacle. Rabbi Chiyah bar Va said: Begin counting from, "Oholiab, the son of Achisamach, from the tribe of Dan" (Exodus 38:23), and continue until the end of the book [of Exodus].

And what is the significance of the seven blessings in the Sabbath Amidah?

Rabbi Yitzchak said: They parallel the seven "voices" in, "Ascribe to God, you sons of the mighty" (Psalm 29).

Rabbi Yudan Antoria said: They parallel the seven times that God's name is mentioned in, "A psalm, a song for the Sabbath day" (Psalm 92).

Talmud Yerushalmi, Berakhoth 4:3.
(Fourth Century).

What do the Eighteen Blessings represent?

Rabbi Hillel, son of Rabbi Shmuel bar Nachmani, said: They represent the eighteen times that David mentioned God's name in the psalm, "Ascribe to God, you sons of the mighty" (Psalm 29).

Rav Yosef said: They represent the eighteen times that God's name is mentioned in the *Sh'ma*.

Rabbi Tanchuma said in the name of Rabbi Yehoshua ben Levi: They represent the eighteen vertabrae in the backbone. Rabbi Tanchum said furthermore in the name of Rabbi Yehoshua ben Levi, "One who prays must bow so as to bend all the joints in his spine..."

Are there then eighteen blessings in this prayer? Actually there are nineteen. Rabbi Levi said, "There was a blessing for the heretics added in Yavneh."

What does this [nineteenth] blessing represent?

Rabbi Levi said: According to Rabbi Hillel, son of Rabbi Shmuel bar Nachmani, it would represent the verse, "The God of glory thunders" (Psalms 29:3). [In this verse, God's name *El* is used, rather than the Tetragrammaton.]

According to Rav Yosef, it would represent the word "One" [in, "Hear O Israel, the Lord is our God, the Lord is One" (Deuteronomy 6:4).]

According to Rabbi Yehoshua ben Levi it would represent the small vertebra (the coccyx) in the backbone.

The rabbis taught:

Shimon the cotton broker arranged the Eighteen Blessings in order before Rabban Gamaliel in Yavneh.

Rabban Gamaliel then said to the sages, "Can any one of you compose a blessing for the heretics?"

Shmuel the Little then stood up and composed it. The next year, he had forgotten this blessing, and it took him two or three hours to recall it...

Talmud, Berakhoth 28b (Fifth Century).

Backbone

More than any part of the body, the Eighteen Blessings represent the spine. The reason for this is because it is written, "All my bones shall say, 'O God, who is like You?'" (Psalms 35:10) The 248 parts of the body parallel the 248 positive commandments of the Torah, and therefore, each part of the body must fulfil the commandments.

For the most part, the commandments are fulfilled by the hands, feet, and the organs of the face which are associated with sight, hearing and speech. The bones of the spine are the most mundane parts of the body, not being directly involved in any observance.

The Eighteen Blessings were therefore composed to represent these spinal bones, so that everyone would remember to place all his strength into his prayers, moving his body, thus fulfilling the verse, "All my bones shall say . . ." The sages therefore also required that one bow until all the joints of his spine bend.

Rabbi Yehoshua Falk (1680–1756),
P'nei Yehoshua (on Berakhoth 28b).

Tabernacle

It is taught that the Eighteen Blessings represent the number of commandments involved in the building of the Tabernacle. This is because we must constantly pray that the Temple be rebuilt. Furthermore, now that the Temple is destroyed, prayer must take the place of sacrifice. The number of blessings therefore parallels the number of units in the Tabernacle.

Rabbi Chanoch Zundle of Bialystok,
Etz Yosef (on VaYikra Rabbah 1:8).

Patriarchs

It is taught that the Eighteen Blessings parallel the eighteen times that the patriarchs are mentioned together in the Torah. This is because the services were first instituted by the Patriarchs.

Rabbi David Abudarham (1274–1341),
Sefer Abudarham, p. 10.

Parallels

The Eighteen Blessings parallel the eighteen verses in the Song of the Red Sea (Exodus 15). They also parallel the eighteen verses in the Ten Commandments.

The Eighteen Blessings are said three times a day, six times a week. They are therefore said eighteen times a week.

Midrash,
quoted in Sefer Abudarham, loc. cit.

Life

The "Life of Worlds" is engraved and impressed in the Eighteen Blessings of prayer. [The Hebrew word for life is *Chai*, which has the numerical value of eighteen.]

Tikkunei Zohar 22 (65b).

Universes

The Eighteen Blessings represent the Life of Worlds. This is the attribute that unifies the land of the living with the highest heavens.

This is the inner meaning of all the reasons given in the Talmud. . . .

They also represent God's eighteen thousand universes. Our sages teach us: God . . . flies through eighteen thousand universes. It is thus written, "God's chariot is twice ten thousand, two thousand angels (*Shinan*)" (Psalms 68:18). Do not read *Shinan*, but *She-ainan*—"which are not."[1] (Rashi: Twice ten thousand, minus two thousand "which are not," yields eighteen thousand.)

The mystery of this is that the highest of the Ten Emanations (*Sefiroth* is so hidden that it cannot even be imagined, and therefore, is not taken into account. We thus only speak of nine Emanations, and since each of these comprise both Love and Justice, we have a total of eighteen. The Eighteen Blessings then unify these eighteen thousand universes.

Rabbi Meir ibn Gabbai (1480–1547),
Avodath HaKodesh, Avodah 12.

The Nineteenth Blessing

In the days of Rabban Gamaliel, the number of Jewish heretics increased, and they troubled Israel, attempting to cause them to abandon the way of God. It was realized that protection againt this was greater than any other human need, so Rabban Gamaliel and his legislative body initiated a blessing which contains a petition that God should destroy these heretics. This was included in the Prayer [of Eighteen Blessings,] so that it would be said by all.

This Prayer therefore actually has nineteen blessings.

Maimonides,
Yad Chazakah, Tefillah 2:1.

The Sabbath Amidah

Of the Eighteen Blessings, only the first and last three praise God. The twelve middle Blessings only involve human needs.

This is why the Sabbath prayer does not contain Eighteen. If a person has a member of his family who is sick, he will recall it when he says, "who heals the sick of His people Israel," and he will be troubled. The Sabbath was given to Israel for holiness, delight and rest, and not for worry. We therefore only say the first three and last three Blessings, with a single Blessing in the middle.

David therefore said, "Seven in the day I will praise You" (Psalms 119:164). These are the seven blessings that one says on the Sabbath, since this is "the day"—the unique day of rest.

Midrash Tanchuma, VaYera 1.

Ordering

Rabbi Yehudah said: A person should not petition for his needs in the first three or in the last three, but only in the middle blessings.

Rabbi Chaninah thus said: In the first three, one is like a slave who is praising his master. In the middle ones, he is like a slave who seeks a portion from his master. In the last three, he is like a servant who has received a portion from his master, and then takes leave and departs.

Talmud, Berakhoth 34a.

Moses did not ask God for Israel's needs until he first began with praise.

This is like an advocate, hired by another to speak on his behalf before the king. Before he speaks for his client, he first praises the king ... and only then does he plead his client's case. He then closes with praise for the king. ...

The Eighteen Blessings ordained by the early sages for Israel also do not begin with a petition for Israel's needs, but with praise for God. ... Then, after we ask God to heal the sick, we conclude with thanksgiving.

Sifrei, VeZoth HaBerakhah 343.

Peace

Rabbi Mani of Shaab and Rabbi Yehoshua of Sikhnin said in the name of Rabbi Levi: Great is peace, since all blessing, good and consolation that God grants to Israel is sealed with peace.

The final blessing of the Sh'ma is therefore, "Who spreads a tent of peace." The last of the Eighteen Blessings is, "Who blesses His people with peace." And the end of the Priestly blessing is, "He will grant you peace" (Numbers 6:27).

Midrash, VaYikra Rabbah 9:9.

The Patriarchs' Blessings

When Abraham vanquished the kings (Genesis 14), God told him, "I am your Shield" (Genesis 15:1). He then composed the blessing, "Shield of Abraham."

When Isaac was bound on the altar to be sacrificed, he heard God's word, "Do not move your hand toward the boy" (Genesis 22:12). He then composed the blessing, "Who brings the dead to life."

When Jacob saw the angels "ascending and descending" (Genesis 28:12) [on the ladder in Bethel], with the Divine Presence over him, praised by all the angels, he composed the blessing, "The Holy God."

Midrash,
quoted in Sefer HaEshkol, (ed. Z.B. Auerbach) Tefillah 10
(page 19).

Rules

Silence

Rav Hamnuna said: Many important rules can be derived from Hannah's prayer:

"She spoke in her heart" (1 Samuel 1:13). This teaches that when one prays he must concentrate in his heart.

"Only her lips moved." This teaches he must articulate the words with his lips.

"Her voice could not be heard." He may not raise his voice in prayer.

"Eli thought that she was drunk." One who is drunk is not permitted to recite the service.

Talmud, Berakhoth 31a.

He who makes his voice heard in prayer is of small faith. (Rashi: as if God does not hear whispered prayer).

He who raises his voice in prayer is counted among the false prophets. (Rashi: As it is written, "And they called out with a loud voice" (1 Kings 18:28).) . . .

Rav Huna said: This is only true when one can concentrate in silence. If he cannot, he is permitted [to pray out loud]. This, however, is only true in private, but not in a public service, since it would disturb the congregation.

Talmud, Berakhoth 24b.

Rabbi Yochanan said in the name of Rabbi Shimon bar Yochai: Why was it ordained that prayer should be whispered? It was so as not to shame the sinners. (Rashi: Those who confess their sins in their prayers.) We thus find that the Torah does not differentiate between the place of the burnt offering and that of the sin offering.

Talmud, Sotah 32b.

There is a slight difficulty, since in one place it appears that prayer should be silent in order not to shame sinners, while in Berakhoth it says that one who makes his voice heard is of small faith. . . .

This difficulty can be resolved, however, since if everyone prayed out loud, one who did so would not be considered to have small faith. But once it was ordained that prayer be silent because of sinners, one who is different and prays out loud is considered to be of small faith.

Rabbi Samuel Eliezer Edels,
The Maharsha (1555–1631),
Commentary ad loc.

The reason why prayer must be quiet is because, "the whole earth is filled with His glory" (Isaiah 6:3). This is especially true of a place designated for prayer. If one raised his voice in prayer, it would appear as if God cannot hear whispered worship. . . .

There is a difficulty, however, since in many places we find that people cried out in prayer. For example, it is written, "Moses cried out to God" (Exodus 8:8).

Daily worship, when there is no trouble, should not be recited in a loud voice, since one can concentrate better when it is said quietly. But when one prays in a time of trouble and suffering, it is impossible for him to pray calmly, because of his anguish. He may therefore cry out in a loud voice, indicating that he is aware of his anguish and trouble, and no one can save him other than God.

Rabbi Moshe of Trani (1505–1585),
Beth Elokim, Tefillah 6.

Jerusalem

If one is riding on a donkey, he should descend and pray. If he cannot, he should turn his face (Rashi: toward Jerusalem). If he cannot turn his face, he should direct his heart toward the Holy of Holies.

Mishnah, Berakhoth 4:5.

Standing

Prayer must be said standing. It is thus written, "Pinchas stood up and prayed" (Psalms 106:30).

Midrash Tehillim 108:1.

Rabbi Yose, son of Rabbi Chanina, said in the name of Rabbi Eliezer ben Yaakov: One should not stand in a high place and pray, but should stand in a low place. It is thus written, "From the depths I call You, O God" (Psalms 130:1).

This is also found in an earlier teaching: One should not stand on a chair, a stool, or any other high place when he prays, but on a low place, since there is no elevation with respect to God.... It is thus written, "A prayer of the poor, when he is enwrapped" (Psalms 102:1).

Talmud, Berakhoth 10b.

One must stand while involved in both prayer and sacrifice. The reason for this is because one of the most visible differences between man and beast is the fact that man stands erect on two feet.... The soul of the animal descends to the earth, and it therefore walks on all four, looking at the place of its origin. But man's soul is hewn out from under the Throne of Glory, and he therefore stands erect and looks upward....

*Rabbi Moshe of Trani,
Beth Elokim, Tefillah 7.*

Feet Together

When one stands and prays, he must keep his feet together.

Two sages, Rabbi Levi and Rabbi Simon, gave reasons for this rule. One derives it from the angels, and the other, from the priests.

One derives it from the priests: "You shall not ascend with steps upon My altar"(Exodus 20:23). This teaches us that the priests would walk with toe touching heel, and heel touching toe.

One derives it from the angels: " Their feet was a straight foot" (Ezekiel 1:7). [The word "foot" is in the singular, indicating that both feet were together, and had the appearance of a single foot.]

Talmud Yerushalmi, Berakhoth 1:1.

One must keep his feet together for two reasons.

First, he should behave as if his hands and feet were tied, so that he is utterly helpless to help or defend himself without God.... This is especially true of the feet, with them one can normally flee from danger and pursue pleasure. The feet must therefore be kept together.

Secondly, one should meditate on the fact that when God created man, it was His intent that he should be perfect in his deeds and recognize God's works, just like the angels. The prophet thus said, "Seek Torah from his lips, for he is an angel of God" (Malachi 2:7).

Furthermore, when one prays, he should resemble an angel. The Talmud derives this from the verse, "Their feet was a straight foot."

The word "foot" in Hebrew (*regel*) also has the connotation of motive. . . . The verse, "Their feet was a straight foot," can therefore be interpreted to mean that their motives are upright and constant, and they do not turn, since they have no lusts swaying them from the truth. When one prays, he should similarly concentrate all of his motives, and make them "straight" for God's service.

Rabbi Shlomo ben Abraham Adret,
The Rashba (1235–1310),
As quoted in commentary on Eyn Yaakov, Berakhoth 54 (Talmud p. 10b).

Wall

Rabbi Yehudah said in the name of Rav, and some say, in the name of Rabbi Yehoshua ben Levi: One who prays should not have anything separating him from the wall. It is thus written, "Hezekiah turned his face to the wall and he prayed" (Isaiah 38:2).

Talmud, Berakhoth 5b.

Deportment

Rava, son of Rav Huna, would put on his fancy boots when he worshiped. He said that it is written, "Prepare to meet your God, O Israel" (Amos 4:12). (Rashi: This means that one should dress well in God's presence).

Rava would take off his fine cloak and clasp his hands when he worshiped. He said, "Like a slave before his master."

Rav Ashi said: I saw Rav Kahana worship, and when there was suffering in the world, he took off his fine cloak and clasped his hands, saying, "Like a slave before his master." But when there was peace in the world, he would wear all his fine clothing in worship, saying, "Prepare to meet your God, O Israel."

Talmud, Shabbath 10a.

Clothing

When one worships, he should wear proper clothing. This means that he should dress neatly and as well as possible. It is thus written, "Worship God in the beauty of holiness" (Psalms 29:2).

Maimonides,
Yad Chazakah, Tefillah 5:5.

Sacrifice

Prayer is in place of sacrifice, as it is written, "We will make up for our bullocks with our lips" (Hosea 14:3).... Therefore, one must be careful that his worship be just like a sacrifice.

One should not think about anything else during worship, since an improper thought can render a sacrifice invalid.

One should stand, just as for the Temple service. It is thus written, "Stand to serve in the name of God" (Deuteronomy 18:5).

One's feet should be together, just like a priest involved in the Divine Service.

One must be in a set place. Each sacrifice had a set place where it was slaughtered and where its blood was sprinkled.

There should be no intervention between the individual and the wall. When an intervention separates a sacrifice from the sacred vessel or the floor, it becomes invalid.

It would be proper that everyone also have fine, special clothing for worship, just as the priest had special garments, but not everyone can afford that....

When a person makes his worship into a sacrifice, it rises as a pleasant fragrance before God, and the angels make it into a crown for their Master....

Rabbi Yaakov ben Asher (1270–1343).
Tur, Orach Chaim 98.

Charity

Rabbi Eleazar would give a coin to the poor, and would then worship. He said: It is written, "I will greet You with charity" (Psalms 17:15).

Talmud, Bava Bathra 10a.

Chapter 5

THE DAILY SERVICE*

Morning

Give ear to my words O God,
    consider my prayer.
Listen to the sound of my cry
    my King, my God,
    for to You I pray
O God, hear my voice in the morning—
In the morning when I utter an order of prayer to You
    and anticipate.

Psalms 5:2–4.

I cry out to You, O God
In the morning my prayer comes to greet You.

Psalms 88:14.

The Yoke of Heaven

Rabbi Yochanan said, "If one wishes to accept upon himself the complete yoke of Heaven, let him relieve himself, wash his hands, put on Tefillin, recite the Sh'ma, and then pray. This is the essence of the yoke of the Kingdom of Heaven."

Rabbi Chiya bar Abba said in the name of Rabbi Yochanan, "When a person relieves himself, washes his hands, puts on Tefillin, says the

Sh'ma and then prays, it is counted as if he built an altar and offered a sacrifice on it."

Talmud, Berakhoth 14b, 15a.

Ashrei

Rabbi Avina said, "Whoever says the psalm, "A Praise of David" (Psalm 145), three times each day, is guaranteed a portion in the World to Come."

What is the reason? If we say that it is because its verses are in alphabetical order, let one say the psalm, "Happy are the upright in the way" (Psalm 119), which contains the alphabet repeated eight times. If we say that it is because it contains the verse, "You open Your hand and satisfy the wants of all life" (Psalms 145:16), let one say the Great Hallel, which contains a similar verse, "He gives bread to all flesh" (Psalms 136:25). But the reason is because [the 145th Psalm] has both.

Talmud, Berakhoth 4b.

Verses of Praise

Rabbi Yose said, "May my portion be among those who complete the Praise (Hallel) each day."

How could he have said this? We have learned, "One who completes the Praise each day is blaspheming and degrading."

When he said this, he was speaking of the Verses of Praise (*Pesukei DeZimra*).

[Rashi: This refers to the two psalms of praise, "Praise God from Heaven" (Psalm 148), and "Praise God in His Sanctuary" (Psalm 150).]

Talmud, Shabbath 118b.

The Verses of Praise consist of all the psalms from "A Praise of David" (Psalm 145) until "Let every soul praise God" (Psalms 150:6).

The Rabbis ordained that a blessing be said before and after these Verses of Praise. [The initial blessing is] "Blessed is He Who Spoke" (*Barukh SheAmar*), [while the concluding blessing is] "May He be Praised" (*Yishtabach*).

One should therefore not speak out between "Blessed is He Who Spoke" and the end of the Eighteen Blessings.

Rabbi Yitzchak Al-Fasi
The Rif (1013–1103),
Code, Berakhoth 23a.

Our sages praised the person who daily recites the psalms from "A Praise of David," until the end of the Book of Psalms. It is also a custom to recite various other verses, both before and after these. They also ordained a blessing before the Psalms, namely, "Blessed be He Who Spoke," and a concluding blessing, namely, "May He be Praised."

After this, one recites the *Sh'ma* and its blessings.

Maimonides (1135–1204),
Yad Chazakah, Tefillah 7:12.

Piercing Barriers

There are troops of evil angels between earth and heaven, making the path between them a place of danger. When a person worships, his prayers must pass through these troops in order to ascend to heaven. If he has merit, they do not encounter these evil angels lying in ambush. But if one does not have merit, then they encounter many Destroyers and Intruders.

This is why King David composed the Songs of Praise (*Zemiroth*). They serve to clear the way for prayer, so that it can pass through all these troops.

All these troops are like clouds, preventing prayer from ascending. They are alluded to in the verse, "You have covered Yourself with a cloud, so that no prayer can pass through" (Lamentations 3:44). King David composed the Songs of Praise, and when a person recites them, the Destroyers, Intruders and Vandals are banished.

These songs are called *Zemiroth*, from the same root as *mazmer*, meaning a "pruning shear."[1] With the *Zemiroth* one cuts through these disturbing forces.

Rabbi Yosef Gikatilla (1248–1305),
(Kabbalist)
Shaarei Orah 1.

Blessings of the Sh'ma

In the morning, one says two blessings before the Sh'ma, and one following it. In the evening, one says two blessings before it, and two following it.

Mishnah, Berakhoth 1:4.

Rabbi Yose bar Avin said in the name of Rabbi Yehoshua ben Levi: These blessings are based on the verse, "Seven each day I will praise You, for Your righteous judgment" (Psalms 119:164). [The three morning blessings, and four in the evening, make a total of seven.]

Talmud Yerushalmi ad loc (1:5).

What are these blessings?

Rabbi Yaakov said in the name of Rabbi Oshaya, "Who forms light and creates darkness" (Isaiah 45:7) . . . This is so that one should recall the attribute of day by night, and the attribute of night by day.

Here [in the morning blessing] we see the attribute of night by day. But where do we find the attribute of day by night? Abaya said, "[In the evening prayer, we say in the first blessing], 'Who rolls away the light before the darkness, and the darkness before the light.'"

What is the second blessing? Rabbi Yehudah said in the name of Shmuel, "With Great Love" (*Ahavah Rabbah*). Rabbi Eleazar likewise taught his son, Rav Pedat, to say, "With Great Love."

This is found in an earlier teaching: One does not say "With Eternal Love" (*Ahavath Olam*), but "With Great Love." But the Rabbis said, "With Eternal Love," as it is written, "With eternal love I have loved you, therefore I drew you to Me with affection" (Jeremiah 31:3).

Talmud, Berakhoth 11a, b.

[As a result of this dispute] it was ordained that "With Great Love" be said in the morning, and "With Eternal Love" at night.

Tosafoth ad loc.

[This is the Ashkenazic custom.] But the Sefardic custom is to say "With Eternal Love" both morning and evening.

Rabbi Yosef Caro (1488–1575),
Beth Yosef, Orach Chaim 60.

Rava, son of Chanina the elder, said in the name of Rav: If one does not say "True and Certain" (*Emeth VeYatziv*) [as the blessing after the Sh'ma] in the morning, and "True and Faithful" (*Emeth VeEmunah*) in the evening, he has not fulfilled his obligation. It is thus written, "To declare Your mercy in the morning, and Your faith by night" (Psalms 92:3).

Talmud, Berakhoth 12a.

Redemption

Rabbi Yochanan said: Who is worthy of the World to Come? One who recites the Blessing of Redemption [which concludes the blessing after the Sh'ma] immediately before the Prayer [of Eighteen Blessings].

Talmud Berakhoth 4b.

Rabbi Zeira said in the name of Rabbi Abba bar Yirmeya: ... The Prayer must follow immediately after the Blessing of Redemption. ...

It is thus written, "May the words of my mouth be acceptable before You, O God, my Rock and my Redeemer" (Psalms 19:15). The very next verse is, "God answer you in the day of trouble" (Psalms 20:2).

Rabbi Ami said: If one does not say the Prayer immediately after the Redemption Blessing, what is he like? He is like a king's friend who comes and knocks on the king's door. But when the king comes out to see what he wants, he sees him leaving. The king then also repulses him.

Talmud Yerushalmi, Berakhoth 1:1.

Meaning

The pious individual realizes the meaning of each blessing, and how it was intended to relate to him.

When he says "Who Forms Lights," [the first blessing before the morning Sh'ma], he should meditate on the order of the celestial world, the greatness of the heavenly bodies, and their usefulness. He should also remain aware that even though the stars appear immense to us ... they are no greater than worms in the eyes of the Creator.

The wisdom and providence that go into the creation of an ant or bee are not less than that in the creation of the sun and planets. Indeed, the ant and bee are all the more wondrous, since, small as they are, they have many faculties and organs. If one keeps this in mind, he will not be tempted to overrate the astronomical bodies and be drawn to the views of those who worship them. . . .

In the blessing, "With Eternal Love," one becomes aware of the relationship between the Divine Power and the community that is fit to receive it—which is like a bright light falling on a clear mirror. One also realizes that the Torah is an emanation of God's will, revealing His authority on earth, just as it is revealed in heaven.

God's wisdom decreed that the earth not be populated with angels, but with human beings, of flesh and blood, torn by many conflicts. . . . When people purify themselves, either as individuals or as a community, then God's light shines over them, directing them with wonders and marvels, and allows them to transcend the bounds of the material world. This results in love and joy.

Nothing in all creation accepted this concept and hearkened to God's word . . . other than the pious human being. From the time of Adam until Jacob, there were just a few such individuals. Then an entire community was formed, accepting this concept in an act of love, where He would be their God.

God arranged them in the desert just like the heavenly spheres. There were four camps, like the four sectors of the zodiac, and twelve tribes, representing the twelve constellations. The Levite's camp was in the center, just as the Book of Creation states, "The Holy Palace is precisely in the middle, and it upholds them all."[2] All this is an expression of God's love.

We praise God for all this [in the blessing preceding the Sh'ma]. This is immediately followed by an acceptance of God's Torah when we recite the Sh'ma itself.

After the Sh'ma, we recite the prayer, "True and Certain." This includes concepts that are important if we are truly to accept the Torah. We clarify these concepts for ourselves, bringing ourselves to clearly understand and recognize them. Then, we bind them as a seal on our soul, testifying that we accept them just as our ancestors did, and that our children will adhere to them forever. We thus say, "For our fathers, for us, for our children, and for all generations, it is a good and enduring thing, a decree that shall not be violated. . . ."

We then tie the knot which binds together all Jewish belief. We confess God's existence, His eternity, His providence over our fathers, His authorship of the Torah, and the testimony to all of this, which is the

Exodus from Egypt. We include all this when we say, "True, You are the Lord our God.... True, Your name is from eternity... the help of our fathers.... And true, You redeemed us from Egypt, O Lord our God...."

When a person recites all this, meditating upon it with total concentration, then he is a true Jew. It is fitting for him to aspire to bind himself to that Godly concept that is bound to the Children of Israel alone among all nations. It is then easy for him to stand and petition before the Divine Presence and be answered.

One must therefore follow the Redemption Blessing immediately with the Amidah (the Prayer of Eighteeen Blessings), with the utmost alertness and enthusiasm....

Rabbi Yehudah HaLevi (1075–1141),
Kuzari 3:17.

Renewal and Rectification

When we recite the Sh'ma, every element of man's being is perfected with the Light of God's unity. As a result, all creation is also rectified.... Because of this concept our sages composed the blessings surrounding the Sh'ma.

All existence is renewed by God each day. This involves two basic concepts.

The first of these involves the world's preservation and continuity. God's abundance must be renewed each day to sustain it and allow it to continue to exist.

The second concept involves the fact that every single day ... has its own separate decree emanating from God. This decree determines the illuminations, influences, entities and states required to complete the cycle and attain the goal of ultimate perfection. Each day is therefore literally a new entity, through which all creation is renewed.

Both of these concepts are included in the words, "He renews the act of creation each day," [which are recited just before the end of the first blessing].

All the blessings and prayers surrounding the Sh'ma are based on this principle. They all make reference to the entirety of creation, which must be renewed each day.

Creation in general is divided into two basic categories. The first consists of the human race as a whole, especially Israel, which is its ultimate realization. The second category includes everything else in the world, both above and below.

The first blessing speaks of all creation other than man. It mentions the angels on high, as well as things in the physical world, speaking of their tasks and functions. It then concludes with the order of day and night, and the astronomical bodies that rule over them.

The second blessing thanks God for the concept of Israel. It speaks of His love for Israel, as well as the manner in which He brought them close to Him by allowing them to serve Him.

These blessings thus include all these concepts in their true light. They are then followed by the Sh'ma itself, [which unifies them all].

This in turn is followed by still another blessing, which speaks of the great miracles that God has done for us. Its main point is the Exodus and its details, arranged according to the mystery of these concepts.

The main concept of these blessings relates to the morning, since this is the time when all existence is renewed. In the evening, however, all creation receives an additional dimension according to the concept of nighttime, which, in a sense, is the conclusion and fulfillment of the daytime aspect.

It was because of this added dimension that the blessings of the evening Sh'ma were composed. They are much shorter than the blessings of the morning Sh'ma, since this new aspect is merely a continuation of what is renewed by day.

Our sages also added a fourth blessing after the evening Sh'ma, which speaks of nighttime rest and sleep, with all its ramifications. This is the blessing, "Let us Lie Down in Peace" (*Haskivenu*).

Rabbi Moshe Chaim Luzzatto (1707–1746),
Derekh Hashem 4:4-10-12.

The Order of Prayer

In the morning, one wakes up and recites the morning blessings. He then reads the prescribed psalms, saying the blessings before and after them. The Sh'ma is then recited, together with the blessings that precede and follow it. . . . When one concludes the blessing, "Redeemer of Israel" [which concludes the blessing after the Sh'ma], he should immediately stand and say the Amidah, so that it be said right after the Redemption Blessing. One must recite the Amidah while standing.

When one completes the Amidah, he should fall on his face in supplication (*Tachanun*). He then raises his head, and recites words of supplication while sitting. "A Praise of David" (Psalm 145) is then recited, after which one prays to God with all his strength, and then goes about his daily affairs.

One begins the Afternoon Service by saying, "A Praise of David" while sitting. The afternoon Amidah is then recited....

In the Evening Service, one recites the Sh'ma, saying the blessings before and after it. Right after the Redemption Blessing, one then recites the Amidah.... Even though another blessing ["Let us Lie Down in Peace"] is recited after "Redeemer of Israel," this is not an interruption between the Redemption Blessing and the Amidah; rather, it is like a continuation of this blessing.

Maimonides,
Yad Chazakah, Tefillah 7:17, 18.

Sacrificial Readings

Rabbi Yitzchak said: It is written, "This is the Torah of the sin offering" (Leviticus 6:18). If a person studies the laws of the sin offering, it is considered as if he had actually sacrificed it.

Talmud, Menachoth 110a.

Abraham said, "When the Temple no longer stands, what will they do?"

God replied, "I have already taught them the order of the sacrifices. When they study this, I will count it as if they actually offered them before Me."

Talmud, Megillah 31b.

Because of this it was ordained that verses dealing with the daily offerings be recited [as part of the daily service].

Rabbi Yaakov ben Asher (1270–1343),
Tur, Orach Chaim 48.

The Spiritual Ladder

The morning service is divided into four general sections. The first

(*Korbanoth*) involves readings associated with the sacrificial system. The second is the Verse of Praise (*Pesukey DeZimra*), consisting of psalms and other Biblical praises. The third is the Sh'ma and its blessings, and the fourth is the Amidah (the Prayer of Eighteen Blessings), and various concluding prayers.

The readings associated with the sacrifices (*Korbanoth*) are meant to purify the world as a whole. They remove all obstacles and barriers that would hold back sustenance from on High.

The Verses of Praise are intended to cause the Light of God's presence to be revealed. God made this depend on the singing of His praises. . . .

All things in creation exist in a sequence of steps, from the highest fundamental forces down to the physical world itself.

The Highest Wisdom decreed that in order for all things to receive God's sustenance, they must first bind themselves to each other. The lowest things must bind themselves to those above them, and these, in turn, to the ones that are still higher, continuing in this manner until reaching the most fundamental Forces, which in turn depend on God Himself. His sustenance is then extended to these Forces, and it spreads downward appropriately to all levels of creation. In this manner, they all arrive at their ordained level and function.

The blessings of the Sh'ma were arranged so that they should relate to these mysteries. Through this liturgy, every level of creation is made to elevate itself, so that each one is bound to the one above it. When they are all bound together and are dependent on God's Light, sustenance can then be transmitted to all of God's handiwork. This in turn is accomplished by the Amidah.

Rabbi Moshe Chaim Luzzatto (1707–1746),
Derekh HaShem 4:6:10.

Four Universes

It is necessary to realize that there are four general universes.

The physical world consists of two parts, the terrestrial and the astronomical. The astronomical is the real of the stars and planets, while the terrestrial is the earth upon which we live. The two together are considered to be a single universe, namely, the physical.

Above this is a second universe, which is the world of angels.

Higher than this is a third universe, which is the world of the highest Forces.... This is called the universe of the Throne.

On a still higher level, we can speak of God's Influence in general. These consist of the revelations of His Light, from which all existence is derived, and upon which all depends.... In figurative terms, these Influences in general can also be said to constitute a universe. This is usually referred to as the Universe of Godly Essence....

Creation as a whole therefore follows the following sequence: The physical world depends on the angels, and the angels in turn depend on the Throne and its Steps, which is above them. The Throne is dependent on God's Influences, and the revelations of His Light, which is the true Root of all things.

The four parts of the daily service parallel this order. The first three parts therefore rectify the lower three universes. The Sacrificial Readings (*Korbanoth*) thus pertain to the physical world, the Verses of Praise (*Pesukey DeZimra*), to the world of angels, and the Sh'ma and its blessings, to the Universe of the Throne. This is followed by the Amidah, which pertains to the Universe of Godly Essence, transmitting the Influences of this Universe according to their various aspects.

Derekh HaShem 4:6:13-14.

Alenu

After each service, we should say *Alenu*.... It is taught that *Alenu* is a great praise, and should therefore be said while standing....

There is a tradition that *Alenu* was composed by Joshua when he conquered Jericho. It contains an allusion to his name.

Kol Bo 16 (Anonymous, 13th Century, New York, 1946, p. 9c).

Alenu was originally composed by Joshua, son of Nun. Rabbi Yochanan ben Zakkai later ordained that it should be said following each service.

Hai Gaon (939-1038), Responsum.[3]

Joshua recited Alenu seven times, backward and forward, and thus broke down the walls of Jericho. It is therefore beneficial for all things, helping for whatever trouble may occur. . . .

Rabbi Moshe ibn Makhir of Safed
(16th Century),
Seder HaYom p. 12d.

I found a manuscript relating a tradition that one should recite Alenu with awe and reverence. . . . All the hosts of heaven hear it, and the Blessed Holy One and His heavenly family rise and respond, "Happy is the one who has all this . . ."

Rabbi Moshe Mat (16th Cent.),
Mateh Moshe.[4]

We conclude the service with Alenu in order to reinforce our faith in the unity of God's kingdom before we return from the synagogue. We thus strengthen our faith that, "He will wipe out false gods from the earth, and all idols will be cut off, so that the world will be rectified in the Kingdom of the Almighty."

Even though we must then go and deal with the gentiles, seeing that they are dominant, our hearts will not be drawn to their gods, and we will not have any sinful thoughts.

Rabbi Yoel Sirkes (1561–1640),
Bayith Chadash, Orach Chaim 133.

Kaddish

[Elijah told Rabbi Yose]: When Israel responds, "May His great Name be blessed" [in the Kaddish], God nods His head and says, "Happy is the King who is thus praised in His house. What does a Father have when He has banished His children? Woe is to children banished from their Father's table."

Talmud, Berakhoth 3a.

Rabbi Yehoshua ben Levi said: If one responds, "Amen, may His great Name be blessed" with all his might, then all decrees against him are torn. . . .

Rabbi Chiyah bar Abba said in the name of Rabbi Yochanan: Even if one is tainted by idolatry, he is forgiven....

Talmud, Shabbath 119b.

Aramaic

People say that Kaddish is said in Aramaic [rather than Hebrew] because it is a beautiful prayer and a great praise. It was therefore composed in Aramaic so that the angels would not be able to understand it, since it would make them jealous.[5] This does not seem to be the true reason, however, since many beautiful prayers were composed in Hebrew.

The Talmud states that the Kaddish was recited after homiletic lectures,[6] and this may provide us with the reason. These lectures were often attended by the ignorant, who knew Aramaic, which was their everyday language, but did not understand Hebrew. It was therefore ordained that the Kaddish be said in Aramaic, in order that everyone should understand it.

Tosafoth, Berakhoth 3a. (12th Century).

In ancient times, there was once a government decree forbidding the Jews to say, "May His great Name be blessed." It was therefore ordained that it be said in Aramaic, so that their enemies would not understand it. Even though the decree was eventually abolished, they did not revert this prayer to Hebrew. The abolishment of the decree involved miracles and wonders, and this would recall them and publicize them.

I found this in the name of the great sage, Rabbi Benjamin ben Avraham the physician.

We say the Kaddish at least seven times each day. The Geonim found support for this in the verse, "Seven each day I will praise You" (Psalms 119:164).

Tanya Rabbati (Anonymous, 13th Cent.).

Kaddish is not like the other sanctifications.... It ascends from all sides, from above, below and every side of faith. It breaks locks and rings of iron, and all evil Husks, elevating God's glory over all.

We say the Kaddish [in Aramaic, which is] the language of the Other Side, and we respond with great strength, "Amen, may His great Name be blessed forever and ever." In this manner, we break the strength of the Other Side, and the Blessed Holy One is elevated over all His glory.

When this Kaddish breaks the strength of the Other Side, the Blessed Holy One raises Himself in His glory, remembering His children recalling His Name.

Since the Blessed Holy One raises Himself in glory in this sanctification, it cannot be said with less than ten men.

This [Aramaic] language is certain to subjugate the Other Side and break its strength, elevating the glory of the Blessed Holy One. It breaks the powerful locks, fetters, chains, and all evil Husks. God then remembers His name and His children.

Zohar 2:129b.

For the Dead

It was ordained that the Kaddish be said for one's father and mother.... This is based on the following account:

A rabbi once came across a dead man who was cutting wood and carrying it on his shoulder. He said, "My son, why are you doing this?"

The other replied, "Rabbi, this is my judgment. I bring this wood to feed the fires of Gehinom, and then I am judged in it."

The rabbi said, "Is there no one who can save you from this suffering?"

The man answered, "Nothing can save me, unless my son says the Kaddish on the Haftarah, glorifying God's name for my sake. If he does that, I know that its merit will stand up for me and protect me."

The rabbi went and told this to the son of the dead man, and the son did all that he said.

The dead man later appeared to the rabbi and said, "May your spirit be at ease, for you have put me at ease."

Because of this, it became a custom for the son of a dead person to say the final Kaddish for twelve months following his death, and also to say the Haftarah.

It is also a custom for such an orphan to lead the evening service each Saturday night. This is the time when sinners are brought back to Gehinom after the Sabbath, and it is possible that the merit of his prayer will protect them.

Rabbi Aaron HaKohen (1266–1334),
Orachoth Chaim, Hilchoth Aivel 31.[7]

If an orphan can, he should lead the weekday services. This is even better than saying the Mourner's Kaddish, since the latter was intended primarily for minors. . . .

It is a custom that Kaddish only be said for eleven months. This is so as not to make one's father and mother appear wicked, since we are taught that "the judgment of the wicked is for twelve months."[8]

Rabbi Moshe Isserles (1525–1572),
Mapah, on Shulchan Arukh, Yoreh Deah 376:5.

Amen

Blessed be God, the Lord of Israel, from eternity to eternity and let all the people say Amen, praise God.

Psalms 106:48.

I shook out my lap and said, "May God shake out every man who keeps not his promise from this house and this labor, even so shall he be shaken out and banished." And all the congregation said "Amen," and they praised God.

Nehemiah 5:13.

Ezra blessed God, the great Lord, and all the people responded Amen,Amen.

Nehemiah 8:6.

Three Implications

Rabbi Yose, son of Rabbi Chanina, said: Amen implies an oath, Amen implies consent, and Amen implies confirmation.

Amen implies an oath, as it is written, "[The priest shall make the woman swear with a maledictory oath, and the priest shall say to the woman, 'God make you for a curse and an oath among your people. . .'] and the woman shall say Amen, Amen." (Numbers 5:22).

Amen implies consent, as it is written, "Cursed be the man who does not uphold all the words of this Torah to do them, and all the people shall say 'Amen'" (Deuteronomy 27:26).

Amen implies confirmation, as it is written, "Jeremiah said, 'Amen, so shall God do, may God uphold your words.'" (Jeremiah 28:6).

Talmud, Shavuoth 36a.

Amen implies an oath. If a person responds Amen after another person's oath, it is as if he himself had expressed the oath.

Amen implies consent. If a person expresses a condition to his neighbor, and his neighbor answers "Amen," he is obliged to keep the condition.

Amen implies confirmation. It is fitting to respond Amen to every prayer and supplication. This implies that one believes the words, and that it should be God's will that the prayer come true.

*Rabbi Shlomo Yitzchaki,
Rashi (1040–1105),
Commentary ad loc.*

Faithful King

What is Amen? Rabbi Chanina said: It consists of the first letters of *El Melekh Ne'eman* ("God Faithful King").

(Rashi: When one responds Amen, he bears witness that God is the faithful King.)

Talmud, Shabbath 119b.

Truth

The root "Amen" implies trust, acceptance and credence. These are derived from faith (*Emunah*), since when one has faith in another, he believes him and assumes that he is true. . . .

In my opinion, the word *Emeth* (truth) is also derived from this root, and is a contraction of *Emen-eth*. . . .

Therefore, when it is written, "Amen, so shall God do" (Jeremiah 28:6), it means, "This is true, and so shall God do."

The verse, ["Cursed is the man who does not uphold all the words of this Torah. . . .] and all the people shall say Amen" (Deuteronomy 27:26), also has this meaning. It means that this is true, and one who violates this will indeed be cursed. It is said as a prayer, or as a confirmation, indicating that they all accept the curse if they violate it.

*Rabbi David Kimchi (1160–1235),
Sefer HaShorashim, Amen (39).*

Confirmation

Amen has the connotation of confirmation. When one responds to a blessing, he confirms the blessing.

> Rabbi David Kimchi,
> Radak on Psalms 41:14.

Belief

When a person says Amen, he should have in mind that the blessing to which he is responding is true, and that he believes in it. This is because Amen has the connotation of confirmation.

> Rabbi Yaakov ben Asher (1270–1343),
> Tur, Orach Chaim 124.

[Some blessings, such as] the middle blessings of the Amidah, imply a petition. When one responds Amen to such a blessing, he should also have in mind, "May it be God's will that this should come true, and may He fulfill our requests. . . ." We confirm his request and pray that God make it come true.

> Rabbi Yoel Sirkes (1561–1640),
> Bayith Chadash, ad loc.

World to Come

When does a child become worthy of the World to Come? . . . Rabbi Meir says, "From the time that he first says Amen."

> Talmud, Sanhedrin 110b.

One should therefore train young children to respond Amen to blessings.

> Rabbi Moshe Isserles (1525–1572),
> Darkei Moshe, Orach Chaim 124:6.

Merit

The ignorant come to synagogue, but do not know scripture, or mishnah, or midrash. Still, they come into the synagogues and study halls, and hear people pronounce the blessings, "He forms the lights," and "He resurrects the dead." . . . These ignorant people then respond Amen, indicating that they indeed believe that God created the world and will resurrect the dead. Even if they have no merit other than this "Amen," it is sufficient for them.

Midrash, Agadath Bereshith 80:1.

Heroes

Rabbi Yose said. "He who responds Amen is greater than he who blesses."

Rabbi Nehorai remarked, "By heaven this is true. The common soldiers begin the battle, and the heroes then come and win it."

Talmud, Berakhoth 53b.

Gematria

The purport of Amen includes two of God's names, YHVH and Adonay. [The numerical value of Amen is 91. This is the sum of the numerical value of the Tetragrammaton (26), and God's name Adonay (65).]

Zohar 2:178a.

"He who responds Amen is greater than he who blesses," since the former confirms the blessing. But the one who says the blessing only mentions God's name once, while the one who says Amen includes two names (YHVH and Adonay,) since it equals the sum of their numerical value.

Rabbi Yehudah HeChasid (1149-1217),
Sefer Chasidim 18.

Traditional Forms

The various blessings and prayers which are well known to all Israel, were composed by Ezra and his legislative body. Therefore no man may add to them or subtract from them. . . .

As a general rule, whoever alters the coin minted by our sages with regard to blessings is in error, and must repeat the blessing. . . .

> Maimonides, (1135–1204),
> Yad Chazakah, Keriath Sh'ma 1:7.

In the Amidah, one should not alter the coin minted by our sages. . . . I have in my possession an ancient manuscript that contains all the prayers of the entire year. It also enumerates the number of words in each prayer and explains their significance.

> Rabbi Asher ben Yechiel (1250–1327),
> Teshuvoth HaRosh 4:20.

Counting Words

My brother, Rabbi Yechiel, said that the saints of Germany used to weigh and count each word in the prayers and blessings. . . .

> Rabbi Yaakov ben Asher (1270–1343),
> (son of the above)
> Tur, Orach Chaim 113,

Mysteries

The Talmud teaches us that Rabban Gamaliel said to the sages, "Is there anyone among you who can compose a blessing for the heretics?"[9]

This clearly indicates that all the blessings and prayers are based upon "foundations of gold," with a set number of words and letters, as mentioned by the *Tur*. This is in addition to the fact that each word contains wondrous mysteries.

If this were not true, what would be the meaning of Rabban Gamaliel's query? Such a prayer would be nothing more than a curse pronounced against the heretics; what then would be the great accomplishment of Samuel the Little in composing this prayer? And when it was forgotten, why did he spend two and three hours trying to recall it?

This is clear evidence that the precise number of letters and words have a great effect on high, both in their own right, and because of the mysteries that they imply. As a result, they can help one's prayer be granted.

This may seem surprising, since our sages taught that one can pray in any language that he wishes, and according to what we have said, one should only be allowed to pray in Hebrew. This is no problem, since "God desires the heart."[10] If one prays with true sincerity, no matter in what language, these prayers can have the same effect as the language ordained by the Great Assembly.

Rabbi Yaakov Yehoshua Falk (1680–1756),
P'nei Yehoshua on Berakhoth 28b.

It is taught that one hundred and twenty elders, among them many prophets, composed the prayer service. Is there any human being alive who could compose such a wondrous rectification? In the regular form of daily prayer, they set up a single rite that can bring about the rectification of all universes, above and below, as well as all parts of the Divine Vehicle.

Each time we recite the service, we bring about new rectifications in the order of the spiritual universes and powers, and we transmit new mental energy to them. Therefore, [even though the words are all the same,] ... no service is really the same as the other. ...

Rabbi Chaim of Volozhin (1749–1821),
Nefesh HaChaim 2:13.

Dissenting Opinions

The Mishnah states, "In a place where they said to say a long blessing, we may not abridge it...."[11]

This does not mean that one may not lengthen or abridge the body of the prayer, increasing or decreasing the number of words. If this were true, they would have ordained the form of every blessing with a fixed number of words and with precise concepts, so that we could know the exact form of each blessing. This is something that we do not find anywhere.[12]

Rabbi Shlomo ben Avraham Adret (1235–1310),
Rashba on Berakhoth 11a.

Some people count the number of words in each blessing of the Amidah. They cite Biblical verses expressing the same ideas as the blessings, and claim that the number of words in these verses should be the same as the number in the blessings.

I also did this at first. But then I began to realize that this does not have any real foundation, since we do not find any place where it states that the Amidah must be said with a set wording. Some people add words, while others omit words, and therefore, such enumerations only help those who are involved with them, but no one else. Therefore, why should we bother the scribes to write them down?

Rabbi David Abudarham (1274–1341),
Sefer Abudarham, p. 105.

Different Rites

Rabbi Yose sent to them, "Even though I have sent you an order [of prayers] for the festivals, do not diverge from the customs of your fathers who have passed on."[13]

Talmud Yerushalmi, Eruvin 3:9.

Twelve Gates

There are various different rites of prayer among the Ashkenazim, the Sefardim, as well as the people of Catalonia and Italy. These different rites do not merely involve poems and prayers that were added on later, but involve the basic form of the service as required by law.

My master [Rabbi Yitzchak Luria, known as the Ari,] said that there are Twelve Gates in heaven, one for each of the Twelve Tribes. The prayers of each different tribe would ascend through its own particular Gate. These are the gates mentioned at the end of the Book of Ezekiel.

Each of these gates is different, and therefore the forms of prayers are also different. Each person should therefore keep the custom of his fathers, since . . . his prayers can only ascend through their own particular gate.

All laws stated in the Talmud, however, are the same for all Twelve Tribes.

Rabbi Chaim Vital (1543–1620),
(Master of Kabbalah),
Pri Etz Chaim, Sha'ar HaTefillah, beginning (Jerusalem 1980, p.1)

The Thirteenth Gate

Our sages teach us that a person entering and leaving the Holy Temple would have to bow thirteen times, once for each of the thirteen gates in the Temple.[14] These gates are alluded to in the Book of Ezekiel, where each tribe will have its own gate when the holiness of Jerusalem is raised to the status that the Temple had in the past.

It is known that the Temple here on earth paralleled the Temple on High. The Holy Temple on High therefore also has a gate for each tribe, as discussed in the writings of the holy Ari.

A person had to bow thirteen times, once for each of these gates. These kneelings involved the transmission [of the spiritual sustenance that flows through these gates], as known to those who delve into the writings of the Ari.

The worship service is therefore [the key] with which each individual enters through his own gate. We are thus taught that prayer is, "the ladder standing on earth, with its head reaching the heavens" (Genesis 28:12). Each gate has its own combination, and it is for this reason that there are different rites of prayer. [Each of the twelve gates has its own liturgy.]

The thirteenth gate, however, is for the individual who does not know from which of the Twelve Tribes he originates. Since he does not know which gate to use, [he can use this one] to enter the King's courtyard. . . .

Knowing the paths of heaven as he did, the godly Ari taught a way for those who do not know from which tribe they originate. It is for this reason that he arranged a special order of prayer, based on all the others, as known to those who are well versed.

Since all are included in the thirteenth, it may be asked why all the other Twelve Gates were needed. Why is the thirteenth gate not sufficient?

But as long as each tribe knew its own particular order of prayer, it was certainly best for each one to enter through its own special gate. . . .

Now that people do not know the tribe of their origin, and we also do not know which customs apply to which tribes, it is best to follow the rite suggested by the Ari, which is universal.

The prophet Ezekiel predicted that in the Ultimate Future, there would only be Twelve Gates in Jerusalem, one for each tribe. The reason for this is that at that time, all people will know their tribe.

Rabbi Dov Baer, Maggid of Mezrich,
Chasidic Master (1704–1772),
Magid Devarav LeYaakov 141 (Jerusalem 1971, p. 43a–b)

An Opposing Opinion

What you quote from the book Likutei Amarim [Magid Devarav LeYaakov] that the Sefardic rite [of the Ari] is intended for those who do not know their tribe, I am not worthy of understanding. If this verse were true, the Kohanim and Levites, who certainly know the tribe of their origin, should not use this rite, but a special liturgy for Levites. [We clearly see that this is not the case].

Furthermore, in the time of the Talmud, people were already ignorant of their tribes of origin, the only ones knowing for sure being the priests, the Levites, and the house of Rabbi [Yehuda the Prince] and the princes. . . . We would therefore have to say that all the Talmudic sages also used the Sefardic rite, and if this were true, from what source have we derived other rites? . . .

We know that all the sages of France, Rashi, the Tosafists, Rabbi Meir of Rothenburg, Rabbi Asher, his son Rabbi Yaakov (authors of the Tur), and many others, all made use of the Ashkenazic rite. Even though they did not know their tribe, their prayers certainly ascended to the heavens.

The Ari himself used the poems that Rabbi Shimon the Great composed for Rosh HaShanah and Yom Kippur, saying that they were composed by one who knew the way of Truth . . . but Rabbi Shimon used the Ashkenazic rite. Rabbi Amram, who arranged the worship service used by all Israel, lived in Mayence, and I myself saw his grave. The same is true of Rabbi Amnon, who wrote the prayer *U'nethane Tokef* [said in all congregations on the High Holy Days], and his house is still there. Shall we then say that the prayers of all these saints were cut off, may the Merciful One protect us?

Rabbi Moshe Sofer (1762–1839),
Teshuvoth Chatham Sofer, Orach Chaim 16.

Heavenly Channels

The Maggid (angelic spokesman) warned Rabbi Yosef Caro to come on time to synagogue, so that he would be able to say the entire service in order. When one skips prayers, he upsets the heavenly channels.

Rabbi Yehudah Ashkenazi (17th Century),
Ba'er Hetev, Orach Chaim 52:1.

The entire order of the service was composed and arranged in its proper order. If one comes late to synagogue, and misses prayers, he disorganizes and changes the order.

Rabbi Yosef Caro,
Maggid Mesharim, BeShalach, Jerusalem 1960, p. 57a.

Chapter 6

CONGREGATION AND SYNAGOGUE

In congregations bless God,
the Lord from the source of of Israel.

Psalms 68:27.

In a multitude of people is the King's glory.

Proverbs 14:28.

Acceptance

Rabbi Yitzchak asked Rav Nachman, "Why did you not come to synagogue?"

"I could not," he replied.

"You should have gathered ten men with whom to pray."

"That would have been burdensome."

"You should have asked the Prayer Leader to inform you when the congregation begins their worship."

"Why is all this necessary?"

"Because Rabbi Yochanan said in the name of Rabbi Shimon bar Yochai: It is written, 'And as for me, my prayer is to You, O God, at a time of acceptance' (Psalms 69:14). When is a 'time of acceptance?' This is when the congregation prays."

Rabbi Yose, son of Rabbi Chanina, said that we can also derive it from the verse, "Thus says God: In an acceptable time I will answer you" (Isaiah 49:8).

Rabbi Acha, son of Rabbi Chanina, said, from here: "Behold God will not despise the multitude" (Job 36:5). It is likewise written, "He has redeemed my soul in peace that none should approach me, for many were with me" (Psalms 55:19).

This is also found in an earlier teaching:

Rabbi Nathan said: How do we derive the fact that God does not reject the prayer of a multitude? It is written, "Behold God will not despise the multitude" and, "He has redeemed my soul in peace..."

God said, "If a person is involved in Torah and acts of kindness, and if he worships with the congregation, then I will count it as if he has redeemed both Me and My children from among the nations."

Resh Lakish said: If a person has a synagogue in his city and does not attend, he is called a bad neighbor. It is thus written, "Thus says God: All My bad neighbors plague the inheritance that I have given to My people Israel" (Jeremiah 12:14). Besides that, they and their children will go into exile, as it is written, "I will pluck them off from their land, and I will pluck up the house of Judah from among them" (Jeremiah 12:14).

Talmud, Berakhoth 7b, 8a.

Heart in Hands

Rabbi Ami said: Prayer is not heard by God unless one places his soul in his hands. It is thus written, "Let us lift up our hearts with our hands" (Lamentations 3:41).

But how can we say this? Shmuel's spokesman expounded the verse, "For their hearts were not steadfast with Him, nor were they faithful to His covenant" (Psalms 78:37). Nevertheless, the very next verse says, "But He, being full of compassion, forgives sin and does not destroy" (Psalms 78:38).

There is no contradiction. Rabbi Ami is speaking of an individual, while Shmuel's spokesman is speaking of a congregation.

Talmud, Taanith 8a.

Iron Walls

Rabbi Yochanan said, "When one worships at home, it is as if he is surrounded with walls of iron.

Talmud Yerushalmi, Berakhoth 5:1.

Whenever we Call

King David said, "As for me, my prayer is to You at a time of acceptance" (Psalms 69:14). David was an individual, and he therefore had to worship in an "acceptable time." But the prayer of a congregation never returns empty-handed, as it is written, "[What great nation is there, that has God so near to them,] as the Lord our God is, whenever we call Him" (Deuteronomy 4:7).

Midrash, Devarim Rabbah 2:7.

Scrutiny

Before the prayer of an individual enters to be crowned in its place, the Blessed Holy One scrutinizes it, gazes at it, and behold the sins and merits of the individual. But this is not true of the prayer of a congregation. Many prayers are not from the righteous, but they still enter before the Blessed Holy One, and He does not look at their sins.

Zohar 1:234b (Tosefta).

Jewels

Rabbi Acha said: What does one who prays with a congregation resemble?

A number of people make a crown for the king. A poor man then comes along and places his portion in it. The king says, "Just because of the poor man, shall I not accept the crown?" The king accepts it, and when he places his crown on his head, the poor man's portion is also included.

Likewise, if there are ten righteous men worshiping, and a wicked person stands among them, God says, "Just because of this sinner, should I not accept their worship?"

Midrash, Eikhah Rabbah 3:8.

A Debate

Rabbi: Only prayers of the congregation are answered. There may have been some individuals who were equal to the congregation, but such individuals no longer exist.

King: Why is this true? Would it not be better for a person to isolate himself? His soul would be pure, and his thoughts undisturbed.

Rabbi: The congregation has many advantages.

First of all, a congregation will not pray for something that may harm an individual, while one individual may pray for something that may injure another.... One of the conditions for prayer to be answered is that it must benefit all, and not imply any injury whatsoever.

Another reason is that there are few who can pray perfectly, without error or misdeed.

It was ordained that the individual should say the same prayers as the congregation [i.e. in the plural], and if possible, his prayer should be in a congregation containing not less than ten men. If some people do not pray perfectly, their deficiency can then be made up by others. As a whole, they say a perfect prayer, with pure intent.

The blessing then rests on them all, and each individual receives a portion of it. This is like rain, which waters an area where the inhabitants are worthy of it. Even though some individuals may not be worthy, they gain because of the majority.

The opposite is also true. Rain can be withheld from a given land because the population as a whole is not worthy of it. There may be worthy individuals in that land, but because of the majority, they also will suffer.

This is God's judgment of the world, and the worthy individuals who suffer are repaid in the World to Come. Even in this world, God can give them other benefits instead, rewarding them in an area where they are set apart from their neighbors.

Still, there are very few who are saved completely when the community as a whole is punished.

One who only prays for his own needs is like one who works to strengthen his house alone, and does not want to help his neighbors strengthen the walls of the city. Even though such a person expends much energy, he still remains in danger. But when one includes himself with the community, he expends little and remains safe.

Each individual's lack is made up by another, and the land then attains the best possible condition. All the people partake in its blessing, with agreement and justice, with little expenditure.

Rabbi Yehudah HaLevi (1075–1141),
Kuzari 3:17–19.

Ten Men

Rabbi Chalafta of Kfar Chananya said: When ten people sit and are engaged in Torah, the Divine Presence is among them. It is thus written, "God stands in the godly congregation" (Psalms 82:1).

Mishnah, Avoth 3:6.

How do we know that a congregation consists of ten men? It is written, "How long shall this evil congregation exist" (Numbers 14:27)? [This group consisted of the twelve spies.] Excluding Joshua and Caleb [who were not wicked, we are left with ten].

Mishnah, Sanhedrin 1:6.

One may not introduce the Sh'ma (Rashi: with Kaddish and Barkhu), conduct a congregational service, say the Priestly Blessing, read the Torah, nor chant the Haftarah . . . in the presence of less than ten men.

Mishnah, Megillah 4:3.

From where do we derive this?

Rabbi Chiya bar Abba said in the name of Rabbi Yochanan: It is written [that God said], "I shall be sanctified among the children of Israel" (Leviticus 22:32). There is no sanctification with less than ten.

How is this indicated?

As Rabbi Chiya taught: The word "among" is found in two places. One has already been quoted, "I shall be sanctified *among* the children of Israel." The second place is, "Separate yourself from *among* the congregation" (Numbers 16:21).

The word "congregation" also occurs in two places. One is here, and the other is, "How long shall this evil congregation exist" (Numbers 14:27)? Just as one consists of ten, so does the other.

Talmud ad loc. (23b).

Rabbi Simon said: Here it is written, "I shall be sanctified *among* the children of Israel." In a second place it is written, "[Joseph's *ten* brothers went down to buy grain from Egypt. But Benjamin, Joseph's brother, was not sent by Jacob . . .] The children of Israel came to obtain provisions *among* those who came" (Genesis 42:3–5). In this case, "among" refers to ten [since of the twelve brothers, Joseph was in Egypt, and Benjamin did not go]. In a similar manner, here it also refers to ten.

Rabbi Yose, son of Rabbi Bun, said to him: If you derive it from the word "among" in this verse, there were many who came to Egypt. But let us say that the term, "the children of Israel" occurs in both verses. Just as it refers to ten men in one case, it refers to ten in the other.

Talmud Yerushalmi ad loc. (4:4).

Wedding Blessings

How do we know that the wedding blessings require ten? It is written, "He took ten men among the elders of the city, and he said to them, 'sit here,' and they sat" (Ruth 4:2).

Talmud, Ketuboth 7a.

Sodom

It is written [that when Abraham was arguing with God to save Sodom, he said], "'What if there be ten there?' and [God] said, 'I will not destroy it for the sake of the ten'" (Genesis 18:32).

Why ten? Because they form a congregation.

Midrash, Bereshith Rabbah 49:13.

Emanations

The Divine Presence comprises the totality of Ten Emanations (*Sefiroth*). It is therefore taught, "There is no sanctification with less than ten."

Tikkunei Zohar 18 (35b).

Sayings

There is no sanctification with less than ten. These are the Ten Sayings with which the world was created.[1]

God blessed His world and sanctified it. But there is no sanctification with less than ten.

God thus made ten canopies in the Garden of Eden. The wedding of the Blessed Holy One and the Divine Presence is "Holy, holy, holy" (Isaiah 6:3). The Seven [Wedding] Blessings are those of the Sh'ma, two preceding it and one following it in the morning, and two preceding it and two following it in the evening, making a total of seven. (HaGra: The three "holy's" and the seven blessings, then make a total of ten.)

Tikkunei Zohar 70 (132a).

Shofar

It was ordained that ten blasts be sounded on the Shofar. . . . These are elevated with the ten. The Divine Presence does not rest where there are less than ten, as it is written, "I will not destroy it for the sake of ten" (Genesis 18:32).

Zohar Chadash, Yithro 34a.

The Bent One

Why is the letter *Yud* bent over? [The numerical value of *Yud* is ten, and] it represents the ten in the synagogue, who are bent over in prayer.

Midrash Rabbi Akiba ben Yosef, Yud.

A Special Place

Rabbi Chelbo said in the name of Rav Huna: When one has a fixed place of prayer, the God of Abraham helps him. . . .

How do we know that Abraham prayed in a set place? It is written, "Abraham woke up early in the morning, to the place where he had stood before God" (Genesis 19:27). "Standing" is nothing other than prayer, as it is written, "Pinchas stood up and prayed" (Psalms 106:30).

Talmud, Berakhoth 6b.

Rabbi Yochanan said in the name of Rabbi Shimon bar Yochai: When one has a fixed place to pray, his enemies fall away before him.

It is thus written [that God said], "I will set a place for My people Israel, and I will plant them so that they may dwell in their own place. They shall no longer be disquieted, and the sons of wickedness will no longer afflict them" (2 Samuel 7:10).

Talmud, Berakhoth 7b.

Rabbi Abba [son of] Rabbi Chiya said in the name of Rabbi Yochanan: One must pray in a place set aside for worship.

Why?

Because it is written [that God said], "In every place where I recall My name [I will come to you and bless you]" (Exodus 20:21). The verse does not say, "every place where *you* recall My name," but "every place where *I* recall My name."

RabbiTanchum bar Chanina said: One must specify a place for himself in the synagogue to pray.

Why?

It is written, "David came to the top of the hill, where he would bow down to God" (2 Samuel 15:32). The verse does not say, "where he bowed down," but "where he *would* bow down." [This indicates that he specified a place where he would always worship.]

Talmud Yerushalmi, Berakhoth 4:4.

Permanence

In order for prayer to be perfect, it must not be something casual.

Prayer implies attachment to God, for it is through prayer that one can bind himself to God. If this attachment is merely casual, it is not considered attachment at all. A casual act is only for the moment or hour, but it is not permanent, but something which is not casual remains permanent. It is fitting that this attachment to God not be casual at all.

It is for this reason that we are taught to have a specific place for worship. When one prays in a set place, his prayer is not a casual act, for such an act does not include anything regular. If a person prayed in different places each time, it would not be something regular. This would not be true attachment to God, but a casual act that is only temporary.

Rabbi Yehudah Loew (1525–1609),
The Maharal of Prague,
Nethivoth Olam, Avodah 4.

Windows and Fields

Rabbi Chiya bar Abba said in the name of Rabbi Yochanan: One should only pray in a room that has windows. It is thus written, "The windows of his upstairs room were open toward Jerusalem, [and he kneeled upon his knees three times a day and prayed]" (Daniel 6:11).

Rav Kahana said: Brazen is one who prays in a valley.

Talmud, Berakhoth 34b.

One should pray in a room with windows, since this will cause him to direct his heart. When he looks up at the heavens, his heart will be humbled.

One should not pray in a valley, since when one is in a closed place, he is beset with the fear of God and his heart is contrite.

Rabbi Shlomo Yitzchaki,
Rashi (1040–1105),
Commentary ad loc.

There is a slight difficulty with this teaching, since it is written, "Isaac went out to commune in the field" (Genesis 24:63), [and we are taught that this refers to prayer].[2]

This "field," however, where Isaac prayed, was actually Mount Moriah. We are thus taught that "Isaac called it a field."[3]

Alternatively, one can say that the "valley" mentioned here refers to a place through which people constantly pass, [and they will disturb one's concentration. Isaac, on the other hand, prayed in a secluded field, and this is permitted.]

Tosafoth (12th Century), ad loc.

It is written that "Isaac went out to commune in the field." Did he not have any room or other place in which to pray? But this was the field that Abraham bought, next to the cave of Machpelah....

Why did Abraham himself not pray there? He had previously set aside a different place in which to pray.

Zohar 2:39b.

The Synagogue

Abba Binyamin said: God only hears prayer in the synagogue. It is thus written, "To hear the song and the prayer" (1 Kings 8:28). Prayer should be in a place of song. (Rashi: This is in the synagogue, since it is there that the congregation sings songs and chants praise in a pleasant voice.)

Rabin, son of Rav Adda, said in the name of Rabbi Yitzchak: How do we know that God is to be found in the synagogue? It is written, "God stands in the godly congregation" (Psalms 82:1).

How do we know that when ten people pray, the Divine Presence is with them? It is written, "God stands in the godly congregation."

Talmud, Berakhoth 6a.

Regularly

Rabin, son of Rav Adda, said in the name of Rabbi Yitzchak: When one regularly attends synagogue, and misses one day, God asks for him. . . .

Rabbi Yochanan said: When God comes to the synagogue and does not find ten people there, He immediately becomes angry. It is thus written, "Why was there no man when I came, why did none answer when I called?" (Isaiah 50:2).

Talmud, Berakhoth 6b.

The First Ten

Rabbi Yehoshua ben Levi said: One should always rise up early so as to be among the first ten. Even if a hundred come later, he receives the reward of them all.

Can we then say that he receives all their reward? But this means that he receives a reward equal to them all.

Talmud, Berakhoth 47b.

Principle and Interest

There are six things which provide merit whose interest can be consumed here in this world, while the principle remains intact for the World to Come. [One of these is] rising to synagogue. . . .

Talmud, Shabbath 127a.

The Little Sanctuary

It is written, "[Thus says the Lord God: Although I have removed them far off among the nations, and although I have scattered them among the peoples,] still, I have provided them with a *little sanctuary* [in the countries where they have come]" (Ezekiel 11:16).

Rabbi Yitzchak said: This "Little Sanctuary" refers to synagogues and houses of study in Babylon.

Talmud, Megillah 29a.

Scholars

A scholar may not live in a city that does not have . . . a synagogue. . . .

Talmud, Sanhedrin 17b.

Immersion

Rabbi Eliezer ben Yaakov quoted the verse, "God is Israel's Mikvah (bath)" (Jeremiah 17:13). Just as a Mikvah cleanses those who are defiled, so God cleanses Israel.[4]

But who should go to whom? Does the Mikvah go to the defiled person, or does the defiled person go to the Mikvah? It is obvious that the defiled person must go to the Mikvah and immerse himself in it. When God cleanses Israel, it must also be in this manner.

God thus said to Israel, "When you pray, you must go to the synagogue in your city.

"If you cannot pray in the synagogue, you should pray in the fields. If you cannot pray in the fields, you should pray in your home. If you cannot pray in your home, you should pray in your bed. If you cannot pray in your bed, you should meditate in your heart."

It is thus written, "Speak in your heart, on your bed, and be still" (Psalms 4:5).

Midrash Tehillim 4:9.

Obligation

The people of a city can compel one another to build a synagogue and to buy a Torah. . . .

Tosefta, Bava Metzia 11:12.

Wherever ten Jews live, they must set up a building where they can come together at all time to pray. Such a place is called a *Beth Kenesseth* (House of Assembly; Synagogue).

Maimonides,
Yad Chazakah, Tefillah 11:1.

Beginnings

From the time of Moses until the Great Assembly, the Divine Presence was revealed where sacrifice was offered, and prophecy still existed in Israel. The prayers and blessings of each individual were heard by God. . . .

In my opinion, this is the reason why Jews did not gather morning, afternoon and evening, in a special place to pray during those times, but each one prayed alone, wherever he happened to be. It is for this reason that in the entire Bible we do not find any mention of congregational prayer. It was only after the destruction of the Temple that the Great Assembly composed the Eighteen Blessings, as well as santifications that required a minimum of ten men.

Moses may have ordained that the Torah be read each Monday and Thursday, and this is among the things that require ten men.[5] Still, there was no standard order of prayer for all, and each one would pray in his own words.

It therefore appears that each individual would pray by himself in a place that he set aside, and his prayer was acceptable as that of a congregation. This was because the Divine Presence was revealed in the place of sacrifice.

It is possible that even from the time of Moses people would congregate in the synagogues to hear the Torah reading. At such times, they may also have prayed together as a congregation, each in his own words. But there was no reader's repetition, and no special form, since each individual knew exactly how to pray for what he needed.

Rabbi Moshe of Trani (1505–1585),
Beth Elokim, Yesodoth 38 (204a).

Chapter 7

ALONE WITH GOD

At Home

There were great people who could not worship in the Holy Temple at all times. They used to pray at home, and God would count it as if they had prayed in the Holy Temple.

Talmud Yerushalmi, Berakhoth 4:4.

Spontaneous Prayer

The Great Assembly composed prayers that are the same for all Israel, as well as an order of service that all should say. Still, each individual must pray to God spontaneously for whatever he needs.

One should not merely trust in his diligence and intellect, for no matter what he thinks, "the counsel of God is what will stand."

For every endeavor, one should therefore pray to God, expressing himself in any way he can. After praying, one can engage in the endeavor, trusting that God will help him.

Rabbi Isaiah Horowitz (1556–1630),
Shnei Luchoth HaBrith (Sheloh),
Inyan Sefer Torah (2:216b).

One must meditate and pray to God in his native language. This is how prayer began. The main form of prayer was an expression of the heart before God in each individual's own words.

Maimonides speaks of this in the beginning of his Code on Prayer.[1] He states that this was originally the main form of prayer, before worship was formalized by the Great Assembly. It was only then that a formal order of prayer was introduced.

But even according to the law, the original form of prayer is still the most important. Even though we follow the order of worship ordained by the Great Assembly, personal prayer, as it originally existed, is still the most beneficial.

Make a habit of praying before God from the depths of your heart, using your own words, in whatever language you know best. Ask God to make you truly worthy of serving Him. This is the essence of prayer.

Rabbi Nachman of Breslov (1772–1810),
Hasidic Master,
Sichoth HaRan 229.

The Path of Saints

Spontaneous personal prayer is the highest level of worship, and is most beneficial. You should set aside a certain time to be alone in a room or in the fields, expressing your thoughts before God. Make use of arguments and persuasion, with words of grace, longing and petition, supplicating God and asking that He draw you to serve Him in truth.

Such prayer should be in the language that you normally speak... It is difficult to express your thoughts in Hebrew, and your heart is not drawn to the words. We do not normally speak Hebrew, and are not accustomed to expressing ourselves in this language. In the language that you normally use for conversation, it is much easier to express yourself, and it is more likely that you will experience true contrition. The heart is drawn after your native language, since it is most familiar.

In your everyday native language, you can express all your thoughts, conversing with God and talking out everything that is on your heart. This can involve regret and repentance for the past, or requests and supplications to come truly close to God from this day forward. Every person can express his own thoughts, each one according to his level.

You should be very careful with this practice, accustoming yourself to do it at a set time each day. The rest of the day should then be filled with joy.

This is a very great practice. It is the best possible advice, including many things. It is good for everything that may be lacking in your relationship with God. Even if you are completely removed from God, you should still express your thoughts to Him, and ask that He bring you back.

Even if your lips are sealed and you cannot open your mouth to God, you can still prepare yourself to do so. Even getting ready to speak to God is in itself very good. Even though you cannot speak to Him, you long and yearn to do so—and this itself is very good.

You can even make a prayer of this. You can cry out to God that you are so far from Him that you cannot even speak. Ask Him to have mercy on you and open your lips so you should be able to express your thoughts to Him.

You should be aware that many great, famous saints said that they only reached their high level though this practice of personal prayer. If you have wisdom, you will understand the importance of this practice, and how it can elevate one higher and higher. Yet, it is something that can be done by every individual, great and small alike. Eveyone can observe this practice and reach the highest levels. Happy is he who does so.

Likutei Moharan B 25.

The Untrodden Path

There are many prayers, supplications and petitions that have already been composed. The Destroyers and Denouncers know of them all, and lie waiting to ambush these prayers.

You can travel on a well trodden path, known and publicized to all. But murderers and robbers also know of this highway, and lie in wait there. But when you travel on an untrodden byway, taking a route that is as yet unknown, robbers are ignorant of your movements.

The same is true here. Your spontaneous prayers before God are like a new route. They are prayers that have been composed in your heart, and are now being expressed for the first time. Therefore, no Denouncers lie in wait for these prayers.

Still, your own prayers are not enough. You should also be very careful to say all the regular services and prayers.

Likutei Moharan B 97.

Alone With God

Among the works of the saintly, godly Kabbalist, Rabbi Yitzchak Luria Ashkenazi, of blessed memory, in a text called *Beth Midoth* ("House of Attributes")—but not the *Beth Midoth* that has been published—I found the following:

"All the discussion regarding fasting and self-mortification found in the earlier texts only apply to one who is not steadily involved in the Torah. But when a person's main occupation is Torah, and when he knows wisdom and fears God, he should not weaken himself and diminish his studies. This then is his rectification:

"One day each week, separate yourself from all people, and meditate, alone with God. Bind your thoughts to Him, just as if you were speaking before Him on the day of judgment. Speak to God softly, like a slave to his master, or a child to his parent."

At the end of a text copied by the eminent Rabbi Shmuel bar Avraham Shkiel, of blessed memory, in Acco from a manuscript written by Rabbi Moshe [Nachmanides], light of the exile, I found a similar concept. These are the author's own words.

"On Sunday, the fourth day of Iyar, I embarked on a journey by sea. On the Sabbath, the tenth of Iyar, in the year 5025 (1265 c.e.), we experienced a great storm at sea with howling winds . . .

"At that time I made a vow that I would meditate each year on the tenth of Iyar. I would not see any human being on that day, but would pray and study, all day by myself. Just as I had had none other than God to help me, so I would see no other man on that day. . . .

"On Saturday night, the third day of Sivan, I arrived in peace and disembarked at Acco. I had been saved from destruction and had reached the Land of Israel. I vowed that this day would be a day of joy . . . for me and my family for all generations. . . ."

In many other texts, we find that meditation, isolation, and attachment to God, were practiced by the saints of Israel.

Rabbi Elazar Azkari (1522–1600),
Sefer Charedim, Tshuvah 3 (p. 214).

Meditative prayer is the root of all. It is a concept that is very great and high, making one worthy of all holiness. . . .

When one prays in this manner, he becomes attached to God, even with regard to his bodily needs.

Rabbi Chaim Yosef David Azulai,
The Chida (1724–1806),
Avodath HaKodesh, Tziporen Shamir 51.

Conversing with God

Converse with God, and consider carefully what is your purpose in life. Delve into yourself, and beg God to help you find Him. Use whatever language you speak best, and argue with God, petitioning Him in every way....

If you set aside a time each day to converse with God, you will be worthy of finding Him. You may do this for days and years with no apparent effect, but in the end you will reach your goal.

Rabbi Nachman of Breslov (1772–1810),
Sichoth HaRan 68.

Tranquility

It is not easy to compose yourself for a given time each day, reviewing your life and regretting what you must. Not everyone can have such mental tranquility each day. The days pass and are gone, and you find that you never once had time really to think.

You must therefore make sure to set aside a specific time each day to review your life calmly. Consider what you are doing, and ponder whether it is worthwhile to devote your life to it.

A person who does not meditate cannot have wisdom. He may be able to concentrate occasionally, but not for any length of time. His power of concentration remains weak and cannot be maintained.

If a person does not compose himself, he also does not realize the foolishness of the world. But when a person develops a relaxed and penetrating mind, he can be aware of what is meaningless.

Sichoth HaRan 47.

Fields of Grass

It is best to meditate and pray in the meadows outside the city. Go to a grassy field, for the grass will awaken your heart.

Sichoth HaRan 227.

When you pray in the field, all the grasses enter into your prayers. They help you and give you strength to pray.

Rabbi Nachman of Breslov,
Likutei Moharan B 11.

A Room

It is very good to have a special room set aside for Torah study and prayer. Such a room is especially beneficial for meditation and conversation with God.

It is very good even to sit in such a room. [The atmosphere itself is beneficial, even if you sit there and do nothing].

Even if you do not have a special room, you can still seclude yourself and converse with God.

You can create your own "special room" under your prayer shawl. Just drape your *Tallith* over your eyes and converse with God as you will.

You can also seclude yourself with God in bed under the covers. This was King David's custom, alluded to in the psalm, "I pray every night on my bed in tears" (Psalms 6:7).

You can also converse with God while sitting before an open book. Let others think that you are merely reading or studying.

There are many other ways in which you can accomplish this if you truly want to express your thoughts to God. Above all else, this is the root and foundation of holiness and repentance.

Rabbi Nachman of Breslov,
Sichoth HaRan 274, 275.

In Time of Trouble

It is written, "And I supplicated myself to God at that time to say" (Deuteronomy 3:23). What did Moses mean when he said, "to say?"

Rabbi Azariah said: This teaches us that in future generations people should pray in time of trouble. Although God had just told Moses, "You shall not cross over the Jordan" (Deuteronomy 3:27), he still immediately began to pray.

Midrash, Devarim Rabbah 2:6.

A Commandment

It is a commandment of the Torah to cry out and sound the horn when any trouble comes upon the community. It is thus written, "For the enemy who attacks you, you shall sound the trumpets" (Numbers 10:9). When any misfortune strikes, such as famine, plague, or locust, you shall cry out and sound the horn.

This is one of the ways to repent. For when misfortune comes and the people cry out and sound the horn, they all realize that it came because of their evil deeds. It is thus written, "Your iniquities have turned away [these things, and your sins have withheld good from you]" (Jeremiah 5:25). Such prayer causes the misfortune to be taken away.

But if the people do not cry out and sound the horn, this indicates that they consider their misfortune to be a natural occurrence and a mere accident. This results in an insensitivity that causes them to adhere to their wicked ways. Their misfortune then brings on still more tragedy.

It is thus written, "If you walk with Me in chance . . . then I will also walk with you in the fury of chance" (Leviticus 26:27,28). That is, I will bring troubles upon you so that you should repent. But if you consider them to be mere "chance," then I will bring such "chance" upon you with fury.

Maimonides,
Yad Chazakah, Taanioth 1:1–3.

Chapter 8

SERVICE OF THE HEART

Habit and Devotion

Rabbi Shimon said, "Be careful to recite the Sh'ma and prayer, but when you worship, do not make your prayer a habitual task, but mercy and supplication before God . . . and do not be evil in your own eyes."

Mishnah, Avoth 2:13.

Since one repeats the same service three times a day, it is very easy for it to become habitual, with his lips speaking and his heart absent. . . . [Rabbi Shimon] therefore warns that even though one must be careful to recite the daily service, it must not be a habitual task devoid of meaning. Every prayer must be a supplication, as if one were pleading for his life before an all powerful king. . . .

The saying concludes, "Do not be evil in your own eyes." Do not think that because of your sins it will be impossible for you to put true feeling into your worship. If you concentrate deeply, every day's worship will be a new experience.

Rabbi Sh'muel Ucedah (1540–1604),
Midrash Sh'muel ad loc.

Supplication

Rabbi Eliezer said, "If one makes his worship a habitual task, his prayer is not a supplication."

Mishnah, Berakhoth 4:4.

Kavanah

Rabbi Yose ben Chanina said: It is written, "Hannah spoke in her heart" (1 Samuel 1:13). This teaches that prayer requires *Kavanah* (concentration).

Talmud Yerushalmi, Berakhoth 4:1.

Rabbi Abahu said in the name of Rabbi Eliezer, "Do not pray as if you were reading a letter."

Talmud Yerushalmi, Berakhoth 4:4.

Toward Heaven

When one prays, his heart should be directed [toward heaven].
Abba Shaul said: This is alluded to in the verse, "You will direct their heart, You will make Your ear listen" (Psalms 10:17).

Tosefta, Berakhoth 3:6.

All Your Heart

It is written, "Serve Him with all your heart" (Deuteronomy 11:13). This teaches that when one prays, his heart should not be divided.

Midrash Lekach Tov ad loc.

One's entire heart should be filled with the words of his prayer.

Rabbi Chaim of Volozhin (1749–1821),
Nefesh HaChaim 2:1.

Body and Soul

Prayer and praise of God involve both the heart and the body. Divest your body of all activity, both for this world and the next, and empty your heart of all thoughts that will disturb your prayer. . . .

Keep in mind to whom you are directing your prayer, what you seek in it, and concentrate on the words that you utter before your Creator.

The words on your tongue are the shell, but your thoughts are the fruit. Prayer is the body; concentration is the spirit.

If you pray while your heart is involved with other thoughts, your prayer is like a body without a soul, like a shell without fruit. Your body is there, but your heart is absent.

This concept is found in Scripture: "These people draw near with their mouth—they honor Me with their lips, but their heart is far from Me" (Isaiah 29:13).

The following parable is appropriate:

A servant's master comes to visit his house. The servant instructs his wife and household to honor the master and do all that he desires. But then the servant himself ignores his master; he is totally involved in his own enjoyment. He does not serve his master or honor him personally in any way. The master is naturally angry, and he rejects all the service and honor, throwing it all back in his servant's face.

[The mind is the person, while the tongue and limbs are merely members of his household]. When a person prays and his heart and mind are empty of all thoughts of prayer, God does not accept the service of his limbs and the motions of his tongue.

At the end of the Amidah, we say, "May the words of my mouth and the meditation of my heart before You be accepted" (Psalms 19:15). If a person thinks of any worldly thing during his prayers, whether permissible or forbidden, and then ends by asking acceptance of, "the meditation of my heart before You," he is scoffing God. He is pleading that he has spoken before his God with his heart and mind, while his heart and mind were actually absent. How can he ask God to accept such a prayer?

Rabbi Bachya ibn Pakudah (1050–1120),
Chovoth HaLevavoth, Cheshbon HaNefesh 3:9.

Filling the Mind

Religious activity such as worship . . . serve exclusively to fill our minds with God's commandments and free them from worldly affairs. It is in this manner that, as it were, we communicate with God, undisturbed by anything else.

When some people pray, they merely turn their faces to the wall and make motions with their lips, but their minds are completely devoid of all thoughts of what they are saying. . . . Such people may as well be digging in the ground or chopping wood, since they do not reflect on the nature of their acts, Who commanded them, and what is their object. This is not the way to attain the highest performance.

*Maimonides (1135–1204),
Moreh Nevukhim 3:51.*

Birds

Prayer should not be an obligation of the body alone. It is easy to stand in prayer for a certain time each day. But if you do not concentrate in your heart, how is your prayer any different than the mindless chirping of birds?

*Rabbi Yitzchak Arama (1420–1494),
Akedath Yitzchak 58 (3:17a).*

Better Little

It is better to pray a little with concentration, than to pray much without feeling. . . .

It is better to praise God with few words and without hurry, than to rush and say many praises.

*Rabbi Yehudah HeChasid (1149–1217),
Sefer Chasidim 315.*

One Blessing

When one worships, his heart must concentrate in all [the blessings of the Amidah]. If he cannot concentrate in them all, he should at least concentrate in one.

Which one? Rav Safra said in the name of a scholar of the school of Rabbi, "In [the blessing of] the Patriarchs, [which is the first blessing in the Amidah].

Talmud, Berakhoth 34b.

Passion

It is written, "From my flesh, I shall see God" (Job 19:26).

My master [the Baal Shem Tov] exlained that physical coupling cannot take place without arousal, passion and joy. The same is true of spiritual coupling.... If prayer is to bear fruit, it must be in a state of arousal, passion and joy.

Rabbi Yaakov Yosef of Polonoye (1704-1794),
Ben Porat Yosef 19d.

Free Samples

The Baal Shem Tov gave the following example:

A person comes into a store where they sell many types of delicacies and sweetmeats. The first thing that the storekeeper does is give him a sample of each kind, in order that the customer should have an idea what to buy. When he tastes it and sees how good it is, he wants to sample more. But the storekeeper says, "You have to pay for what you take. We do not give away anything for free."

The "free sample" is the Light that a person experiences when he begins to draw close to God. Through this taste of light, he should subjugate all evil and bring everything back to the good. This is the "free sample" that he is given, so that he will realize the taste of true worship. A taste of this remains after the light is withdrawn, so that he will know what to seek.

Rabbi Yitzchak Isaac of Komarno,
Chumash Heichal HaBracha, Otzar HaChaim, Naso 33c.

Attachment

Our main link to God is through words—words of Torah and prayer.

Every single letter in these words has an inner spiritual essence. You must attach your thoughts and innermost being to this essence....

When you draw out a word and do not want to let it go, you are in such a state of attachment to God.

Rabbi Israel Baal Shem Tov (1698-1760),
Kether Shem Tov 44.

Every word of prayer is a complete concept. You must therefore place all of your feeling into it. If you do not, it remains incomplete.

Rabbi Israel Baal Shem Tov,
Tzava'ath HaRivash.

You can sometimes pray very fast. This is because the love of God is burning in your heart very strongly. The words then leave your lips of their own accord...

When you attach yourself on High, you can be worthy of being lifted still further by the very same prayer. Our sages thus teach, "When one comes to purify himself, he is helped from on High."[1]

Through such prayer, you can bind your thoughts on High. From the power of such prayer, you can then reach even higher levels. Then, even when you are not praying, you can be attached to the spiritual.

Tzava'ath HaRivash.

Soul

Sometimes you can worship in thought, with your soul alone....

Sometimes you can pray with love and awe and with great intensity without moving at all. Someone else looking on would think that you are merely reciting the words without any feeling whatsoever. For when you are very closely bound to God, you can serve Him with great love, with the soul alone.

This is the best type of worship. It moves quickly to bring you closer to God than prayer that is outwardly visible. This prayer is all inside, and cannot be grasped by the evil Husks.

Tzava'ath HaRivash

Lights

Rabbi Israel Baal Shem Tov said that a person can read and see lights in the letters, even though he does not follow the proper punctuation [he does not understand fully what he is reading]. Since he is reading with great love and enthusiasm, God does not pay attention to the fact that he may not be reading correctly.

This is like a child who is very much loved by his parents. Even though he cannot speak well, his parents have great delight when he asks for something.

Rabbi Dov Baer (1704–1772),
The Maggid of Mezrich,
Likutim Yekarim 3.

Before Whom You Stand

When Rabbi Eliezer became ill, his disciples came to visit him. They said, "Rabbi, teach us the ways of life, so we will be worthy of life in the World to Come."

He said, "Respect the honor of your friends . . . and when you pray, know before whom you stand."

Talmud, Berakhoth 28b.

Rabbi Chana bar Bizna said in the name of Rabbi Shimon Chasida: When you pray, see yourself as if the Divine Presence is in front of you. It is thus written, "I have placed God before me at all times" (Psalms 16:8).

Talmud, Sanhedrin 22a.

Before the King

Arouse your concentration and remove all disturbing thoughts from your mind, so that when you pray, your thoughts will be pure.

If you were speaking to an earthly king, who is here today and tomorrow in the grave, you would be careful with your words, concentrating on each one, lest you say something wrong. When you pray, you are speaking before the King of kings, the Blessed Holy One. You must concentrate all the more. God probes all thoughts, and before Him, thought is the same as speech.

Pious men of deed used to meditate and concentrate in prayer until they divested themselves of the physical. They attained a spiritual strength almost on the level of prophecy.

Rabbi Yaakov ben Asher (1270–1343),
Tur, Orach Chaim 98.

From the Depths

Rabbi Hezekiah opened with the verse, "From the depths I call You O God" (Psalms 130:1). Whoever prays before the Holy King must worship and pray from the depths of his heart. His heart must be perfect with the Blessed Holy One, and he must concentrate with his heart and mind. [This is the meaning of, "From the depths I call You]."

But King David had already said, "I sought You with all my heart" (Psalms 119:10). Why did he have to reiterate, "From the depths?"

This teaches us that every person who petitions the King must direct his mind and will to the Root of Roots, so as to transmit blessing from the greatest depths. Blessing then flows outward from the Source of all.

Zohar 2:63a,b.

Words and Letters

When you utter a word of prayer, meditate on the word, with its form and letters. Have in mind that with that word, you can increase the strength of holiness, make it fruitful, and enhance the light of the supernal universes.

Prayer is therefore called, "that which stands in the highest places."[2] Each word, with its actual form, is a universe on High. One can elevate each word to its source and root, and thus accomplish wondrous rectifications.

Rabbi Chaim of Volozhin (1749–1821),
Nefesh HaChaim 2:13.

Heart

At the Red Sea, the people first purified their hearts, and only then did they sing out to God. It is thus written, "They believed in God and in Moses His servant" (Exodus 14:31), and only after this, "Then sang Moses and the children of Israel" (Exodus 15:1).

Each individual must first purify his heart, and only then should he pray.

Midrash, Sh'moth Rabbah 22:3.

It is written, "You hear prayer, to You shall all flesh come" (Psalms 65:3). The verse does not say "all men," but "all flesh." This teaches that one's prayer is not heard unless he makes his heart like flesh.

Midrash Tehillim 65:2.

Self Motivation

Rabbi Yose and Rabbi Hezekiah were going to see Rabbi Shimon in Kapudkeia. Rabbi Hezekiah said, "It is taught that a person should first offer praise to God, and then pray. But if a person's heart is troubled and he wants to pray, or if he is disturbed and cannot offer praise, what should he do?"

Rabbi Yose replied, "If one's heart and mind cannot concentrate, should God's praise be reduced? Let him offer praise to God, even though he cannot concentrate, and let him then pray."

Zohar 1:243b.

There are times when you feel that you cannot pray. Do not give up trying that day. Instead, strengthen yourself all the more and arouse your reverence for God.

A king in battle must clothe himself in battle gear [and cannot be recognized, as usual by his royal garments]. Those who are wise are able to recognize the king by his movements. Those who are less wise can still recognize the king, since he is always surrounded by extra guards.

When you cannot pray with feeling, you should realize that the King is there, but you are encountering His extra guards. Because of this extra protection, you cannot come close to the King.

You must therefore fortify yourself with reverence, great strength and additional intensity in order to break through to God. If you are successful, you will then be able to pray with the greatest possible feeling.

Rabbi Israel Baal Shem Tov (1698–1760),
Tzava'ath HaRivash.

You must force yourself to pray. Some people say that prayer must be totally spontaneous, without being forced, but they are wrong. You must force yourself to direct all your power into your prayer.

Nevertheless, when you pray with true devotion, binding thought to word and listening carefully to your own words of prayer, then strength will automatically enter your worship. All your faculties will anticipate their being drawn into words of holiness. When you focus your mind on your prayers, this strength enters the words.

Merely concentrate on the words, and strength will enter your prayers without your having to force it.

Rabbi Nachman of Breslov (1772–1810),
Sichoth HaRan 66.

Sometimes your prayers may be devoid of enthusiasm. Still, you must compel your emotions and make your heart burn with the words.

A person sometimes works himself up and actually makes himself angry. People then say, "He is working himself up into a rage." You must do the same during prayer. Like the person working up a rage, you must work yourself up, and bring all your emotions into your worship.

Enthusiasm may be forced at first, but eventually it will become genuine. Your heart will burst aflame with God's praise, and you will be worthy of praying with real fervor.

Sichoth HaRan 74.

You will sometimes try very hard, and still not be able to pray. Never become discouraged. This is the most important rule of all.

Force yourself to say each word of the service. Recite it with the simplicity of a child just learning how to read, and simply say the words. In most cases, God will then touch your heart with a flame, and it will be aroused to pray with feeling.

Nevertheless, do not make a test of this. Deep inside, you are very far from true worship. Prayer is very high, even above the study of Torah. How can you consider yourself worthy of making a test of such a lofty concept?

Just do your part. Simply begin reading the words of the service... Listen to every word you utter, concentrate, and do not let your thoughts stray. Simply keep your mind on the words of the service.

Follow the order of the service, even without feeling. Continue word by word, page by page, until God helps you achieve enthusiasm and feeling.

Sichoth HaRan 75.

Extraneous Thoughts

It is taught in the writings of the Ari that the essence of one day's prayers is not the same as that of the next day.... Our sages therefore say, "If one's prayers are fixed, this is not a supplication."[3]

I heard from my master [the Baal Shem Tov] that this is evidenced by the extraneous thoughts that enter one's mind during worship.... These thoughts enter one's mind during worship in order that he should rectify and elevate them. The extraneous thoughts of one day, however, are not at all like those of the next. The evidence should be obvious to one who considers it.

Rabbi Yaakov Yosef of Polonoye (1704–1794),
Toledoth Yaakov Yosef, VaYakhel (Warsaw 1881, p. 150a).

We are taught, "When one comes to purify himself, he is helped from on High."[4] This is somewhat difficult to understand, for it does not seem to apply to all who wish to purify themselves.

Sometimes you may want to pray with great enthusiasm before God. You make many preparations so your prayers should be just right. Still, when you are in the depths of prayer, you are disturbed by extraneous thoughts.

You may wonder, where is this help from on High? You have made every possible preparation, cleansing your mind so you would pray in purity. Why then are you disturbed by such thoughts?

But actually, this itself is God's help ... God sends you these thoughts in order that you elevate them.... These thoughts do not come by chance, but in order that you elevate them to their Root.

You may have a thought involving some unworthy love or fear. You must push aside this thought and bind yourself to the love and fear of God completing your prayers with great enthusiasm. You can then elevate the Spark of holiness that is in that unworthy thought.

The thought itself is therefore the help given to you from on High.

Rabbi Dov Baer (1704–1772),
The Maggid of Mezrich,
Magid Devarav LeYaakov 232 (Jerusalem 1971, p. 78a).

You may be distracted by many disturbing thoughts when you pray. Ignore them completely.

Do your part and say all the prayers in order, ignoring all disturbing thoughts. Do what you must and disregard these thoughts completely.

These disturbing thoughts actually benefit our prayers. Without them, our prayers could not enter on High.

Extraneous thoughts disguise our prayers so that they are ignored by the Outside Forces. Our prayers are then not denounced and can enter on High.

God knows our innermost thoughts. We may be distracted, but deep in our hearts, our thoughts are directed only toward God. God is aware of this.

When you pray, your innermost thoughts are always directed toward God. He knows what is in your heart and sees this innermost desire. Even though it is disguised, He sees through it and accepts your prayer with love.

Rabbi Nachman of Breslov (1772–1810),
Sichoth HaRan 72.

Thoughts that disturb your prayers can be an atonement for your sins. . . .

When you are not suspicious of God and believe that He certainly wants to draw you close and accept your prayers—that the only thing that brings about these confusing thoughts are your own sins—when you are pained by these thoughts and flee from them with all your strength—this is an atonement for your sins.

If you were able to do this truly and fully, all your sins would be forgiven, and all troubling thoughts removed. This is alluded to in the Talmudic teaching, "One who sins and is ashamed of it, is forgiven for everything."[5]

Rabbi Nachman of Breslov,
Shivchei Moharan, Avodath HaShem 138.

Joy and Reverence

It is written, "Worship God with joy" (Psalms 100:2). But it is also written, "Worship God with reverence" (Psalms 2:11). If there is joy, how can there be reverence, and if there is reverence, how can there be joy?

Rabbi Evo said, "One should rejoice in his prayer, and have reverence for God."

Another explanation: One might think that joy should exclude reverence. It is therefore written, "with reverence."

Midrash Tehillim 100:3.

I heard from my master [the Baal Shem Tov] that in worldly matters, where there is joy there can be no reverence, and where there is reverence there can be no joy. But in worship, love always accompanies reverence.

Rabbi Yaakov Yosef of Polonoye (1704–1794),
Toledoth Yaakov Yosef, BeChukothai 127b.

Humility

Do not rise to worship except with a heavy head (Rashi: humility).

The first saints used to wait an hour before praying in order to direct their hearts to God.

Mishnah, Berakhoth 5:1.

Joy of Devotion

Do not rise to worship in the midst of conversation, levity, frivolity, or idle chatter, but only in the midst of the joy that comes when you observe a commandment.

Tosefta, Berakhoth 3:21.

Pray with great joy. This is certainly more acceptable before God than prayer with sadness and tears.

This can be understood with a parable. When a poor man asks something from the king, he is only given a small sum, no matter how much he cries. But a prince praises the king, and in the midst of this also makes his request. The king then gives him generous gifts, as befits a prince.

The Baal Shem Tov (1698–1760),
Tzava'ath HaRivash.

The root of all prayer is a joyous heart before God. It is thus written,

"Glory in His holy name, rejoice you hearts that seek God" (1 Chronicles 16:10). It is for this reason that King David accompanied all his prayers and psalms with the harp. This filled his heart with joy and the love of God.

Rabbi Yehudah HeChasid (1149-1217),
Sefer Chasidim 18.

Mysteries

Rabbi Shimshon of Kinon . . . would pray with the simple intent of a child and not involve himself in mysteries.

Rabbi Yitzchak ben Shesheth (1334-1408),
Teshuvoth Rivash 157.

I heard from my master [the Baal Shem Tov] that even after Rabbi Nehuniah ben Hakanah[6] had mastered all the kabbalistic meditations associated with prayer, he would still pray like a little child.

Rabbi Yaakov Yosef of Polonoye,
Kethoneth Passim (New York 1950, p. 436)..

Elevation

When you pray, have in mind to arouse the letters with which were created heaven and earth, all creatures above and below, and all universes. If you do this, then all the universes and all creation will join you in your worship.

When you do this, you arouse these letters, which are the lifeforce of all creation, and they join your prayers. Thus your thoughts can elevate all creation, and earth alike. . . .

The Baal Shem Tov once told his disciples, "You must even pray for a bird that might be flying by and singing."

Rabbi Zechariah of Jaroslaw,
Darkei Tzedek 39.

Spiritual Ascent

In prayer, you must place all your strength into the words, advancing from letter to letter until you completely forget the physical. Thinking of how the letters unite and combine with each other, you will have great delight. You can feel this delight even physically, and it is certainly a great spiritual delight.

This is the Universe of Formation, [the world of speech].

The letters then enter your thoughts, and you do not even hear the words that you speak. This is the Universe of Creation, [the world of thought].

You then come to the level of Nothingness, where all your senses and faculties are nullified. This is the Universe of Nearness, the attribute of Wisdom.

Rabbi Dov Baer (1704–1772),
The Maggid of Mezrich,
Magid Devarav LeYaakov 97 (Jerusalem 1971, p. 236).

Chapter 9

ADDRESSING GOD

Any Language

These may be said in any language:. . . . The Sh'ma, prayer, and the Grace after Meals. . . .

Mishnah, Sotah 7:1.

In prayer one seeks mercy, and he can express himself as he wishes.

Can prayer then be in any language? We are taught that Rabbi Yehudah said, "One should never pray for his needs in Aramaic. Rabbi Yochanan taught that the angels do not pay attention to it, since they do not recognize Aramaic."

There is no contradiction. A congregation may pray in any language, but not an individual.

Talmud ad loc. 33a.

Since one seeks mercy in prayer, he can pray in the language that he knows best.

An individual's prayer needs the help of angels, and therefore should not be in Aramaic. A congregation does not need such help, as it is written, "God does not reject the multitude" (Job 36:5). That is, He does not reject the prayer of a multitude.

Rabbi Shlomo Yitzchaki,
Rashi (1040–1105), ad loc.

The Sick

In the case of the sick, [one may also pray in any language,] since the Divine Presence is with him.

Rabbi Anan thus said in the name of Rav: How do we know that the Divine Presence supports the sick? It is written, "God will support him on his sickbed" (Psalms 41:4).

Talmud, Shabbath 12b.

When one prays for the sick, he does not need the angels to pay attention and bring his prayer inside the veil.

Rashi ad loc.

Angels

The holy angels do not recognize Aramaic. We cannot say that they do not know it, since we know that Gabriel taught Joseph the seventy languages, and one of these languages is Aramaic. But they know it and do not recognize it. They do not pay attention to it or heed it, for it is more repulsive to them than any other language.

Zohar 1:89a (Sithrei Torah).

Discussion

The Talmud seems to conclude that an individual's prayers should not be said in any language other than Hebrew. This is very surprising, since women have the same obligation to pray as men, and it is a universal custom for them to pray in other languages. According to this, they should not pray in any language other than Hebrew.

The French rabbis resolve this in the following manner. When an individual recites prayers that are usually said by the congregation, this is the same as a congregational prayer, and it can be said in any language. When Rabbi Yehudah says that one should not pray for his needs in Aramaic, he is speaking of spontaneous prayer, such as when one prays for the sick or any other personal trouble.

The service usually recited by the congregation, however, is always considered a congregational prayer, even if said at home. Therefore, if one does not know Hebrew, he can fulfill his obligation by praying in any language.

A congregation can pray in any language, since it does not require any angel as its advocate before God. An individual, on the other hand, requires such an advocate, as it is written, "If he has an angel as his advocate" (Job 33:23).

Rabbi Yonah Gerondi (1192–1263),
Commentary on Rif, Berakhoth 7a.

I do not see any difficulty here, since Rabbi Yehudah is only speaking of Aramaic, and not any other language.

This also answers the question of Tosafoth, how can we say that angels do not understand Aramaic, when they even know man's thoughts? But the meaning is that they despise Aramaic, and do not pay attention to it.

Rabbi Asher ben Yechiel (1250–1327),
Rosh, Berakhoth 2:2.

Aramaic is worse than other languages since it is a corruption of Hebrew.

Rabbi Yom-Tov Lipman Heller (1579–1654),
Maadanei Yom Tov ad loc. #7.

Hebrew

If someone who is Godfearing and does not know Hebrew approaches you ... tell him that he should learn the services in a language that he understands. Prayer is nothing but the heart's communication. If the heart does not understand what the mouth utters, what good is it? It is therefore best to pray in a language that one understands.

Rabbi Yehudah HeChasid (1149–1217),
Sefer Chasidim 588.

It is better to pray and recite the Sh'ma and its blessings in a language that one understands, rather than pray in Hebrew and not understand it. It is thus written, "The writ is delivered to one who is not learned, saying, 'read this please,' and he replies, 'I am not learned.' And God said, 'Since this people draw near, and honor Me with their lips and mouth, but their hearts are far from Me, and their reverence a mere habit'" (Isaiah 29:12,13). This refers to one who reads the service and prays, but does not know what he is saying.

Sefer Chasidim 785.

It is not fitting that we pray and weave the crown of the Life of worlds in any language other than Hebrew, the Holy Tongue with which the universe was created.

The only exception is the person poor in knowledge, who does not know Hebrew, he should express his thoughts before God Himself. God sees into the heart, and has more pleasure from contrite prayer in other languages than from prayer without feeling, even though it may be said in Hebrew. It is obvious that it is impossible to have feeling unless one understands what he is saying.

*Rabbi Menachem Azariah Da Fano
Kabbalist (1548–1620),
Asarah Maamaroth, p. 173a.*

If ten Jews do not know Hebrew, and do not have anyone who can say the Amidah in Hebrew for them, then one of them can act as a prayer leader and say the *Kaddish* and *Kedushah* in any language.

*Rabbi Shmuel Aboav (1621–1694),
Teshuvoth D'var Shmuel 321.*

In our times, since no one is capable of translating Hebrew with absolute accuracy, even one who does not understand Hebrew well and wants to say the service in another language, is admonished not to separate himself from the ways of the community. It is the custom of all Jewish communities from time immemorial to say the prayer service only in Hebrew.

One can fulfill his obligation even if he does not understand the service.... He can easily learn the general meaning of the prayers, even if he doesn't understand each word. If even this is too difficult, he should still pray with the congregation in Hebrew. He can later repeat the service in any other language that he understands.

*Rabbi Efraim Zalman Margolioth of Brody (1762–1828),
Yad Efraim, on Magen Avraham 101:5.*

There is a clear decision in the Talmud that one may pray in any language. This, however, only speaks of the minimal fulfillment of one's obligation.... It cannot be compared to praying in Hebrew, in the very same words that stand in the highest places of the universe.

Rabbi Chaim of Volozhin (1741-1829),
Nefesh HaChaim 2:13 in note.

Long and Short

A disciple descended before the pulpit in the presence of Rabbi Eliezer and prayed at great length. The other disciples said, "Master, see how profuse he is!" He replied, "Is he any more profuse than Moses, who prayed for 'forty days and forty nights' (Deuteronomy 9:25)?"

In another instance, a disciple descended before the pulpit in the presence of Rabbi Eliezer and prayed very briefly. The other disciples said, "Master, how brief he is!" He replied, "Is he any briefer than Moses, who prayed, 'O God heal her' (Numbers 12:13)?"

Talmud, Berakhoth 34a.

God told Moses, "There is a time to pray at length, and a time to be brief."

Mekhilta to Exodus 14:15.

When Moses prayed for all Israel, he prayed at length, but when he prayed for his sister, he was very brief.

Zohar 2:244b (Hekhaloth).

At Length

Rabbi Chanin said in the name of Rabbi Chanina: When one prays at length, his prayer does not return empty.

How do we know that? From Moses, as it is written, "[I fell down before God for forty days and forty nights...] and I prayed to God" (Deuteronomy 9:25,26). It is then written, "God listened to me at that time" (Deuteronomy 10:10).

Is this true? Rabbi Chiya, son of Abba, said in the name of Rabbi Yochanan: When one prays at length and scrutinizes it (Rashi: to see if it is answered), he will eventually suffer anguish in his heart. It is thus written, "Hope deferred makes the heart sick" (Proverbs 13:12).

There is no contradiction. One case speaks of praying at length and anticipating an answer, while the other speaks of praying at length and not anticipating an answer.

Rabbi Chama bar Chanina said: If a person sees that he prays and is not answered, he should pray again. It is thus written, "Look forward to God, be strong and of good spirit, and look forward to God" (Psalms 27:14).

Talmud, Berakhoth 32b.

Rabbi Levi said: It is written, "Even when you make many prayers [I will not hear]" (Isaiah 1:15). From here we see that when one makes many prayers he is usually answered. . . .

Rabbi Chiya said in the name of Rabbi Yochanan, and Rabbi Shimon ben Chalafta said in the name of Rabbi Meir: It is written, "It came to pass as she prayed much before God" (1 Samuel 1:12). From here we see that whoever prays much is answered.

Talmud Yerushalmi, Berakhoth 4:1.

Rav Yehudah said: Three things prolong a person's life. . . . prolonging worship.

Talmud, Berakhoth 54b.

How long must one stand in prayer? Rabbi Yehudah said, "Until his heart aches."

Midrash Tehillim 61:2.

Forty Days

Rabbi Berachiah and Rabbi Chelbo said in the name of Rabbi Shmuel ben Nachmani, "Moses did not leave over a single corner in heaven in which he did not pray." . . .

An ordinary person may pray for an hour or two. If he is exceptionally pious, he may pray for an entire day. But Moses prayed for forty days and forty nights.

Midrash Tehillim 90:6.

Brevity

Rav Huna said in the name of Rav, quoting Rabbi Meir; "A person's words should always be few before God."

It is thus written, "Do not rush your lips nor hurry your heart to speak a word before God; for God is in heaven and you are on earth, therefore, let your words be few" (Ecclesiastes 5:1).

Talmud, Berakhoth 61a.

The prayers of the righteous are brief.

Mekhilta on Exodus 15:25.

Knowing When

Moses knew the ways of his Master better than anyone else in the world. When he had to pray at length, he did so; and when he had to be brief, he was brief....

It is taught that whoever prays at length will suffer anguish in his heart. But at the same time it is also taught that whoever prolongs his prayers will have his days prolonged.

Sometimes a person is profuse when he must be brief. He then suffers anguish in his heart....

But there are other times when one must pray at length. Then when he does so, God accepts his prayer, and this is God's glory. His prayer is then a unification that creates bonds on High, increasing blessing both on High and down below.

Zohar 2:259b.

One Word

Make it a habit to seclude yourself in prayer, expressing your thoughts before God each day. If all you can say is a single word, it is still very good.

If you can only say one word, repeat it over and over again. Even if you spend many days repeating this word, it is also good.

Repeat the word innumerable times. God will eventually have mercy and open your lips so that you will be able to express yourself.

Rabbi Nachman of Breslov (1772–1810),
Likutei Moharan B 96.

Extravagant Praise

An individual was praying in the presence of Rabbi Chanina. He said, "O God, great, mighty, fearsome, extolled, powerful, revered, strong, forceful, certain and honored."

Rabbi Chanina waited until he had finished, and said, "Have you now completed the praise of your Master? We say three praises ['the Great, Mighty and Fearsome']. If Moses had not uttered them in the Torah,[1] and if the Great Assembly had not included them in the Amidah, we could not even make use of these praises. How can you say so many praises?"

What is this like? A mortal king has millions of bars of gold, and someone praises him because he has silver. Would this not be an insult?

Talmud, Berakhoth 33b.

Rabbi Yochanan and Rabbi Yonathan were traveling to make peace in a number of cities in the south. They came to a certain place, and heard the cantor chant, "O God, great, mighty, fearsome, powerful and tremendous." They made him stop, saying, "You have no right to add to the coin minted by the sages in blessings."

Rav Huna said in the name of Rav: It is written, "The Almighty, whom we cannot find out, is excellent in power" (Job 37:23). We cannot find out the strength and power of the Blessed Holy One.

Rabbi Abahu said in the name of Rabbi Yochanan: It is written, "Is it told Him when I speak? If man says something, he is swallowed up" (Job 37:20). If a human being wishes to speak of God's greatness, he is swallowed up out of the world.

Rabbi Shmuel bar Nachman said: It is written, "Who can express God's greatness?" (Psalms 106:2). Only those who are like me and my companions.

Rabbi Abon said, "Who can express God's greatness?"

When Yaakov of Kfar Neburaya was in Tyre, he spoke on the verse, "To You praise is hushed, God in Zion" (Psalms 65:2). The sum of all praise is silence. A priceless jewel is blemished by praise.

Talmud Yerushalmi Berakhoth 9:1.

Rabbi Eleazar said: It is written, "Who can express God's greatness, proclaim all His praise?" (Psalms 106:2). Who is able to express God's greatness? Only one who can proclaim all His praise.

(Rashi: And since no mortal can proclaim all of God's praise, one should not compose praise beyond that ordained by the sages.). . . .

When Rav Dimi arrived, he said: In the Land of Israel they say, "A coin for a word, two for silence."

Talmud, Megillah 18a.

A Philosopher's Interpretation

Consider how repulsive and annoying the profusion of all these attributes was to the sages. They taught that if we followed our reason alone, we could neither compose nor utter any praise at all.

In order to provide some idea in people's minds, however, some words must be expressed. It is in this vein that our sages said, "The Torah speaks in the language of man."[2] We therefore describe God with adjectives that express elements of perfection to us.

The only three adjectives that are mentioned [are "great, mighty and fearsome"]. These are the only ones that we may use, and then, we should not use them as names of God, except when we read them in the Torah. Since they were prophets, the men of the Great Assembly were also able to introduce these expressions into the Amidah. This, however, does not give us the right to introduce any other adjectives describing God into our prayers.

The main lesson that we derive from this is that there are two reasons why we use these adjectives in our prayers. First, they occur in the Torah; and secondly, the Prophets introduced them into the Amidah. If not for the first reason, they could not be used at all. If not for the second, we would have no right to copy them from the Torah and recite them in our prayers. How then can we approve the use of numerous other adjectives?

We can also learn from this that we should not even use all the adjectives applying to God in the Bible for our prayers. The Talmud thus does not just say, "If Moses had not uttered them," but also a second condition, "And *Anshei Knesseth Hagedolah* came and introduced them in our prayers."

We cannot approve of the foolish people who, desiring to approach God, compose prayers and write hymns that are extravagant in praise and abundant in adjectives. Having absolutely no knowledge of the great important principles, not accessible to ordinary human intelligence, they describe God in terms that would be offensive even if applied to a human being.

Treating the Creator with undue familiarity, they speak of Him and describe Him with any expressions that they think proper. They are elaborate with such praise, thinking that they can thereby produce an effect on Him and influence Him.

If these people find phrases suited to their object in the words of the Prophets, they feel even more free to make use of them. Even though such texts require deep explanation, they make use of them in their literal sense, deriving new expressions, building numerous variations, and founding entire compositions upon them.

Such license is frequently encountered in the compositions of singers and preachers, as well as those who consider themselves able to write poetry. In many cases, such authors write things that are nothing less than heresy. The rest is such folly and absurdity that people should laugh at it, but at the same time they should feel grieved at the thought that such words can be uttered in reference to God. . . .

There is absolutely no need to use many adjectives in order to make God appear greater in your thoughts. You need not go beyond that which the men of the Great Assembly composed in our regular prayers and blessings. This is sufficient for all purposes—and even more than sufficient—as the Talmud quotes Rabbi Chanina as saying.

Adjectives found in the Bible should only be used when we are actually reading it. But one must keep in mind . . . that these are either descriptions of God's actions, or expressions implying the negation of their opposite. . . .

We will conclude with an explanation of Rabbi Chanina's wise words. As an example, he does not say, "A king possesses millions of gold bars but is praised for having hundreds." This would imply that even though God's perfections are greater than those ascribed to man, they are still of the same kind. This is not true at all. Rabbi Chanina speaks of "a king who has gold bars, and is praised for having silver." This implies that even though such adjectives express perfections with regard to us, this is not true with respect to God. In relation to Him, all such adjectives would be defects. This is distinctly suggested by his conclusion. "Would this not be an insult?"

Maimonides (1135–1204),
Moreh Nevukhim 1:59.

Blessings

Rabbi Yochanan and Resh Lakish both said: Whoever recites an unnecessary blessing violates the commandment, "You shall not take God's name in vain" (Exodus 20:7).

Talmud, Berakhoth 33a.

Beyond [the Eighteen Blessings] it is forbidden to speak of God's praise.

Talmud, Megillah 18a.

One may not include any additional praise in a blessing.

Rabbi Shlomo Yitzchaki,
Rashi (1040–1105), ad loc.

Codification

Some say that only adjectives such as [those mentioned in the Talmud] should not be said at length. But if one wishes to praise God for doing miracles and wonders, such praise is not forbidden.

In my opinion, however, even in such a case, one should not be overly profuse in adding praise above that composed by our sages. It is thus taught, "Whoever speaks too much of God's praise is torn out of the world."[3]

Alternatively, one can say that the prohibition only exists when one includes such praise in a blessing, since in doing so, one is making this an actual attribute of God. . . . But if one does not seal such praise with a blessing, there is no prohibition.

If one wishes to praise God at length and not become involved in this question, the best thing to do is to recite such praise in the form of Biblical verses. Since he is then merely reading scripture, no fault could be found.

Rabbi Yonah Gerondi (1192–1263),
Commentary on Rif, Berakhoth 23b.

The prohibition only applies to the Amidah, where one may not add anything to the form composed by the Great Assembly. It does not apply at all to spontaneous prayer.

Rabbi Asher ben Yechiel (1250–1327),
Rosh, Berakhoth 5:16.

It is forbidden to include any other praise in the Amidah. But if one wishes to recite hymns and praises all the rest of the day, he is praiseworthy.

> Rabbi Yehudah HeChasid (1149–1217),
> Sefer Chasidim 95.

We see that one may say as much as he desires in spontaneous prayer, since the entire Book of Psalms is filled with such praise.

> Rabbi Eliahu, the Gaon of Vilna (1720–1797),
> Gloss on Shulchan Arukh, Orach Chaim 113:9.

Just Beginning

King David composed 147 Psalms praising God, as it is written, "My mouth will speak the praise of God" (Psalms 145:21). He praised God with every part of his body, as he said, "All my bones will say, O God, who is like You" (Psalms 35:10)? There was not a limb in his body that did not utter God's praise.

But King David said, "Just because I have praised God in so many ways, have I then touched even a millionth of His praise. Now I am just beginning."

It is thus written [toward the end of the Book of Psalms], "I *will* exalt You, O My God, the King" (Psalms 145:1).

> Midrash Tehillim 104:2.

Above all Praise

It is written that God is "fearsome in praise" (Exodus 15:11). Rabbi Yudin said, "God is fearsome above all His praise. People may praise a mortal king, saying that he is rich and powerful, but he may be weak. They may say that he is merciful, but he may be cruel. But this is not true of God. However one praises Him, He is higher than all praise.

> Midrash Tehillim 106:2.

Including Everyone

Abaye said: One should always include himself with the community. He should therefore say, "May it be Your will, O God *our* Lord, that You bring *us* in peace...."

Talmud, Berakhoth 29b, 30a.

One should not say a short prayer in the singular, since when he says it in the plural form, his prayer is heard.

Rashi ad loc.

The Sick

Rabbi Yose said: When one comes to visit the sick, he should say, "May God have mercy upon you among all the sick of Israel."...

This is the same as Rabbi Chanina's teaching: One who prays for a sick person in his household should include him among all the sick of Israel.

Talmud, Shabbath 12a, b.

When one includes him among others, his prayer is heard in the merit of the multitude.

Rashi ad loc.

Answers

Some pray and are answered, while others pray and are not answered.

One is not answered because he is not concerned with his neighbor's pain and suffering. It is therefore fitting that he not be answered. He should have thought, "If I suffered the same anguish as this person, I would pray for it"—and it is written, "You shall love your neighbor as yourself" (Leviticus 19:18). Since he does not feel the pain of others, it is not fitting that his prayer be answered.

It is for this reason that all prayers and supplications are said in the plural form: "Heal *us*," "See *our* troubles."

It is thus written, "I will teach you mercy and I will have mercy on you" (Deuteronomy 13:18). We are also taught, "He who shows mercy is shown mercy."[4]

Rabbi Yehudah HeChasid (1149–1217),
Sefer Chasidim 553.

Plural Form

All prayers and blessings were composed in the plural form. For if they were said in the singular [and not answered for the individual,] they would appear to be vain prayers.

Sefer Chasidim 839.

A Single Body

All Israel collectively form a single body.... Therefore, even if an individual has never committed a particular sin, he should still confess it before God. For if another Jew has committed this sin, it is the same as if he himself had done so. It is also for this reason that the confession is in the plural form.

Even when a person prays for forgiveness at home, he must say, "we have sinned" in the plural. All souls are interconnected, and when any Jew sins, it is counted as if all Israel had participated.

*Rabbi Yitzchak Luria (1534–1572),
Kabbalist Master,
Likutei Torah, Taamei HaMitzvoth on Leviticus 19:18.*

Codification

When an individual takes upon himself to fast, he should say the prayer, "Answer *Us*" in the plural rather than in the singular. We are thus taught that "one should include himself with the community."

But if he adds personal supplications and petitions for his own needs ... it is proper for him to say them in the singular form.

*Rabbi Shlomo ben Avraham Adret (1235–1310),
Teshuvoth Rashba 25.*

Only prayer composed for the masses must be said in plural form.

*Rabbi Avraham Abele of Gombin (1635–1683),
Magen Avraham 110:10.*

How can one use the plural form when one is praying for himself? It is impossible that someone else in the world not have the same need.

Magen Avraham 565:1.

Recalling Patriarchs

It is written, "You plucked a grapevine out of Egypt" (Psalms 80:9). Why is Israel likened to a grapevine? Just like a grapevine rests on dead trees, so Israel, who live and survive, depend on the dead—the Patriarchs.

Elijah said many prayers on Mount Carmel, asking that fire should descend, as it is written, "Answer me, O God, answer me" (Kings 18:37). Still, he was only answered after he said, "O Lord, God of Abraham, Isaac and Israel" (1 Kings 18:36).

The same is true of Moses. When Israel sinned with the Golden Calf, he prayed on their behalf for forty days and forty nights, but he was not answered. But as soon as he recalled the dead, he was immediately answered. It is thus written, "Remember Abraham, Isaac and Israel" (Exodus 32:13), and immediately afterward, "God regretted the evil that He had said He would do to His people" (Exodus 32:14).

Midrash, Sh'moth Rabbah 44:1.

Voice

It is written, "Honor God with your talents" (Proverbs 3:9). If you have a pleasant voice, use it to lead the service.

Chiya bar Adda, Bar Kapara's nephew, had a pleasant voice. Bar Kapara used to tell him, "My son, use it to lead the service."

Pesikta DeRav Kahana (ed. Buber) 97a.

One who leads the service . . . must have a pleasant voice.

Talmud, Taanith 16a.

Whoever wishes to praise God with song must have a pleasant voice, that others wish to hear. Otherwise, he should not stand and raise his voice.

Zohar 1:249b.

Showing Off

If a cantor rejoices because he can praise God with a pleasant and beautiful voice, rejoicing with reverence, then he is praiseworthy. It is required that the one leading the service have a pleasant voice, as we find in the Talmud. . . .

But if the cantor's intent is to show off his voice and be complimented for it, he is despicable. Regarding his like, it is written, "She has raised her voice against Me; therefore I hated her" (Jeremiah 12:8).

In any case, it is not correct to draw out the service. In numerous places our sages teach us to make the service brief so as not to overburden the congregation.

Rabbi Shlomo ben Avraham Adret (1235–1310),
Teshuvoth Rashba 215.

Tears

Thus says God . . . "I have heard your prayer, I have seen your tears."

2 Kings 20:5.

You have counted my wanderings,
Place my tears in Your bottle,
are they not in Your book?

Psalms 56:9.

Rabbi Eleazar said: Since the Temple was destroyed, the gates of prayer have been sealed. It is thus written, "When I cry out and call for help, He shuts out my prayer" (Lamentations 3:8).

But even though the gates of prayer have been shut, the gates of tears are never shut. It is thus written, "Hear my prayer, O God, listen to my cry, You will not ignore my tears" (Psalms 39:13).

Talmud, Berakhoth 32b.

Rabbi Eliezer once decreed thirteen fasts for the community, and still rain did not fall. When the people began to leave, he said, "Have you prepared graves for yourselves?" The people's eye streamed with tears, and only then did rain fall.

Talmud, Taanith 25b.

There is no barrier that tears cannot penetrate.

Zohar 2:12b.

Tears and Joy

It is written, "Serve God with gladness, come before Him with song" (Psalms 100:2). No sadness may be shown.

What if a person feels pain and anguish? He cannot rejoice in his heart, and must seek mercy from the supreme King in the midst of his troubles. Should he desist from praying, since he cannot do so without sadness? He cannot make his heart rejoice and enter in gladness. What can such a person do?

We are taught that other gates may be opened or closed, but the gate of tears is never closed.

Tears are only the result of sadness and anguish. Those who oversee the ways of prayer break down all locks and bars, and bring in these tears. That person's prayer is then admitted before the Holy King.

Zohar 2:165a.

Throne of Mercy

All the people lifted their voices with weeping until their cry ascended on high and God heard the sound of their weeping. At that time, God's mercy was aroused, and He rose from His Throne of Judgment and sat on the Throne of Mercy.

Midrash, Esther Rabbah 9:5.

Stars and Constellations

When one weeps in his prayers, the stars and constellations weep with him, and his prayers are heard.

Rabbi Yehoshua Boaz (1487–1554),
Shiltei Giborim, on Mordechai, Berakhoth 4:5 (end).

Motions

Rabbi Yehudah said: This was the custom of Rabbi Akiba. When he prayed with the congregation, he would be brief, so as not to burden the congregation. But when he prayed by himself, he would be left in one corner and be found in the other—because of his bending and bowing.

Tosefta, Berakhoth 3:7.

One must shake during prayer, since it is written, "All my bones shall say, O God, who is like You" (Psalms 35:10). This is the custom of the righteous.

Midrash,
Quoted in Menorath HaMaor 3:3:1:13 (103).

King: I would like to ask you, why do Jews shake when they read Hebrew?

Rabbi: Some say that it is because of their emotional nature. But in my opinion . . . it was because many of them would read together, ten or more by one book, therefore their books were very large. Each of these ten would have to bend over to look carefully at the script, and he would then return. Since the book was on the ground, he would continuously lean over and return in this manner.

This was the original cause. Later it became a regular custom practiced by all.

Rabbi Yehudah HaLevi (1075–1141),
Kuzari 2:79,80.

It is written, "The people saw and they quaked" (Exodus 20:15). The Torah was given with fear, trembling and quaking. It is for this reason that people shake when they study.

Rabbi Yaakov ben Asher (1270–1343),
Baal HaTurim, ad loc.

Rabbi Yose said: . . . I asked [Rabbi Shimon], Why is it that of all the peoples in the world, only Israel shakes in prayer? When they study the Torah, they sway to and fro, and cannot remain still. From where is this derived, since they do not learn this from any other people?

He said to me, "This reminds me of a very high concept, but people are ignorant of it." He then sat for a while and wept.

He then spoke up and said: Woe is to those people who are without understanding, like the animals of the field. Through this alone, we can recognize the difference between the souls of the heathens and the holy souls of Israel.

The souls of Israel are hewn from a holy burning lamp, as it is written, "The lamp of God is the soul of man" (Proverbs 20:27). When this lamp is lit by the flame of the supernal Torah, it cannot remain still for even a moment. . . .

When a fire takes hold of the wick, the flame cannot remain still, but shakes from side to side. When an Israelite says a word of Torah, the lamp is lit, and he also cannot remain still, but moves to and fro, like the fire of a lamp.

Zohar 3:218b.

We are also taught that man is likened to a tree, as it is written, "Man is a tree of the field" (Deuteronomy 20:19). . . . The root is the first part of the tree, and similarly, the head, which is the abode of the soul, is the root of man. Just like the earth strongly grasps a tree's roots, so the heavens strongly attract man's head. It is for this reason that man stands upright.

When a person studies Torah and prays, he is bound to this spiritual influence, and his body shakes. When rain falls and waters the earth, a tree's branches move to grasp the earth, which is their element. Similarly, when God's holy spirit is revealed in man's intellect, his entire body receives lifeforce, and he shakes so as to receive this influence.

Rabbi Menashe ben Israel (1604–1657),
Nishmath Chaim 3:1.

Prayer is like attaching oneself with the Divine Presence. At the beginning of coupling there is much movement; and similarly, there is motion in prayer. Later, one can stand without moving, attached to the Divine Presence with a powerful bond.

Rabbi Dov Baer (1704–1772),
The Maggid of Mezrich,
Likutim Yekarim 18.

Rabbi Israel Baal Shem Tov said that when a person is drowning, and thrashes about to save himself, people will certainly not make fun of him. Similarly, when a person makes motions during his worship, one should not laugh at him. He is saving himself from drowning in the Waters of Insolence, which are the Husks coming to prevent him from concentrating in his prayers.

Likutim Yekarim 167.

The motion that one makes during prayer are the mystery of "hands writing secrets."

Rabbi Nachman of Breslov (1772–1810),
Sichoth HaRan 75 (end).

Concentration

Shaking in prayer causes one to lose concentration, while standing motionless enhances it. The verse, "All my bones shall say. . ." is speaking of other prayers, but not the Amidah, where one must stand motionless. We see in practice that standing motionless enhances one's meditative concentration.

Rabbi Isaiah Horowitz (1556–1630),
Sh'nei Luchoth HaBrith, Amud HaTefilah 2:203a.

Uplifted Hands

Whatever prayer or supplication may be made by any of Your people Israel ... let him spread his hands toward this Temple.

1 Kings 8:38.

I will bless You as long as I live,
In your name I lift up my hands.

Psalms 63:5.

Every day I call You, O God,
I spread forth my hands to You.

Psalms 88:10.

Spreading one's hands alludes to the fact that the *Shechina* is transmitting sustenance from on high.

Rabbi Moshe Cordovero (1522–1570),
Pardes Rimonim 15:3.

It is forbidden to stand for more than three hours with one's hands spread out to heaven.

Bahir 138.

Today

One should not pray with his hands raised, even though this was once the best way of worship. But now, since the nations of the world worship in this manner, we no longer do so.

Our sages likened it to the verse, "You shall not raise up a monument, which the Lord your God hates" (Deuteronomy 16:22). Even though this was something loved by God in the time of the patriarchs, when it became an idolatrous custom of the Canaanites, it became hated.

Rabbi Yisachar Baer Eilenberg (1551–1623),
Beer Sheva, p. 111a.

When a person stands in prayer, he must place his feet next to each other, and cast his eyes downward, as if he were looking at the ground.

His heart should be directed on High, as if he were standing in heaven. He should place his hands over his heart, right on left, standing like a slave before his master, with fear, awe and reverence.

Maimonides,
Yad Chazakah, Tefillah 5:4.

Kneeling

[Solomon] kneeled down on his knees ... and he spread forth his hands toward heaven.

2 Chronicles 6:13.

I fell on my knees and spread my hands toward the Lord my God, and I prayed.

Ezra 9:5.

To Me shall every knee bend.

Isaiah 45:23.

He kneeled on his knees three times a day, and prayed and gave thanks to his God.

Daniel 6:11.

One should kneel on his knees for an hour each day, with his hands spread out to heaven, and he should confess his sins to God, and ask for mercy and help in repenting.

Rabbi Moshe of Coucy (1192–1260),
Sefer Mitzvoth Gadol, positive 16 (99a).

Even though this is in itself a valid way to worship, we no longer worship on our knees, because of what the Talmud says in Taanith 14, that one should not pray in a fallen position unless he is as sure of being answered as Joshua.

Rabbi Yaakov Chagiz (1620–1674),
Halakhoth Ketanoth 1:94.

Chapter 11

HOW TO PRAY

Action and Prayer

It is written, "God said to Moses, 'Why are you crying out to Me? Speak to the children of Israel, and let them move!'" (Exodus 14:15).

Rabbi Eliezer said: The Blessed Holy One said to Moses, "My children are in trouble. The sea is closing upon them and the enemy pursues—and you are busy saying lengthy prayers! Why are you crying to Me?"

Mekhilta of Rabbi Yishmael ad loc.

When people are in trouble, one should not pray at length.

Rabbi Shlomo Yitzchaki,
Rashi ad loc.

Do not pray, even for necessities, if you can obtain them yourself. Our sages teach that if one has even enough bread for a single meal and asks, "What shall I eat?" he is a person of small faith.[1] Certainly, then, one should not pray to God when he can obtain food by himself.

David thus said, "Help us against the enemy, for vain is the help of man" (Psalms 60:13). If we cannot help ourselves in a natural manner, and all our own efforts are in vain, then God must help us against the enemy. But if we can help ourselves in a natural manner, then we should not ask God for miraculous intervention.

Rabbi Moshe of Trani (1505–1585),
Beth Elokim, Tefillah 1 (5a).

Small Things First

Rabbi Shimon said: How skillfull are the Israelites in enticing their Creator!

Rabbi Yudin said: They are like the Cuthites, who are expert beggars. One of them once went to a woman and said, "Please give me an onion." Upon obtaining this, he said, "What good is an onion without bread?" When she gave him bread, he said, "How can one eat without something to drink?" He thus obtained an entire meal.

[The righteous thus first ask for a small thing, and only then do they ask for more].

Midrash, VaYikra Rabbah 5:8.

Two Things at Once

In the days of Rabbi Shmuel bar Nachman there was a famine and a plague. The people said, "What can we do? It is impossible to pray for both. We will pray regarding the plague, and will tolerate the famine."

Rabbi Shmuel bar Nachman said to them: Pray for mercy regarding the famine, and when He grants mercy, it will be the living whom He will feed. It is thus written, "You open Your hand, and satisfy the wants of all *life*" (Psalms 145:16).

How do we know that we should not pray for two things at once? It is written, "We will fast and pray to our God for *this*" (Ezra 8:23). It is evident that there was other trouble, [but at that time they did not pray regarding it].

The sages of the west, in the name of Rabbi Chaggai derived it from another verse, "They pray for mercy from the God of heaven concerning this secret" (Daniel 2:18). It is evident that there was also something else to pray for.

Talmud, Taanith 8b.

When Rabbi Chaggai proclaimed a fast, he would say, "My brothers, even though you have many pains in your hearts, pray only for this."

Talmud Yerushalmi Taanith 4:3.

Codification

If a community has two troubles, they should only pray for mercy concerning one of them. . . . They should say, "Even though we have many troubles in our hearts, we have come to pray for this."

Rabbi Yosef Caro (1488–1575),
Shulchan Arukh, Orach Chaim 576:15.

But where there is only one trouble, one can mention other troubles as well. We find this in many *Selichoth* and *Piyyutim*.

Rabbi Avraham Abele of Gombin (1635–1683),
Magen Avraham 576:11.

Before Troubles Come

Rabbi Eleazar said, "Pray before troubles come."

Talmud, Sanhedrin 44b.

He said, "Honor your Physician before you need Him."

Talmud Yerushalmi, Taanith 3:6.

Even though God hears prayer in time of trouble, it is more acceptable before trouble arrives.

Rabbi Yitzchak Aboav (14th Century),
Menorath HaMaor 3:3:1:14 (104).

Say a psalm, and put it aside for when you need it.

Rabbi Nachman of Breslov (1772–1810).
Sichoth HaRan 271.

Vain Prayers

If one cries out regarding something that has already happened, this is a vain prayer.

For example, if one's wife is pregnant, and he says, "May she give birth to a son," this is a vain prayer.

Similarly, if one is coming from a journey and hears a cry in the city, and says, "May this not be my household," this is a vain prayer.

Mishnah, Berakhoth 9:3.

Give thanks for the past and pray for the future.

Mishnah, Berakhoth 9:4.

If one prays for the sex of his unborn child, is this a vain prayer? Do we say that supplication does not help?

It is written, "After that, [Leah] had a daughter, and she named her Dinah" (Genesis 30:21). Rabbi Yosef asked, "What is the meaning of 'after that'?"

Rav said: This was after Leah [was pregnant] and made a judgment (*Din*) of herself. She said, "Twelve tribes are supposed to emanate from Jacob. Six have come from me, and four from the handmaids, making ten. If this child is a male, then my sister [Rachel] will have even fewer [children] than one of the handmaids." The child was immediately changed into a girl. . . .

[This does not contradict our teaching, since] we do not consider miraculous acts.

Talmud ad loc. 60a.

Hidden Things

Rabbi Yitzchak said: Blessing only exists in things hidden from the eye. It is thus written: "God will command His blessing in your hidden stores" (Deuteronomy 28:8).

The house of Rabbi Yishmael taught: Blessing only exists in that which the eye cannot penetrate . . .

The Rabbis taught: One who goes to measure his grain should say, "May it be Your will O God that You send a blessing in the work of our hands." As he begins to measure, he should say, "Blessed is He who sends a blessing in this pile of grain."

If one has measured and then says the blessing, it is a vain prayer. Blessing does not rest on something that has been weighed, measured or counted, but only on that which is hidden from the eye. . . .

Talmud, Bava Metzia 42a.

Miracles

One day, the workers of Rabbi Yose of Yukrat were plowing in the field. It was getting late, and no food had been brought out to them. They complained to his son that they were hungry.

At the time, they were sitting under a fig tree. The son said, "Fig tree, fig tree, give forth fruit and let my father's workers eat." Fruit appeared on the tree, and they ate it.

Before long, his father came and said, "Do not be angry at me for being late. I was delayed because I had to do an important good deed." The workers replied, "May God feed you like your son fed us!" They then told him the whole story.

He said, "My son, you have bothered your Creator to bring forth figs before their time. You, too, shall die before your time."

Talmud, Taanith 24a.

Do not pray for the impossible. Even though God has the power, do not ask Him to alter the laws of nature. . . .

It is forbidden to pray that God should do something that would change the ways of nature. . . . as in the case of the son of Rabbi Yosi of Yukrat.

Rabbi Yehudah HeChasid (1149–1217),
Sefer Chasidim 794.

Do not ask God to do something that is impossible, as for a stillborn child to live, or to be transported to a far away land. Even though God can do this, it is still a vain prayer.

Sefer Chasidim 95.

Only pray for that which is fitting. Do not say that it is possible from God's viewpoint, since He can do everything. Also be sure that it is possible on your side, that you are able to receive the favor.

If it is something that you cannot accept because it is not in your nature, do not pray for it. You may want to pray that you become king of the world, since it is within God's power to grant this. Still, it is not in your nature to receive such a great favor. For the likes of this, it is not suitable to pray.

Rabbi Yosef Albo (1380–1435),
Sefer HaIkkarim 4:17.

The Sick

A person was fasting and praying that his friend should live. Just before the festival, a man came from his friend's town, and this person asked him, "How is my friend doing? I have been praying for him for many days now."

The man did not know what to answer, so he deferred and asked a sage, "What shall I do? If I tell him that his friend died, he will suffer on the festival. But if I do not tell him, he will fast and pray for him in vain."

The sage replied, "After the festival, have a slave or gentile inform him. But do not tell him now, so as not to diminish the festival."

Rabbi Yehudah HeChasid
Sefer Chasidim 801.

It is said that when Rabbi Zalman was in Neustadt, he would not permit them to say a public prayer for a sick person who was in another city, lest he had already died or recovered.

Rabbi Yaakov Moellin (1360–1427),
Sefer Maharil, Semachoth 83a.

We must dispute the opinion [of Rabbi Zalman]. As long as we have no proof to the contrary, we must assume that the patient is still ill and in need of our prayers.

Rabbi Shmuel ben David HaLevi (1624–1681),
Nachalath Shiv'ah, Teshuvah 39.

Generalities and Particulars

If you hear that people from a certain town are coming to do you evil, do not pray, "Save me from the people of that city." Rather, you should pray, "Save me from them and from all my enemies," since there may be others with them.

It is thus written, "Give this people into my hand" (Numbers 21:2). They did not know if they were Canaanites or Amalekites, so they prayed in general, mentioning "this people."

Rabbi Yehudah HeChasid,
Sefer Chasidim 789.

It is written [that Jacob prayed], "Save me from my brother Esau, for I am afraid, lest he strike me, along with mother and child" (Genesis 32:12). From here we see that one who prays must specify things properly ... and not speak in generalities.

Zohar 1:169a.

All Needs

It is written, "For this shall all the pious pray, in found time" (Psalms 32:6).

Rabbi Chanina says, "This refers to praying for a wife..."

Rabbi Nathan said, "This means that one should pray for Torah...."

Rabbi Nachman bar Yitzchak said, "This is for a good death...."

Rabbi Yochanan said, "This is for a grave...."

Rabba, son of Rav Shela, agreed and said, "There is a proverb, 'Pray for mercy until the last shovelful rests.'"

Talmud, Berakhoth 8a.

It is written, ["The young lions roar for prey,] seeking their food from God" (Psalms 104:21). This is Israel, who pray to God for their needs."

Midrash Tehillim 104:17.

Nothing happens to a person that is not decreed by God. It is thus written, "Shall there be evil in a city, and God not cause it?" (Amos 3:6).

Each person must therefore pray for all things that God decrees upon him, that it should come out for the sake of heaven. Be careful in prayer that you do not stumble.

Rabbi Yehudah HeChasid,
Sefer Chasidim 748.

Since everything comes from God, we have an obligation to pray to Him for all our needs. No matter what you need, at any time, say a short prayer and "cast your burden on God."

Rabbi Isaiah Horowitz (1556–1630),
Sh'nei Luchoth HaBrith, Tefillah (2:217a).

Food

Rabbi Yose opened with the verse, "You open Your hand and satisfy the desire of all life" (Psalms 145:16). Immediately preceding this it is written, "The eyes of all look toward You, and You give them their food on time."

Everyone in the world raises their eyes for this. All believers must pray to God each day for food.

Why? Because when one prays to God for his food, he brings a blessing to the tree which contains the food of all. Even when one has food, he must request it from God, praying for food each day. This brings about a blessing on high, this being the meaning of, "Bless God each day," (Psalms 68:20).

Zohar 2:62a.

Therefore, even if one is wealthy, he should still pray for his food.

Rabbi Avraham Abele of Gombin,
Magen Avraham 119:1.

All Things

Accustom yourself to pray for all your needs, whether it be livelihood, children, or healing. The best advice is to believe in God and pray to Him. God is good to all, healing, providing livelihood, and giving all you need.

Rabbi Nathan Shternhortz of Nemerov (1780-1844),
Likutei Etsoth, Tefilah 25.

You must pray for everything. If your garment is torn and needs replacing, pray to God for a new one. Do this for everything.

Make it a habit to pray for all your needs, large and small. Your main prayers should be for fundamentals, that God help you in your devotion, and that you be worthy of coming close to Him. Still, you should also pray even for trivial things.

God may give you food, clothing and everything else you need, even though you do not ask Him for them. But then you are like an animal. God gives every living thing its food without being asked. He can also give it to you in this manner.

But if you do not live through prayer, then you are like a beast. For a human being must draw all his necessities of life, only through prayer.

Rabbi Nachman of Breslov (1772–1810),
Sichoth HaRan 233.

The Trivial

Is it beneath your dignity to pray to God, even for a trivial thing?

Sichoth HaRan 233.

A Different Opinion

Do not pray for that which is not necessary. As it were, you then bother your Creator unnecessarily.

The acceptance of prayer is a miraculous thing, beyond the realm of the natural. If you have much merit, you can be saved through prayer.

Rabbi Moshe of Trani,
Beth Elokim, Tefillah 1 (5a).

The Unusual

When anything unusual happens, say a prayer regarding it. Thus, for example, if your wife gives birth to twins, pray that they both live.

Rabbi Yehudah HeChasid,
Sefer Chasidim 792.

Injuries

If you are sick, do not say that it is because of something you ate or drank, and not from God. Even if wicked people injure you, it is from God. It is thus written, "I have set each man against his neighbor" (Zechariah 8:10). It is likewise written, "Shall there be evil in a city, and God not cause it?" (Amos 3:6). [When Joseph's brothers found the money that Joseph had placed in their sacks,] they said, "What is this that God has done to us?" (Genesis 42:28).

You should therefore pray to God regarding all types of injuries, whether from heaven or from man.

Sefer Chasidim 751.

Formal Petition

Nachum of Medea said: One should pray for his needs [in the Amidah, in the blessing], "Who hears prayer." . . .

Rabbi Yehudah, son of Rav Shmuel bar Shelath, said in the name of Rav: Even though it is taught that one should ask for his needs in the blessing, "Who hears prayer," if one wants to add a prayer to any pertinent blessing [in the Amidah], he may do so.

Rabbi Chiya bar Ashi said in the name of Rav: Even though it is taught that one should ask for his needs in the blessing, "Who hears prayer," if one has a sick person in his house, he should pray for him in the blessing, "Who heals the sick." If he needs livelihood, he should pray for it in the blessing, "Who blesses the years."

Rabbi Yehoshua ben Levi said: Even though it is taught that one should ask for his needs in, "Who hears prayer," if one wishes to pray after the Amidah, he can say as much as is recited in the Yom Kippur service.

Talmud, Avodah Zarah 7b,8a.

When the Talmud says that one may add a short prayer in any blessing [of the Amidah] it is speaking of an occasional practice. It does not mean that one may make a regular daily practice of adding such a prayer There is no evidence to permit . . . any regular addition to the coin minted by our sages.

Rabbi David ben Shmuel HaLevi (1586–1667),
Turei Zahav, Orach Chaim 122:2.

Godly Things First

Do not ask for your own needs until you ask for those of heaven. Thus, in the Amidah, they first ordained prayers for knowledge, return to the Torah, and forgiveness of sins, and only then did they include prayers for worldly needs.

Rabbi Yehudah HeChasid,
Sefer Chasidim 752.

When you pray for your needs, your intent should not be that God give you riches, honors and physical enjoyment. Rather, ask that God give you your needs so that you should be better able to serve Him.

Rabbi Yehudah Loew (1525–1609),
The Maharal of Prague,
Nethivoth Olam, Avodah 2.

Self Improvement

It is written, "Be gracious to me, O God, be gracious to me, for in You will my soul take refuge" (Psalms 57:2).

"Be gracious to me," that I not stumble in sin. "Be gracious to me," that if, God forbid, I sin, "in You will my soul take refuge,"—I should be able to repent.

Midrash Tehillim 57:1.

If you pray for something that honors God, such as the ability to study Torah, and really pour out your heart, God will listen to your prayer, even if you do not have any merit.

Rabbi Yehudah HeChasid,
Sefer Chasidim 131.

At every moment, constantly have this prayer on your lips: "Master of the universe, direct me on the way of truth."

Rabbi Pinchas of Koretz (1726–1791),
Chasidic Master,
Midrash Pinchas 17 Jerusalem 1971, (p. 12a.)

One may ask, How can a person pray that God should bring him close to His worship? Many of the earlier saints composed such prayers, asking that they be saved from the Evil Urge, and come close to love and fear God. The Great Assembly likewise included the prayer, "Return us to Your Torah" in the Amidah.

At first, this seems difficult to understand, since we are taught, "All is in the hand of heaven, except the fear of heaven."[2] Since God gives such things over to our free will, how can we pray for them?

But actually, this itself depends on our free will. Without prayer, it is impossible to attain perfection, repulse evil, choose God, and attain what man must in this world through free will. One must make use of many prayers, supplications, and conversations with God, asking that he be worthy of approaching Him in worship. This is the main concept of prayer.

Rabbi Nathan Sternhartz of Nemerov (1781–1844),
Disciple of Rabbi Nachman of Breslov,
Likutei Halakhoth (Choshen Mishpat), (as adapted in Hishtapchuth HaNefesh, 93). Pikadon 3:7,9.

Conquering God

There are times when you must even conquer God. You may feel that God has rejected you because of your sins. You may think that you are still not doing His will. But remain strong and throw yourself before God. Spread your hands to Him and beg that He have mercy and let you continue to serve Him.

[It may seem that God is rejecting you, but cry out], "No matter what, I still want to be a Jew!" This is the way you conquer God. God has great joy when you conquer him this way.

Rabbi Nachman of Breslov (1772–1810),
Sichoth HaRan 69.

Help in Prayer

Rabbi Yochanan said: At the beginning [of the Amidah] one should say, "O God, open my mouth, that my lips may speak of Your praise" (Psalms 51:17).

Talmud, Berakhoth 4b.

This verse was not part of the Amidah when it was first composed by the Great Assembly. The verse, "O God, open my mouth," was only added later ... as a prayer that we should be able to pray.

In earlier generations, worship was pure, and such a prayer was not needed. But in the course of time, our hearts were reduced, and a special prayer was added that our worship be pure.

There are thus two concepts of prayer. One is prayer itself, and the other is a petition that we should be able to pray.

Rabbi Levi Yitzchak of Berdichov (1740–1809),
Kedushath Levi, VaEthchanan, p. 244.

It is written, "I set my face toward God in prayer and supplication" (Daniel 9:3). Is not prayer and supplication the same? But the righteous supplicate God that He should hear their prayers.

Midrash Tehillim 108:1.

It is written, "Hear my prayer O God" (Psalms 143:1). David said, "When I pray to You, I pray that You should answer me."

Midrash Tehillim 143:1.

Praying for God

It is written, "He will call Me and I will answer him, I am with him in affliction" (Psalms 91:15).

God said, "When trouble comes to Israel and they seek Me, they should make themselves partners with My glory, and I will answer them immediately. It is thus written, "He will call Me and I will answer him." Why? Because, "I am with him in affliction."

Rabbi Yudin provided the following parallel: A woman in childbirth became angry at her mother, and her mother went upstairs. She began screaming, and when her mother heard her voice, she also began to scream. Her neighbors asked, "Why are *you* screaming? Are you giving birth along with her?" She replied, "Is it not my daughter who is in pain? I cannot stand her cries, so I scream with her. My daughter's pain is also my pain."

Midrash Tehillim 20:1.

Levels

There are many levels of prayer, one higher than the next, as I have learned from my teachers and the sacred texts.

The lowest level of prayer is when a person prays for his own needs. This is the level of the masses. Regarding this it is written, "All flesh is grass, and all its kindness is like the clover of the fields" (Isaiah 40:6). It is also taught, "All the good that they do is only for themselves."[3]

A higher level is when one has in mind to rectify the needs of the Divine Presence. His own needs down below are then automatically rectified when their roots are rectified on High, since all things on High and down below parallel each other. Nevertheless, one should not have in mind that he will accomplish things for himself by rectifying things on High. If one does this, he is "tearing out his planting," and causing a separation. This I heard from my master [the Baal Shem Tov].

There is also a higher level than this. On this level, a person works to rectify things on High, without any thought of his own needs whatsoever. He does not even seek that his own requests be fulfilled. . . . This is the highest level, "serving God so as not to receive reward."[4]

Rabbi Yaakov Yosef of Polonoye (1704–1794),
Toledoth Yaakov Yosef, Sh'lach (Warsaw 1881, p. 287b).

A Drop in the Sea

Do not pray for your own needs, for then your prayer will not be accepted. But when you want to pray, do so for the Head. For whatever you lack, the Divine Presence also lacks.

This is because you are a "portion of God from on High." Whatever any part lacks affects the Whole, and the Whole feels the lack of the part. You should therefore pray for the needs of the Whole.

The Baal Shem Tov (1698–1760),
Tzava'ath HaRivash.

Think of your soul like part of the Divine Presence, like a drop in the sea. Then pray for the needs of the Divine Presence.

You can be sure that your prayer will benefit the Divine Presence. Then, if you are properly attached to the Divine Presence, this influence will also be transmitted to you.

When a person is happy, he unconsciously claps his hands. This is because his joy spreads through his entire body. The same is true of the Divine Presence. Each influence is transmitted to all of its parts.

Rabbi Dov Ber (1704–1772),
The Maggid of Mezrich,
Magid Devarav LeYaakov 66 (Jerusalem 1971, p. 156).

Think of yourself as nothing, and totally forget yourself when you pray. Only have in mind that you are praying for the Divine Presence.

You can then enter the Universe of Thought, a state that is beyond time. Everything in this realm is the same, life and death, land and sea.

... But in order to enter this Universe of Thought, you must totally disregard yourself and forget all your troubles.

You cannot reach this level as long as you attach yourself to physical, worldly things. For then you are bound to the division between good and evil, which is included in the seven days of creation. How can you then approach a level above time, where absolute unity reigns?

If you consider yourself to be "something" and ask for your own needs, God cannot clothe Himself in you. God is infinite, and no vessel can hold Him at all, except when a person makes himself like Nothing.

Magid Devarav LeYaakov 159 (p. 49a).

Good Soldiers

When you pray, your entire intent should only be to increase the strength of Holiness. A king's soldiers throw aside all their own needs and wants, willingly sacrificing all for the king's honor, conquering lands, and enhancing his reign. The upright person should likewise concentrate and meditate in prayer only to give strength to the holy universes on High.

With your voice, you should arouse the supernal Voice, transmitting from it blessing and light to all, removing the spirit of corruption from the world, and perfecting God's kingdom on earth. Do not think of your own wants or needs at all.

This is obvious in the entire Rosh HaShanah service, from beginning to end. It speaks only of God's glory, that the world should be rectified as it was before Adam's sin. The same is true of the daily prayers for the entire year. Even though their simple meaning appears to involve mundane needs, it is certainly clear to all who understand that the men of the Great Assembly intended more than this simple meaning.

The services were ordained to parallel the daily sacrifice. This sacrifice consisted of burnt offerings, where the entire sacrifice was offered to God, with nothing remaining for the mundane.

Even though the Talmud clearly states that one can add petitions regarding his own needs to the service, the intent should not be for one's own purposes. This is not the proper way for those upright in heart.

Actually, it is very surprising that one should pray to God to alleviate his suffering. In the practice of medicine, the physician often prescribes bitter medicines, and if necessary, may even amputate a limb so that the infection not spread. Should the patient beg that he not be given these medicines, or that his limb not be amputated? Is it not for this very reason that he went to the physician?

How can a person pray to God to remove his suffering? Is this suffering not a vital medication, to atone for one's sins? Our sages teach, "There is no suffering without sin."[5] If not for this suffering, how could one's sins be forgiven?

The main intent should therefore be for the needs of heaven. When Israel is in trouble, when they are repressed and subjugated, this is a desecration of God's name. They say, "These are God's people, and they were driven from their land" (Ezekiel 36:20). We must therefore pray and pour out our hearts before God regarding the desecration of His name. He will then do it only for the sake of His name.

The same is true of the anguish of the individual. Even though there is no desecration of God's name, when a person is in pain, there is also anguish on High, and one should pray regarding this. Our sages thus teach, "When a person is in pain, the Divine Presence says, 'My head aches, My arm aches...'"[6]

When a person feels so much suffering for the anguish of the Divine Presence that he cannot feel his own pain, this itself is an atonement for all his sins.

Rabbi Chaim of Volozhin, (1749–1821),
Nefesh HaChaim 2:11.

No Reproach

Levi decreed a fast, but no rain came. He prayed, "Master of the universe: You ascended and sit on High, and You do not have mercy on Your children." It then rained, but Levi became lame.

Rabbi Eleazer said: "Never reproach the One on High. A great man did this, and he became lame."

Talmud, Taanith 25a.

Rabbi Yochanan said, "God does not owe anything to any creature. Even Moses, master of all prophets, only came asking for a free gift.

Midrash, Devarim Rabbah 2:1.

God Knows the Heart

It is written, "Listen to my words, O God, understand my meditation" (Psalms 5:2). . . . King David said, "Master of the universe: When I have the strength to stand before You in prayer and express my words, listen to me. But when I do not have the strength, understand what is in my heart."

Midrash Tehillim 5:6.

If you are so ill that you cannot pray, at least say the prayers in your mind. It is thus written, "Speak in your heart, on your bed."

Rabbi Moshe Isserles (1525–1572),
Mapah, on Orach Chaim 94:6.

Like a Child

It is written, "Is Ephraim a darling son to Me, is he a dandled child? For as often as I speak to him, I will remember him still, therefore My heart yearns for him, and I will have compassion upon him" (Jeremiah 31:19). In the Midrash, one opinion states that a "dandled child" is like a two or three year old, while another opinion states that he is a four or five year old.[7]

The commentaries explain that even though a child of two or three cannot speak, but only makes signs and speaks broken words, his father still delights in his words and does what he requests. . . .

This gave me great encouragement. . . . Even when you cannot speak at all to God, and cannot express yourself well, it is still precious to God. Even if you only speak with gestures and broken words like a two or three year old, your Father still delights in it and often will help you find more eloquent words.

Rabbi Nathan of Nemerov (1780–1844),
Alim LiTerufah 254 (Jerusalem 1968 p. 217).

Chapter 12

HELPING OTHERS

Answered First

One who prays for his neighbor and needs the same thing is answered first.

Rava asked Rabba bar Mari, "From where do we derive this?"

He replied: It is written, "God changed Job's fortune when he prayed for his friends" (Job 42:10).

The other said: This may be your derivation, but I have another. It is written, "Abraham prayed to God, and God healed Abimelekh, his wife, and his maids, and they bore children" (Genesis 20:17). Immediately afterward it is written, "God remembered Sarah as he said . . . and Sarah conceived and bore Abraham a son" (Genesis 21:1,2). "As he said," means as Abraham had spoken in prayer regarding Abimelekh.

Talmud, Bava Kama 92a.

Sometimes one can pray for others and be answered, while his prayers for himself are not. We are taught "Whoever prays for others also sees his own desires fulfilled."

So why do we see that one who prays for others is answered, and for himself he is not? We find this to be true in the case of Rabbi Chiya—as soon as he arrived in the Land of Israel, the flax there no longer suffered from blight. His own flax had been blighted, but in his merit, the flax of others was spared.[1] In a similar manner, when one prays for others, his prayer may be answered, while when he prays for himself, it does not help.

The reason for this may be because, "a prisoner cannot free himself from jail."[2] It is thus written, "In all their affliction, He was afflicted"—and it needed that, "the angel of His presence save them" (Isaiah 63:9).

Actually, the fact that the prayers of Abraham and Job helped them personally does not contradict this. In both these cases, the people for whom they prayed were like enemies, and they should normally have rejoiced in their downfall. ... Therefore, the fact that they prayed for them was a very high act of charity.

But the reason this does not apply when praying for other Jews is because we are taught, "All Israel are responsible, one for the other."[3] Therefore, when one individual suffers, all must feel it and pray for him. It is thus written, "When they were sick, my own clothing was sackcloth," and the verse concludes, "so may my prayer return to my own bosom" (Psalms 35:13). [Thus praying for another Jew is considered praying for oneself].

Rabbi Yehudah HeChasid,
Sefer Chasidim 753.

When a person prays for himself, it is obvious that he is motivated by thoughts of his own gain; therefore, his prayer is not perfectly sincere. But when one prays for others, his intent is not to gain benefit, but to demonstrate clearly that none can fulfill the desire of each individual other than God. It is for this reason that God first fills the needs of the one who prays, and only then fills those of the one for whom he prays.

Rabbi Moshe of Trani,
Beth Elokim, Tefillah 12 p. 15b.

Obligation

Rabba bar Chinana the elder said in the name of Rav: If one has the opportunity to pray for another and does not do so, he is called a sinner. It is thus written, "Far be it for me that I sin against God by not praying for you" (1 Samuel 12:23).

Talmud, Berakhoth 12b.

An elder said that from the lectures of Rava he had learned: "They were punished because they should have prayed for their generation and neglected to do so."

This is similar to the case when a lion ate a man within three leagues of Rabbi Yehoshua ben Levi, and Elijah did not speak to him for three days.

Talmud, Makkoth 11a.

Pray for your neighbor first.

Rabbi Avraham Abele of Gombin,
Magen Avraham 130:2.

Atonement

Seek atonement for your own sins, then seek atonement for others.

Talmud, Horayoth 13a.

Pray for yourself and then pray for others. It is thus written, "He should atone for himself, for his household, and for all the congregation of Israel" (Leviticus 16:17). First, "for himself," and then, "for all the congregation of Israel."

Zohar 1:94b.

Heart's Desire

Rabban Gamaliel once visited Rabbi Chelbo in Keruyah and said, "Pray for me." He responded, "May God give you your heart's desire."

Rav Huna, son of Rabbi Yitzchak, said, "This is not what he said. Actually, he said, 'May God fill all your requests' (Psalms 20:6)."

But this is not a prayer that one should say regarding anyone. Sometimes there lurks in a person's heart an intent to steal, sin or do evil even though this is not befitting of him. How can one pray, "May God give you your heart's desire?" But Rabban Gamaliel's heart was perfect with his Creator, and therefore such a prayer could be said for him.

Midrash Tehillim 20:9.

By Name

Rabbi Yaakov said in the name of Rav Chisda: When one prays for his neighbor, he need not mention his neighbor's name. Moses thus prayed for Miriam, "O God, heal her" (Numbers 12:13), and did not mention her name.

Talmud, Berakhoth 34a.

When you stands next to a sick person and pray for him, you need not mention his name. We see this in Moses' prayer for Miriam. . . . But when you say a prayer for him and are not in his presence, you should mention his name.

Rabbi Yaakov Moellin (1360–1427),
Sefer Maharil, Semachoth 83a.

A neighbor of Rabbi Chanina ben Dosa was building a house, and found the beams to be too short. She came to him and said, "I have built a house, but now the beams that I bought do not reach from one wall to the other."

He asked, "What is your name?"

She said, "Ikhu."

He exclaimed, "Ikhu, let your beams expand!"

It is related that the beams expanded a cubit on each side. Some say that branches sprouted out of them.

Talmud, Taanith 25a.

Saints

Rabbi Ami said: It is written, "If the copper one bites without a whisper, there is no advantage to the master of the tongue" (Ecclesiastes 10:11).

When the skies become the color of copper and do not give forth rain, it is because that generation is "without a whisper" of prayer.

What is the remedy? They should go to one who knows how to whisper in prayer. It is thus written, "Let his friends speak up for him" (Job 36:33).

"There is no advantage to the master of the tongue." If one can pray and does not do so, what advantage does he have?

If he prays and is not answered, what is the remedy? They should go to the greatest saint of their generation (*Tzaddik HaDor*), and ask him to pray for them. It is thus written, "Let him command one to pray for him" (Job 36:32). . . .

If one prays, is answered, and boasts about it, he brings anger to the world. It is thus written, "For boasting, he gains anger" (Job 36:33).

Talmud, Taanith 8a.

The Circle Drawer

The people once came to Choni the Circle Drawer and asked him to pray for rain. He said, "Bring the Passover ovens indoors so they should not be softened by the rain." (Rabenu Nissim: He was so sure that he would be answered.) He then prayed, but no rain fell.

He then made a circle and stood in the middle. He said, "Lord of the universe: Your children look toward me, for I am like a member of Your household. I swear by Your great Name that I will not move from here until You have shown mercy to your children."

A few drops of rain fell. He said, "This is not what I requested. I want rain to fill the pits, cisterns and caves."

Rain then began to torrent in a flood. Again he said, "This is not what I requested. I want rain of blessing, charity and desire."

The rain then fell normally. But it continued until it forced the inhabitants to seek refuge on the Temple Mount. The people said to him, "Just as you prayed for the rain to come, pray for it to stop."

He replied, "Go see if the stone of Toim [a high stone in Jerusalem, where people announced objects they had found] in dissolved yet." (Rabenu Nissim: Just as the stone cannot be dissolved, so one cannot pray for an overabundance of good to go away.)

Simon ben Shetach sent him the following message: "If you were not Choni, I would excommunicate you. But what can I do when you pester God and He does your will, just as a child pesters his father and gets what he wants. Regarding you it is written, 'Your father and mother shall rejoice, and those who bore you shall be glad' (Proverbs 23:25)."

Mishnah, Taanith 3:8.

For the Sick

Rabbi Pinchas bar Chama preached: If you have a sick person in your household, ask a sage to pray for him. It is thus written, "The King's anger is an angel of death, but a wise man can undo it" (Proverbs 16:14).

Talmud, Bava Bathra 116a.

Even though the Talmud only quotes this in passing [among other quotes from Rabbi Pinchas bar Chama], I am citing it. It is the custom here in France that when a person is sick, the rabbi who heads the Academy is asked to bless him.

Rabbi Yosef Chabiba (14th Century),
Nimukei Yosef ad loc. (Rif. 53a).

It appears that [Rabbi Yosef Chabiba's statement] is the source of the custom in all our lands to bless the sick in the synagogue, and pray for them.

Rabbi Moshe Isserles (1525–1572),
Darkei Moshe, Yoreh Deah 335:2.

One's Own Prayer

The prayer of the sick person himself is best of all.

Midrash, Bereshith Rabbah 53:14.

It is best when one prays for his own suffering, because "God is close to those broken in heart" (Psalms 34:19).

Rabbi Shmuel Yaffe (16th Century),
Yafeh Toar ad loc.

It is written, "God head the voice of the young boy" (Genesis 21:17). From here we see that the prayer of the sick person himself is better than that of others who pray for him, and it is accepted first.

Rabbi Shlomo Yitzchaki,
Rashi (1040–1105), ad loc.

There is a slight question here. The Talmud says, "A prisoner cannot free himsef from jail."[4]

But the only time one cannot free himself is when he cannot concentrate on his prayers. If he can, however, his own prayers are best.

Rabbi Eliahu Mizrachi (1452–1526),
Commentary ad loc.

In the case of prayer, we do not say that "a prisoner cannot free himself," since it is God who frees him.

Rabbi Yehudah Loew (1525–1609),
The Maharal of Prague,
Gur Aryeh ad loc.

Sinners

A number of scoffers lived in Rabbi Meir's neighborhood, and they used to bother him very much. So annoyed was he that he wanted to pray that they die.

His wife Beruriah said to him: "Do not pray for an end to sinners, but for an end to sin. Pray that they repent. . . ."

Rabbi Meir did so, and eventually they repented.

Talmud, Berakhoth 10a.

[The rabbis asked Abba Chilkia, grandson of Choni the Circle Drawer, to pray for rain. His prayers were not answered, but those of his wife were. When asked the reason, he replied,] "There were scoffers in our neighborhood, and I prayed that they should die. My wife prayed that they should repent, and they did.

Talmud, Taanith 23b.

It is written, "He interceded for sinners" (Isaiah 53:12). This is speaking of Moses, who prayed that sinners should repent.

Talmud, Sotah 14a.

It is a virtue to pray for the wicked that they should improve and not end up in Gehinom. It is thus written, "I put on sackcloth for their sickness" (Psalms 35:13)...

It is forbidden to pray that the wicked die. Terah was a wicked idolator, but if God had taken his life, Abraham would never have been born, the tribes of Israel, King David, and the Messiah would never have existed, the Torah would never have been given, and all the righteous, pious, and prophets, would never have been.

Zohar 1:105a (Midrash Ne'elam).

Rabbi Moshe Alshekh had a son who became an apostate. My master [Rabbi Yitzchak Luria, the Ari,] taught him a prayer that would cause him to repent. He made use of it, and his son eventually returned.

Rabbi Chaim Vital (1543–1620),
Shaar Ruach HaKodesh, p. 76.

Why?

The question arises, how can we pray for someone to repent? Are we not taught, "All is in the hand of heaven, except for the fear of heaven?"[5]

But God includes all souls, and whatever is in the Whole is also in each part. Each soul therefore includes all other souls.

When you yourself repent, you can also bring your neighbor to repent. This is because you are included in your neighbor, and your neighbor is included in you.

Rabbi Pinchas of Koretz (1726–1791),
Midrash Pinchas 21 (Jerusalem 1971, p. 19a).

Enemies

Pray that even your enemies serve God.

When you say in the Amidah, "grant knowledge," "return us," and "forgive us," have in mind to include all Israel, friends and enemies alike.

Anonymous,
Orechoth Tzadikim, Simcha, (Jerusalem 1967 p. 68).

Life

David prayed, "Save me that I not be killed by Saul's hand, and save me that he not be killed by mine."

Midrash Tehillim 7:18.

Judging Others

Rabbi Yitzchak said, "Three things recall one's sins: Standing under a leaning wall, looking forward to an answer for prayer, and asking God to judge another."

Rabbi Chanan said, "If you pray that another should be judged, you are punished first." . . .

Talmud, Rosh HaShanah 16b.

One may not ask God to judge another. But this is only true if justice can be obtained in an earthly court.

Talmud, Bava Kama 93a.

Codification

It is forbidden to pray that evil befall another. One may not seek judgment from heaven if justice can be obtained on earth.

If one prays against his neighbor, he is punished first.

Some say that if one cannot obtain justice in an earthly court, he should not seek justice from heaven unless he first informs his adversary.

Rabbi Moshe Isserles (1525–1572),
Mapah on Choshen Mishpat 222:1.

Advice

Sometimes you hate your neighbor because of some insult, and you wish to pray for him to die. But if he actually died, you would be very sorry. It is therefore better to make peace with him and become friends. . . .

If someone did you so much wrong that you cannot forgive him, do not rush to pray that he be punished. First measure yourself, and consider if you would be in the other's place, if you had wronged others in a similar manner, then would it be proper for you to be punished for the same thing for which you are praying?

Rabbi Yehudah HaChasid,
Sefer Chasidim 750.

Shaking Fists

Rabbi Tanchuma said in the name of Rabbi Chiya the Great, and Rabbi Berachiah said in the name of Rabbi Chiya: Whoever shakes a fist at the Attribute of Justice does not emerge from its hand unscathed. Sarah should have lived as long as Abraham, but when she said to him, "May God judge between me and you" (Genesis 16:5), thirty-eight years were taken away from her life.

Midrash, Bereshith Rabbah 45:5.

The Dead

God first created Libra (the scales), since all deeds are weighed on a scale.
He then created Scorpio (the scorpion). If a person is found to be sinful, he is cast into Gehinom.
He then created Sagittarius (the archer). One might think that when one is cast into Gehinom, he has no remedy. But as soon as people pray for him, he is shot out of Gehinom, like an arrow from a bow.

Midrash, Pesikta Rabbati 20 (p. 95b).

If you give charity for the sake of the dead, tell the recipient, so that he should pray for your dead. Moses thus prayed for Judah's bones, "May God hear Judah's voice" (Deuteronomy 33:7).

Rabbi Yehudah HeChasid,
Sefer Chasidim 241.

The dead are helped when the living pray for them, or give charity for their sake. It is thus written, "Charity saves from death" (Proverbs 11:4)—from death in this world, and from death in the next.

Sefer Chasidim 1172.

Our sages have a tradition that one can pray for the dead, even if they were wicked, and God listens.... It is therefore a custom in all Israel to bless the dead and pray for them.

Chasdai Crescas (1340–1410),
A major Jewish philosopher,
Or HaShem 3b:1:1 (83b).

Children

Rabbi Yishmael said: The righteous would bless their children just before they died.

Isaac thus said to Esau, "I will bless you before God before I die" (Genesis 27:4). For the same reason, when Jacob was close to death, Joseph brought his two children to his father for a blessing.

Midrash Tanchuma, VaYechi 5.

Chapter 13

OPENING DOORS

As long as the righteous pray, their prayers are answered.

Talmud, Yoma 29a.

Answering No

Sometimes one prays and is answered, but sometimes the answer is no.

No one prayed harder than Moses did to enter the promised land, but still God refused him.

Midrash, Koheleth Rabbah 9:12.

Sometimes God is seen, and sometimes He is not. Sometimes He listens, and sometimes not. Sometimes He can be sought, and sometimes not. Sometimes He can be found, and sometimes not. Sometimes He is near, and sometimes far.

Midrash Tanchuma, Haazinu 4.

Rabbi Yehudah said: There is nothing as beloved to God as the prayers of the righteous. Even though He accepts their prayers, sometimes He fulfills their requests, and sometimes the answer is no.

Zohar 2:15a.

Partial Answers

Our sages teach us that the prayer of the congregation is never returned empty. Still, we pray for the redemption every day and our prayers are not answered.

One answer is that even though congregational prayers are never rejected, this does not mean that God must fill the request entirely. He may answer it only partially—and it is through this that we can survive. . . .

Another answer is that God does not reject their prayers, but accepts them as an offering. . . . It is not necessary that the request be fulfilled, since God knows what is best for us.

Rabbi Yaakov Zvi Jolles (1752–1825),
Kehillath Yaakov, Tefillath Tsibbur.

Highest Places

The Talmud speaks of, "Things that stand in the highest places of the universe, but are taken lightly by man."[1]

The results of prayer are often not manifest here in the physical world, but only in the "highest places of the universe." People therefore think that their prayers are in vain, and prayer is therefore "taken lightly by man." Actually, however, all prayer has some effect.

The Baal Shem Tov (1698–1760),
Kether Shem Tov 138.

Waiting

There are prayers that are answered after forty days. We learn this from Moses, as it is written, "I fell down before God for forty days. . ." (Deuteronomy 9:18).

There are prayers answered after twenty days. We learn this from Daniel, as it is written, "I ate no pleasant bread for three weeks. . ." (Daniel 10:3), and only then did the vision come to him.

There are prayers answered after three days. We learn this from Jonah, as it is written, "Jonah was in the fish's belly for three days . . . and he prayed to God from the fish's belly" (Jonah 2:1,2).

There are prayers answered the same day. We learn this from Elijah, as it is written, "Elijah approached and prayed ... and God's fire descended ... (1 Kings 18:36,38).

There are prayers heard in their time. We learn this from David, as it is written, "May my prayer to You be in a time of acceptance; answer me with the truth of Your salvation" (Psalms 69:14).

There are prayers answered by God before they leave the lips, It is thus written, "Before they call, I will answer them" (Isaiah 65:24).

Midrash, Devarim Rabbah 2:10.

Merit

When you share your bread with the hungry,
    Bring the outcast poor to your house,
When you see the naked and clothe them,
    Hide yourself not from your own flesh...
Then you shall call, and God shall answer,
    You shall cry out, and He will say, "I am here."

Isaiah 58:7,9.

O God, hear my plea for justice
    give my cry a hearing
    listen to my prayer
For it is innocent of all deceit.

Psalms 17:1.

I call with my whole heart,
    answer me O God,
    I will keep Your decrees.
I have called You, save me,
    And I will observe Your testimonies.

Psalms 119:145,146.

God is far from the wicked,
But He hears the prayer of the righteous.

Proverbs 15:29.

Deeds

Rabbi decreed a fast, but no rain fell. Ilfa, and some say Rabbi Ilfai, approached the ark to pray. He said, "He makes the wind blow," and the wind blew—"He makes the rain fall," and rain fell.

Rabbi asked him, "What are your deeds?"

He replied, "I live in a very small village, where there is no wine for Kiddush and Havdalah. I bring the people wine for Kiddush and Havdalah so they can fulfill their obligation to God."

Rav once came to a certain place and decreed a fast, but no rain came. The prayer leader descended to the ark and said, "He makes the wind blow," and the wind blew; "He makes the rain fall," and it immediately rained.

Rav asked him, "What are your deeds?"

He replied, "I am a teacher of small children. I teach the children of the poor exactly the same as the children of the rich. If someone cannot pay, I take nothing from him.

"I also have a fish tank, and when a child does not want to learn, I bribe him by letting him play with it. This makes him feel good so that he will come learn."

Rav Nachman decreed a fast and prayed for mercy, but no rain came. He said, "Take Nachman and throw him from a tower to the ground." He was very contrite, and then rain came.

Rabba decreed a fast and prayed, but no rain came. The people said to him, "But Rabbi Yehudah decreed a fast and brought rain!"

He replied, "What shall I do? If it is because of scholarship, we know more than they do. . . . Still, when Rabbi Yehudah took off one shoe [in preparation for the fast], it rained, while we pray all day, and no heed is given us.

"If it is because of deeds, is there anyone who has seen me do wrong? But what shall leaders do when their generation is not worthy?"

Talmud, Taanith 24a,b.

Once Rabbi Eliezer descended to the ark and said twenty-four prayers, but was not answered.

Rabbi Akiba then followed him, and said, "Our Father, our King, we have no King other than You. Our Father, our King, have mercy on us for Your own sake." Rain immediately began to fall.

The rabbis began to murmer [against Rabbi Eliezer]. A heavenly voice then declared, "One is not greater than the other. But one overlooks wrong done to him, and the other does not."

Talmud, Taanith 25a.

Noblemen and Servants

Once Rabbi Chanina ben Dosa went to study Torah with Rabbi Yochanan ben Zakkai. Rabbi Yochanan ben Zakkai's son became sick, and he said, "Chanina my son, pray for him that he should live."

Rabbi Chanina placed his head between his knees and prayed, and the son lived.

Rabbi Yochanan ben Zakkai said, "If ben Zakkai had placed his head between his knees all day long, no heed would have been given to him."

His wife asked, "Is Chanina then greater than you?"

He replied, "No, but he is like a servant before the king, and I am like a nobleman before the king."

Talmud, Berakhoth 34b.

A servant is a member of the king's household, and can enter and leave without permission. A nobleman, on the other hand, does not usually visit the king.

Rabbi Shlomo Yitzchaki,
Rashi ad loc.

By tradition, the acceptance of prayer depends on the attachment of the individual to God. One can be on a higher level of worship, even if he is not as great in wisdom. . . .

Rabbi Yochanan ben Zakkai was certainly on a higher level of wisdom than Rabbi Chanina ben Dosa. But Rabbi Chanina separated himself from all worldly things and worshiped constantly, and his prayer was therefore accepted.

Rabbi Chasdai Crescas (1340–1410),
Or HaShem 3b:1:2(83b).

Shmuel the Little decreed a fast, and it rained before sunrise. The people boasted of the merit of the congregation. He said, "I will give you an example. A slave seeks a prize from his master. The master says, 'Give it to him, and let me hear his voice no longer.'"

At another time, Shmuel the Little decreed a fast, and rain fell after sunset. The people again boasted about the merit of the congregation. He said, "I will give you an example. A slave seeks a prize from his master. The master says, 'Make him wait until he pines and suffers, and then give it to him.'"

When then is a congregation praiseworthy? If they can say, "He makes the wind blow," and have wind blow; and "He makes the rain fall," and have rain fall.

Talmud, Taanith 25b.

Once the world needed rain, and Rabbi Eliezer decreed forty fasts without result. He prayed and prayed, but there was no rain. Then Rabbi Akiba stood up and prayed. He said, "He makes the wind blow," and a strong wind began to blow. He then said, "He makes the rain fall," and it began to rain.

Rabbi Eliezer felt very discouraged, and Rabbi Akiba was aware of it. He stood up before all the people and said:

"I will give you an example of what this is like. Rabbi Eliezer is like a beloved friend of the king. When he comes before the King, the King is very pleased. The King wants to hear him speak, so his request is not granted quickly, in order that he not leave.

"But I am like one of the King's slaves, making a request. The King does not want me to enter his palace, and certainly does not wish me to speak to Him. He therefore says, 'Give him his request right away, and let him not enter.'

"Rabbi Eliezer is like the King's friend, and I am like a slave. The King wants to hear him all day, but does not even want me to enter his palace."

When he said this, Rabbi Eliezer felt better.

Zohar 2:15a.

The Poor

Rabbi Yehudah bar Shalom said in the name of Rabbi Eleazar: In the case of flesh and blood, when a poor man comes to speak, he does not listen. But if a rich man comes, he immediately admits him and listens. But in the case of the Blessed Holy One, all are alike: rich, poor, man, woman, or slave.

We thus see that Moses, the master of all prophets, is treated the same as the poor man. In the case of Moses it is written, "A prayer of Moses" (Psalms 90:1), and by the poor it is also written, "A prayer of the poor" (Psalms 102:1). Both are called prayer, indicating that both are equal before God.

Midrash, Sh'moth Rabbah 21:4.

The poor man's prayer comes to God before all the other prayers in the world. It is thus written, "He does not despise nor abhor the poverty of the poor, nor does He hide His face from him, but when he cries to Him, He hears" (Psalms 22:25). . . . The "prayer of the poor" is a prayer bound to his poverty—when one has nothing of his own. . . .

Every man's prayer is a prayer. But the poor man's prayer stands before the Blessed Holy One. It breaks down gates and doors, and enters before Him to be accepted.

Zohar 1:168b.

Barriers

Rabbi Yehoshua ben Levi said. . .: When people sin, they are not answered. It is thus written, "I called and they did not listen—they shall call and I will not listen" (Zechariah 7:13).

Midrash Tanchuma, BeChukothai 2.

Robbery

Job said, "There is no robbery in my hands, my prayer is pure" (Job 16:17).

Rabbi Yehoshua the Priest, son of Rabbi Nehemiah, said: Can a prayer be impure? When one's hands are filthy with robbery and he calls God, he is not answered. Why? Because his prayer is accompanied by sin. . . .

Rabbi Chama, son of Rabbi Chanina said: When one has illegal gain in his hands, his prayer is impure. It is thus written, "When you lift up your hands, I will hide My eyes from you, though you say many prayers, I will not hear." Why? Because, "your hands are filled with blood" (Isaiah 1:15).

But when one keeps himself from unjustly gain, then his prayers are heard. It is thus written, "Clean of hand and pure of heart. . . . He will receive a blessing from God" (Psalms 24:4,5).

Midrash, Sh'moth Rabbah 22:3.

Rabbi Yehudah said in the name of Rabbi Levi: If a person uses his money for good deeds, his prayers are heard. It is thus written, "My charity shall answer for me" (Genesis 30:33). If not, then it speaks up and condemns him. It is thus written, "Perversion speaks up," (Deuteronomy 19:16), and Rabbi Yochanan said, "This is the judgment of robbery."

Rabbi Shimon bar Abba said in the name of Rabbi Yohanan, "Out of a basket of sins, robbery occurs first of all."

Midrash, Koheleth Rabbah 1:34.

The Miser

If one stops up his ear so as not to hear the cry of the poor, even when he cries out in a loud and bitter voice, then God does not help him. It is thus written, "If one stops his ear to the cry of the poor, he too shall call out and not be answered" (Proverbs 21:13).

Othioth DeRabbi Akiba, Daleth.

Torah

Rava saw Rav Hamnuna praying at great length. He said, "You are leaving eternal life and grasping temporal life!" (Rashi: Torah is eternal life. But prayer is for the needs of temporal life, for healing, peace and food.)

Rav Hamnuna maintained that there is a time for prayer and a time for Torah study.

Rav Yermiya was sitting before Rav Zeira and studying a Torah lesson. It became late, and he hurried to leave for his prayers. Rav Zeira quoted the verse, "He who turns from hearing Torah, his prayer is also an abomination" (Proverbs 28:9).

Talmud, Shabbath 10a.

Rabbi Chanina bar Pappa similarly said, "When one turns his ear from hearing words of Torah, then his prayers are rejected."

Midrash, Devarim Rabbah 10:1.

Seven Reasons

There are seven reasons why prayer is not accepted.

The first is because one prays after the decree has already been sealed. We learn this from Moses, who had been told that he would not enter the promised land. Moses said, "I supplicated God at that time" (Deuteronomy 3:23), but God answered, "Enough, do not speak to Me any more regarding this matter" (Deuteronomy 3:26).

The second is because the prayer is not from the heart. It is thus written, "They beguiled Him with their mouths . . . but their hearts were not steadfast with Him" (Psalms 78:35,36).

The third reason is that one does not want to hear words of Torah. It is thus written, "He who turns from hearing Torah, his prayer is also an abomination" (Proverbs 28:9).

The fourth is because he ignores the cry of the poor. It is thus written, "If one stops his ear to the cry of the poor, he too shall call out and not be answered" (Proverbs 21:13).

The fifth is because one allows oneself forbidden gain. It is thus written, "They eat the flesh of My people, and flay the skin from them . . . then they cry out to God, but He will not answer them" (Micah 3:3,4).

The sixth is because the prayer is not said in purity. It is thus written, "When you say many prayers, I will not hear you, your hands are filled with blood" (Isaiah 1:15).

The seventh reason is because one has many sins, and does not repent in his prayer. It is thus written, "I called and they did not listen— they shall also call, and I will not listen" (Zechariah 7:13).

Saadia (ben Yosef) Gaon (882–942),
Emunoth VeDeoth 5:6.

Aids

Rabbi Yoshua of Sakhnin said in the name of Rabbi Levi: God told

His people, "If you listen to My commandments, then I will also listen to your prayers."

Midrash, Devarim Rabbah 7:4.

Self Sacrifice

If you are self sacrificing for the commandments, fulfilling God's decrees and ignoring those of man, what is your reward?

When God decrees to bring troubles to the world... and you pray to annul the decree, God will hear your prayer. He will ignore His own decree in the merit of the fact that you ignored the decrees of man to obey the decree of God.

Midrash, BeMidbar Rabbah 14:17.

Concentration

If you do God's will and direct your heart in prayer, He will listen to you both in this world and the next.

Midrash, Sh'moth Rabbah 21:3.

Rabbi Shmuel bar Nachmani said: If you can direct your heart in prayer, you can be sure that God hears it. It is thus written, "You direct their heart, Your ear listens" (Psalms 10:17).

Midrash Tehillim 108:1.

Sacrifice of Spirit

Rabbi Yehoshua ben Levi said: When the Temple stood, one could bring a sacrifice and have the merit of that particular offering. But if one is humble in spirit, God counts it as if he had brought all the sacrifices. It is thus written, "The sacrifices to God are a broken spirit" (Psalms 51:19). Also, his prayer is not rejected, as the verse concludes, "God will not reject a broken and contrite heart."

Talmud, Sanhedrin 43b.

Repentance

Rabbi Yehudah said, "Repentance does half, and prayer does all."

Rabbi Yehoshua ben Levi said, "Repentance does all, and prayer does half."

Midrash, VaYikra Rabbah 10:5.

Fluency

If a person makes a mistake in his prayer, it is a bad sign for him. If the prayer leader makes a mistake, it is a bad sign for the entire congregation. [He is the agent of the congregation,] and a person's agent is like himself.

It is told that when Rabbi Chanina ben Dosa prayed for the sick, he would say, "This one shall live," and, "This one shall die."

The people asked him, "How do you know?"

He replied, "If the prayer is fluent in my mouth, then I know that it is accepted. If not, I know that it is torn away."

Mishnah, Berakhoth 5:5.

Once Rabban Gamaliel's son was sick. He sent two sages to Rabbi Chanina ben Dosa, asking him to pray for the boy. As soon as he saw them approach, he went upstairs and prayed for him. When he came down he said, "Go back, for his fever has broken." They said to him, "Are you then a prophet?" He replied, "I am neither a prophet nor the son of a prophet. But I have a tradition that if my prayer is fluent, I know that it is accepted. . . ."

Talmud, Berakhoth 34b.

How did he know this? Rabbi Yehoshua ben Levi said: It is written, "A healthy sound on the lips, 'Peace, peace, to those far and near,' says God, and He will heal him" (Isaiah 57:19).

Talmud, Berakhoth 34b.

Prayer is accepted when it is fluent. The words are well ordered and flow quickly, without any stammering. One can pray as long as he desires, and the words surge up from his heart to his mouth.

Rabbi Shlomo Yitzchaki,
Rashi, Ibid.

If prayer becomes stuck and is expressed with difficulty, then it is torn away. This is because an adhesion in the lung renders something torn away (*Tref*).

Zohar 3:228a (Raya Mehemna).

Deja Vu

In order to understand this, another question must first be discussed. How can a righteous person pray for the sick and cause him to be healed? This seems to involve a change in God's mind. God, however, is a Simple Unity; heaven forbid that we should even think such a change possible.

But the concept is this. At first, before the universe was brought into being, all worlds, together with everything that was to be created, had potential existence in the Infinite Being. When His simple will decided to create, He brought them from potential to realization.

Everything that would ever be therefore had potential existence in the blessed Infinite Being.

Therefore, when a person is healed as the result of prayer, there is no change. All this already existed potentially in the Infinite Being. The entire sequence existed there: The individual would be sick, a righteous person would pray for him, and the prayer would have a beneficial effect.

God longs for the prayers of the righteous. Through his prayers, the righteous person attaches himself to God, and this is a great delight.

We find that two complete strangers can sometimes meet and immediately be attracted together very strongly, even though they had not known each other before. But as soon as they meet and come together, they immediately become attached with a strong bond of love.

This is because both of them were together in the Garden of Eden, where souls exist before birth. Therefore, when they come together, this original love that existed in the Garden of Eden is reawakened.

This explains Rabbi Chanina ben Dosa's remark, "If the prayer is fluent in my mouth, I know that it is accepted." The prayer would then be familiar, like something with which he was already acquainted.

The reason is exactly the same as before. The episode, the prayer, and the righteous person saying it, all existed potentially in the Infinite Being. They are therefore just like the two individuals who are attracted to each other because they were together in a previous existence.

In such a case, Rabbi Chanina knew that the prayer would be accepted. It already existed potentially in the Infinite Being, and nothing changes before Him.

If the prayer was not fluent, however, then this prayer did not have any potential existence in the Infinite Being. Instead, it was now being composed for the first time. In such a case, he knew that it was cut off.

Rabbi Elimelech of Lizensk (1717-1787),
Chasidic Master,
Noam Elimelekh, VaYechi (Lemberg, 1788, 27a).

God's Name

Rabbi Pinchas ben Yair said: Why does Israel pray in this world without being answered? Because they do not know God's Specific Name (*Shem HaMeforash*). But in the Future World, God will reveal His Name to them, as it is written, "My people will know My Name" (Isaiah 52:6). They will then pray and be answered, as it is written, "He will call and I will answer" (Psalms 91:15).

Rabbi Yitzchak said in the name of Rabbi Chiya: If they seek Me when troubles come on them, I will immediately answer them. It is thus written, "He will call Me and I will answer him, I will be with him in trouble, I will rescue him and bring him honor" (Psalms 91:15). It is also written, "Call Me in the day of trouble, I will rescue you and you will honor Me" (Psalms 50:15).

Midrash Tehillim 91:8.

When the sages say that we do not know how to pray with God's Specific Name, they are only speaking of [prayers for the redemption]. Israel is in exile, and the Divine Presence is with them, but they do not know how to awaken the love. The channels that arouse this love are now plugged up, since Israel is bound by an oath not to arouse God, as it is written, "I bind you by an oath, O daughters of Jerusalem, that you will not arouse, that you will not awaken it, until there be desire" (Song of Songs 2:1).

With regard to all other prayers, however, there is no question that they are answered. Prayer is what has allowed both ourselves and our fathers to survive since the beginning of the exile.

Rabbi Moshe ben Nachman (Nachmanides),
The Ramban (1194–1270),
HaEmunah VeHaBitachon 5.

Before we Pray

"Before they call, I will answer; while they are still speaking, I will hear."

Isaiah 65:24.

Rabbi Eleazar ben Pedat said, "If a mortal hears a person's words, he can judge him, but if he does not, he cannot judge him correctly." This is not true of God. Before a person prays, God knows what is in his heart."

Midrash, Sh'moth Rabbah 21:3.

King David said to God. . ." "When Israel calls upon You, answer their prayers at once." He therefore wrote, "When I call, O God, answer me" (Psalms 4:2).

God replied, "Why do you say, 'When I call, answer me?' By your life, even before you call Me, I will answer you." It is thus written, "Before you call, I will answer" (Isaiah 65:24).

Midrash, Devarim Rabbah 2:6.

This is because when one prays, his intent is not to inform God of our troubles, or to make His ear hear them, but only to fortify his own heart and improve his deeds. Our sages thus declared, "Our brothers, it is not the sackcloth and ashes that help, but repentance and good deeds."[2]

Rabbi Yitzchak Arama (1420–1494),
Akedath Yitzchak 58 (3:15b).

Intent

In the days of Rabbi Zeira, a decree was issued against the Jews, and it included a clause that they should not be allowed to fast. He said, "Let us accept upon ourselves the fast now, and when the decree is repealed, we will actually fast."

The people asked him, "How do we know that it will help?"

He replied, "We know it from the verse, 'He said to me: Do not be afraid, Daniel; from the first day that you made up your mind to understand and to mortify yourself before your God, your prayers were heard'" (Daniel 10:12).

Talmud, Taanith 8b.

"Before they call"—when they are still making mental preparation to pray and fast, even before they are actually accomplished—"I will answer." "While they are still speaking"—about these preparations—"I will hear"—even before they actually pray.

Rabbi Yosef Albo (1380–1435),
Sefer HaIkkarim 4:17.

When a city is under siege, or when an individual is being pursued . . . they are not allowed to fast and pray, for this may sap their strength. Instead, they should immediately accept upon themselves to fast and pray when they are saved, and do so later.

Rabbi Yosef Caro (1488–1575),
Shulchan Arukh, Orach Chaim 571:3.

Two Levels

Sometimes God answers before they call, and sometimes while they are still speaking.

Rabbi David Kimchi (1160–1235),
Radak on Isaiah 65:24.

It is written, "God is close to all who call Him, to all who will call Him in truth" (Psalms 145:18).

One may wonder why the same concept is apparently repeated twice in this verse. Furthermore, why is the first part in the present tense, while the second is in the future? Also, why does the expression "in truth" only occur in the second part?

This can be explained on the basis of the verse, "Before they call, I will answer; while they are still speaking, I will hear" (Isaiah 65:24).

There are some saints who are answered by God even before they call. Regarding these it is written, "Before they call, I will answer." Others are on a lower level, and must actually pray, but while they are still praying, God answers them. Regarding this second group it is written, "While they are still speaking, I will hear."

The Psalmist therefore says, "God is close to all who call Him"—beginning with those on the lower level. ... Even though they are not worthy, God is still close to them, since they call out and pray. But there is also a higher level, regarding which it is written, "God is close to ... all who *will* call Him"—in the future tense. Even though they have not yet called out, God is already close to them.

If one wishes to be in this group, he must always pray from the heart. He must call God "in truth," and not just from the lips outward. Regarding this second group, the verse therefore says, "in truth."

Rabbi Yitzchak Luria (1534–1572),
The Ari, Kabbalist Master,
Shaar HaPesukim ad loc.

Anticipating Answers

Rabbi Chiya bar Abba said in the name of Rabbi Yochanan: If you pray at length and anticipate an answer, you will eventually experience anguish and pain in your heart. It is thus written, "Hope deferred makes the heart grow sick" (Proverbs 13:12).

Talmud, Berakhoth 32b.

Rabbi Yitzchak said, "When a person anticipates an answer to his prayers, ... his sins are recalled."

Talmud, Berakhoth 55a.

When one anticipates an answer, his deeds are scrutinized [on high]. They say, "This person thinks that he has much merit. Let us check it carefully."

Tosafoth, Rosh HaShanah 16b.

This is measure for measure. This person scrutinizes God improperly for an answer to his prayers. His deeds are therefore also scrutinized and all his sins recalled.

Rabbi Yehudah Loew (1525–1609),
The Maharal of Prague,
Nethivoth Olam, Avodah 6.

Just because you pray for something, do not anticipate that God will grant your request. This is among the things that recall your sins. Rather, you should hope for God's mercy. The reason why we must pray to Him is to remind our own hearts of how much we are dependent on Him. We need God for all things, and no one else can fulfill our requests.

Rabbi Yitzchak of Corbeil (1214–1280),
Sefer Mitzvoth Katan 11.

Unbending

We are forbidden to be unbending in anything. Do not be stubborn in your prayers, demanding that God do exactly as you ask. This is like taking something with force, almost like robbery. But pray with humility, seeking God's mercy. If He gives what you request, He gives it; and if He does not, He does not.

Rabbi Nachman of Breslov (1772–1810),
Likutei Moharan 196.

Gentile and Jew

King Solomon prayed, "If a Jew prays for something, if it is fitting, give it to him, but if not, do not give it to him." It is thus written, "You shall give every man according to his ways, as You know his heart" (1 Kings 8:39).

"But if a gentile prays for something, give him what he asks for." It is thus written, "Also the stranger..." (1 Kings 8:41).

Midrash Tanchuma B, Toledoth 14 (134).

From Themselves

It is God's way to listen to all who call upon Him, whether for good or for bad. Our sages thus say, "Even in his hiding place, a thief calls out to the Merciful One."[3] This being so, what is the difference between the righteous and the wicked?

The Baal Shem Tov explained that when the thief is later caught, he cries out to God again. But since he chose the wrong way, he is no longer answered.

This is not true in the case of the righteous. When he prays for something that God knows is not good for him, He still fulfills his request. It is thus written, "He fulfills the desire of those who fear Him" (Psalms 145:19). But later, when this righteous man sees that this is really not good for him, he cries out again to God. Then, as the verse concludes, "He hears their cry and saves them."

Rabbi Yaakov Yosef of Polonoye (1704–1794),
Toledoth Yaakov Yosef, Shoftim (Warsaw 1881, p. 372).

Never Give Up

Rabbi Chama, son of Rabbi Chanina said "If you pray and are not answered, pray again."

Talmud, Berakhoth 32b.

Rabbi Yochanan and Rabbi Eleazar both said, "Even if the sword is on your neck, do not stop praying for mercy."

Talmud, Berakhoth 10a.

God had told Moses, "Enough, do not speak to Me any more" (Deuteronomy 3:26), but still he did not stop praying for mercy. This is all the more true of all other people.

Sifrei, VaEthchanan 29.

Many days and years may pass, and it may seem that you are accomplishing nothing with your prayers. Do not give up, for every word makes an impression.

It is written, "Water wears away stone" (Job 14:19). It may seem that water dripping on a stone will not make any impression, but after many years, it can actually make a hole in the stone. This can actually be demonstrated.

Your heart may be like a stone. It may seem that your words of prayer make no impression on it whatsoever. Still, as the days and years pass, even your heart of stone will be penetrated.

Rabbi Nachman of Breslov (1772–1810),
Sichoth HaRan 234.

Chapter 14

EFFECTIVENESS

Prayer is powerful, for it can break a decree.

Midrash, Bereshith Rabbah 71:2.

Two Cases

Rabbi Meir said, "Two people can be laid up with the same illness, or two people can be on trial for their life for the same offense. One recovers and the other does not; one is spared and the other is not. One prays and is answered; and the other prays and is not answered.

"Why is one answered and the other not? If one prays with perfect concentration, he is answered; but if one does not pray perfectly, he is not."

Rabbi Eleazar said, "In one case the decree has not yet been sealed on High, and in the other case it has."

Rabbi Yitzchak said, "Crying out is good, both before the decree is sealed and afterward."

Talmud, Rosh HaShanah 18a.

Three Things

Rabbi 'Lazer said, "Three things annul an evil decree: Prayer, charity and repentance.

Talmud Yerushalmi, Taanith 2:1.

A Rake

Rabbi Yitzchak said, "Why is the prayer of the righteous likened to a rake? Just like a rake turns grain from one place to another, so the prayers of the righteous turn God's attributes from wrath to mercy."

Talmud, Yevamoth 64a.

A rake turns over grain, first from below to on top, and then above to below. Similarly, when the righteous pray, their thoughts first ascend higher and higher. God then transmits sustenance from on High to down below.

Rabbi Bachya ben Asher (1269–1340), Commentary on Genesis 25:21.

The Wicked

A person may not be worthy that his prayers be answered and that he be granted mercy. But if he prays and says many supplications, God will act merficully toward him.

Midrash Tanchuma, VaYera 1.

King David prayed, "Lord of the universe: When even the most wicked Israelite calls upon You, answer him immediately. Let not the nations say that all deities are the same."

God replied, "By your life, even before he calls Me I will answer him."

It is thus written, "Call Me in a day of trouble, I will rescue you, and you will honor Me" (Psalms 50:15). It is also written, "He will call Me and I will answer him" (Psalms 91:5), and, "Before they call, I will answer" (Isaiah 65:24).

Still, it is necessary that the call be in truth. It is written, "God is close to all who call" (Psalms 145:18). One might think that this applies to any prayer. The verse therefore concludes, "to all who call Him in truth."

Midrash Tehillim 4:5.

Powerful Supplications

Some people are not worthy that God accept their prayers, but because of their powerful supplications and constant weeping before God, He accepts their prayer and fulfills their request, even though they do not have merit.

Rabbi Yehudah HeChasid (1149-1217),
Sefer Chasidim 130.

Free Mercy

God has the power to grant free mercy, whether the recipient is deserving of it or not. All that one must do is prepare himself with prayer.

We find this true in many cases, particularly in the case of Manasseh, son of Hezekiah, king of Judah. He was absolutely wicked, and none was more infamous for wrongdoing, either before him or afterwards.

Still, with regard to him it is written, "When he was in distress, he beseeched the Lord his God ... and prayed to Him. God let Himself be entreated and heard his supplication, and He brought him back to Jerusalem his kingdom" (2 Chronicles 33:12,13).

We learn two things from this. First, that even though the one who prays is as evil as Menasseh, he can still find God's mercy through prayer. Secondly, we learn that one who prays is heard, even though he only prays because of his troubles. The scripture explicitly states that he prayed, "when he was in distress." God is not like a human being, who would say, "Why are you coming to me only when you have troubles?"

Rabbi Yosef Albo (1380-1435),
Sefer HaIkkarim 4:16.

Confidence

Abba Yudin of Sidon said in the name of Rabbi Gamliel, "Do not say, I am unworthy of praying for the Holy Temple and the Land of Israel." It is thus written, "I will surely hear his cry" (Exodus 22:22).

Mekhilta of Rabbi Shimon bar Yochai,
Mishpatim p. 211

God's Child

It is very good to pour out your thoughts before God, as a child pleads before his father. God calls us His children, as it is written, "You are children to the Lord your God" (Deuteronomy 14:1). It is good to express your thoughts and troubles to God, as a child complains and pesters his father.

You may think that you have done so much wrong that you are no longer one of God's children. But remember, God still calls you His child. We are thus taught, "Whether you are good or evil, you are always called God's children."[1]

Let us assume that God has dismissed you and actually told you that you are no longer His child. Still, you must say, "Let Him do as He wills. I must do my part and still act like His child."

How very good it is when you can awaken your heart and plead until tears stream from your eyes, and you stand like a little child, crying before its Father.

Rabbi Nachman of Breslov (1772–1810),
Sichoth HaRan 7.

Galbanaum

I may be far from God because of my many sins. Let it be. If this is so, there can be no perfect prayer without me.

The Talmud teaches that every prayer that does not include the sinners of Israel is not a true prayer.[2] Prayer is like an incense offering. The Torah requires that the incense contain galbanaum, even though, by itself, it has a vile odor.[3]

If I consider myself a sinner, then I am an essential part of every worship service. No prayer is perfect without me.

I, the sinner, must strengthen myself even more to pray to God and trust that in His mercy He will accept my prayer. I am the perfection of prayer—the galbanaum in the incense.

Just like the vile smelling galbanaum is an essential ingredient of the fragrant incense, so my tainted prayer is a vital ingredient of the prayers of all Israel. Without it, prayer is deficient, like incense without galbanaum.

Sichoth HaRan 295.

Good Points

When you look at yourself, you may see yourself as far from good and filled with sin. You can then fall and not be able to pray at all. You must then seek out and find some good in yourself. It is impossible that you have never done any good since you were born. . . . Find some good points in yourself, and use them to give yourself the strength to pray.

Rabbi Nathan of Nemirov (1780–1844),
Likutei Etsoth, Hithchazkuth 26
(based on Likutei Moharan 282).

Chapter 15

INTERCESSION

Rabbi Yose said, "Israel is beloved, since the Torah does not require them to make use of any emissary."

Talmud, Yoma 52a.

Each individual can pray for himself. It is thus written, "Each man knows the plagues of his own heart, and he shall spread forth his hands. . ." (1 Kings 8:38).

Rabbi Shlomo Yitzchaki,
Rashi ad loc.

Patrons

Rabbi Yudin said: When a person has a mortal patron, and has needs and troubles, he cannot suddenly come to his patron. He must stand at his patron's door, and call his servants or members of his household, and then be announced. The patron may then decide to let him in, or he might leave him standing outside.

This is not true of God. When a person has troubles, he does not call out to Michael or Gabriel; he calls out to God and is immediately answered. It is thus written, "Whoever calls in God's name will be saved" (Joel 3:5).

Talmud Yerushalmi, Berakhoth 9:1.

Petitions

King David prayed before God, "Lord of the universe: When a petition is sent to a mortal king, others receive it for him. But when I petition You, I pray that You take it Yourself." It is therefore written, "O God, take my prayer" (Psalms 6:10).

Midrash Tehillim 6:10.

God said, "Behold, I will send an angel before you. . . . Take heed of him, and hearken to his voice; do not rebel against him; he will not pardon your sin, for My name is in him" (Exodus 23:20,21).

You shall not put this angel in My place. You might say, "This is our guardian angel, and therefore we should worship him and he will forgive our sins." This is not so, for, "he will not pardon your sin." He is not like Me, for only regarding Me is it written, "He forgives sin and overlooks rebellion" (Micah 7:18). But he cannot forgive your sins.

Furthermore, if you pray to him, you will cause My name to be removed from him. It is thus written, "My name is in him."

Midrash, Sh'moth Rabbah 32:4.

A Principle of Faith

Whoever combines the name of Heaven with something else is torn out from the world.

Talmud, Sanhedrin 63a.

I believe with perfect faith that it is only proper to pray to God, and that it is not proper to pray to anything else.

Thirteen Principles of Faith #5.

The fifth principle teaches us that God is the only one whom we may serve and praise. Only His greatness may we sing, and only His commandments may we obey.

We may not act in this manner toward anything beneath Him, whether it be an angel, a star, one of the elements, or any combination of them. All these have a predetermined nature; therefore, none can have authority or free will. Only God has these attributes.

It is not proper to serve these things or to make them intermediaries to bring us closer to God. All our thoughts should be directed only toward Him, and nothing else should even be considered.

This principle forbids all forms of idolatry, and it consitutes a major portion of the Torah.

Maimonides (1135-1204),
Commentary on Mishnah, Sanhedrin 10:1.

Saints

Throughout the entire Bible we find cases when Israel was in trouble and would go to a prophet to pray for them. . . . Actually, it seems that it should be forbidden to ask another person to pray for someone else. When a person prays for another individual or for his entire generation, there is no difficulty. But when others ask him to pray, it would appear that they are making an intermediary between them and God, and this is forbidden. . . .

It therefore appears that the prohibition only applies to the angels and other supernal overseers. To them we may not pray, making them intermediaries between ourselves and God. But when we go to the righteous, who deserve that their prayers be accepted, this is not forbidden.

This is permitted for two reasons.

First, because the denezins of the supernal worlds are so lofty, if people prayed to them as intermediaries, it is possible that they would mistakenly accept them as deities. One could then think that they themselves have the ability to do good or evil, and it is therefore fitting to pray to them in their own right. With mortal saints, it is impossible to make such an error, since they are human beings, made up of the same elements as other people. . . .

The second reason is that the supernal beings are not subject to the accidents and limitations of this world, and therefore, they themselves have no need to pray to God for anything. All they must do is praise and glorify His great Name, each according to its own perception. Therefore, if people prayed to them, they would erroneously think that just as these beings are exempt from the accidents and limitations of this world, so they have the ability to fulfill the desires of all people.

But in the case of human beings, even if they are saints, they are still subject to the accidents and events of this world. Therefore, even if people ask them to pray for them, there is no possibility of confusion, since the same thing could happen to these saints.

Rabbi Moshe of Trani (1505–1585),
Beth Elokim, Tefillah 12, p. 16b.

Angels

If there be for him an angel, an intercessor, one among a thousand, to vouch for a man's uprightness, then He is gracious to him.

Job 33:23,24.

Resh Lakish said, "When one strengthens himself in prayer below, he does not have any enemies on High."

Rabbi Yochanan said, "One should always pray that all should strengthen his power, and that he should not have any enemies on High."

Talmud, Sanhedrin 44b.

One should pray that the angels should help him seek mercy, and that none on High should denounce him.

Rashi ad loc.

Rabbi Pinchas said in the name of Rabbi Meir, and Rabbi Yirmeya said in the name of Rabbi Chiya bar Abba: When Israel prays, they do not all pray at once. Each congregation prays by itself, first one, then another. After all the congregations have finished their services, the angel overseeing prayer takes all the prayers said in all congregations, and makes them into a crown, placing it on the head of the Blessed Holy One.

Midrash, Sh'moth Rabbah 21:4.

Sandalfon

The angel in charge of prayer is Sandalfon. He takes all prayers and weaves them into a crown for the Life of Worlds.

Zohar 1:167b.

Akraziel

When Moses prayed to enter the promised land, he put on sackcloth, covered himself with ashes, and stood in prayer and supplication before God until heaven and earth trembled.... What did God do then? In the gate of each heaven, and in each heavenly tribunal, He proclaimed that Moses' prayer should not be accepted nor brought up to Him, since the decree had already been sealed.

The name of the angel in charge of proclamation is Akraziel (Proclaimer of God). At that moment, God called him hastily, and told him to proclaim to all angels, "Seal all the gates of heaven. The sound of Moses' prayer is very powerful on High."

Midrash, Devarim Rabbah 11:10.

Discussion

If found in the name of Rabbi Avigdor, of blessed memory, that [when we ask angels to bring our prayers in before God] there is no prohibition of "combining the name of heaven with something else." He brings evidence for this from the Talmudic teaching, "One should always pray that all should strengthen his power on High."

In a Midrash on the Song of Songs, we find the following:

There are angels who stand by the gates of prayer and the gates of tears. The congregation of Israel said to them, "Bring our prayers and tears in before God, and be an advocate for us, that He should forgive us for our sins." It is thus written, "If he has an angel, an advocate, one out of a thousand...." (Job 33:23).

[In the *Selichoth* service, we make such a request of the angels] in Aramaic... Even though our sages say that the "Angels are not bound to Aramaic," this is only true in the case of an individual, but not for a congregation....

Each individual's guardian angels understand only the languages that he speaks. But angels who are set over a community understand all languages.

Anonymous (13th Century),
Tanya Rabbati, Rosh HaShanah 72 (77d).

The simplest way to explain this is as a lesson that one should pray with devotion, and not as mere habit. In one's prayer, he should have in mind that God should overwhelm all forces that oppose him, and the angels that oversee these forces are then also subjugated to the will of their Master.

Heaven forbid that we think that we must pray to any angel to bring our prayer to God. God Himself hears prayer, and He commands the angel in charge of a particular force opposing this person to do away with this opposition. When one prays with proper devotion, "He does the will of those who fear Him" (Psalms 145:19). If one prays in Aramaic, in which he is accustomed [to speak casually], this is not strong enough devotion to ensure the subjugation of the angels and forces, so that his request be granted.

Hebrew, however, is the language with which the world was created and which the angels speak. Therefore, when one prays in Hebrew, it is fitting that his prayer be accepted, and that the angels themselves guide it and bring it inside the veil. . . .

The angels do not pay attention to Aramaic, since it is a common language, and such a prayer is apt to be uttered in a casual manner. The angels know the thoughts of our hearts, and our intent in prayer is engraved on the tablets of our hearts. Deep intent is not to be attained when one prays in a common language like Aramaic.

Rabbi Yaakov Chabib (1450–1515),
HaKothev in Eyn Yaakov, Shabbath 7.

The concept of prayer is somewhat difficult to understand. It is written, "The whole earth is filled with His glory" (Isaiah 6:3). We are similarly taught that, "There is no place empty of Him." Wherever man exists, God's glory is there.

It is therefore very difficult to understand why prayer is accepted through angels. Why do angels bring our prayers from one chamber on High to another?

God ordained this so that man should realize how far he is from God. He can then try to come closer.

Before the sounding of the Shofar one year, the Baal Shem Tov gave the following example:

A very wise king once wanted to test his subjects' loyalty and devotion. Making use of of optical illusions, he made barriers, walls, towers and gates, and ordered that large sums of money be deposited near each gate. He then commanded that his subjects come to him, through these gates and towers.

There were some people who went through one gate, found the money, took it, and went home immediately. Others went through two or three gates, but they too were eventually tempted by the treasures, so they also did not go all the way into the king's chamber.

The king's beloved son, however, strived very hard to come to his father, and would not be satisfied with anything less. When he finally arrived in the king's chambers, he saw that there was really no barrier, and it was all just an optical illusion.

The parallel is obvious. God hides Himself with many Garments, behind many barriers. But it is know that, "The whole earth is filled with His glory," and that every thought and movement comes from Him. Likewise, every angel, and every chamber, and everything that exists, as it were, is made of God's own Essence. It is like the case of a snail, "who is both contained in, and consists of, his garment." There is thus really no barrier separating man from God.

When a person realizes this, "all the workers of iniquity crumble away."

Rabbi Yaakov Yosef of Polonoye (1704-1794),
Ben Porath Yosef 70c.

In many places in the Zohar, we find that many angels oversee prayer, receiving and elevating it. This is because it is impossible for man's physical voice to ascend on High and be included in its Source in the Infinite Light, except through angels.

This is very much like the soul, which cannot garb itself in man's physical body, except through an intermediary, the blood. "which is the soul." Even though the blood is physical, it has the power to give rise to spiritual essence. It is through this that man's abilities and the functions of his soul are unified.

Similarly, it is impossible for the Infinite Light to be garbed in voice and speech except through angels, which are an aspect of messengers. They are therefore the vessels of the Infinite Light, which acts and functions through them according to His will.

Rabbi Schneur Zalman of Liadi,
The Alter Rebbe (1745-1812),
Likutei Torah New York 1973, BeMidbar 11a.

It is somewhat difficult to understand how prayer can be elevated so high. Does prayer not pertain to a physical, mortal human being?

It is for this purpose that angels are appointed in each chamber on High. They receive each prayer and elevate it from one level to the next. The *Zohar* states that an angel takes each prayer, hugs it and kisses it, and then elevates it to the next higher universe. This process continues until it reaches the highest level.

When an angel "kisses" the prayer, he brings his innermost breath and spirit into that prayer. . . . Through this, it is divested of the letters emanating from physical human speech, and it becomes an aspect of angelic speech, which is like pure thought in physical man. . . . The letters of prayer contain its intent and meaning, and with this kiss, they become included in the spirit of the angel. The prayer then pertains to the perception and speech of the angel.

When the angel then "hugs" the prayer, he transmits Enveloping Light to it, from his own envelopment. . . . It is in this manner that prayer ascends, level by level . . . to the very highest state.

Rabbi Schneur Zalman of Liadi,
Siddur, Shaar HaChanukah (273a).

You can pray to God that you should not have any adversaries on High, but it is not proper to pray to the angels that they themselves should not be your adversaries. You should only pray to God. . . .

Even though it is permissible to ask another human to pray for you, this is only true of a mortal. You can do a favor for your neighbor, and later, he may ask you to do him a favor and pray for him. But this cannot be said with regard to the angels. Here one is actually praying to them, and heaven forbid that we should do this.

Rabbi Yehudah Loew (1529-1609),
The Maharal of Prague,
Nethivoth Olam, Avodah 12.

The Dead

Why do we go to the cemetery to pray? There is a dispute between Rabbi Levi bar Chama and Rabbi Chanina.

One says, "It is as if to say, 'We are helpless like the dead before You.'"

The other says, "In order that the dead should pray for us."

Talmud, Taanith 16a.

[When the spies went to survey the Promised Land] it is written, "They went to the south, and *he* came to Hebron" (Numbers 13:22). Actually, the verse should have said, "and *they* came to Hebron."

Rava said: This teaches us that Caleb separated himself from the other spies, going to Hebron to supplicate on the graves of the Patriarchs. He said to them, "My fathers, pray for me that I be saved from the wicked counsel of the other spies."

Talmud, Sotah 34b.

Rabbi Mani, son of Rabbi Yonah, was troubled by the house of the Patriarchate. He supplicated himself on his father's grave and said, "Father, father, these men are troubling me!"

One day, these men of the Patriarchate rode by Rabbi Yonah's grave. The feet of their horses became caught, and they could not loosen them until they agreed not to trouble him any more.

Talmud, Taanith 23b.

When the world is in anguish, and people go to pray at the graves, all the dead are aroused. . . . . The souls speak up to God, and He has mercy on His world.

Zohar 1:225a.

We find that the dead pray for their children.

Rabbi Yehudah HeChasid (1149–1217),
Sefer Chassidim 1171.

Discussion

There is some difficulty, since the Talmud teaches that the dead know nothing.[1] From the conclusion, it appears that this is even true of the Patriarchs.

We must therefore say that when a person prays, the dead are told about the prayer.

Tosafoth, Sotah 34b (12th Century).

The saints are buried in the cemetery, which is therefore a holy and undefiled place. Since it is holy ground, prayer is more acceptable there.

When one prays on the graves of saints, he should not direct his prayers toward the dead who are buried there. Rather, he should ask that God grant mercy in the merit of the saints who lie in the dust.

Rabbi Yaakov Moellin (1360–1427),
Sefer Maharil, Taanith 37a.

We do not ask the dead to pray for us; instead, we go to the cemetery to join with them. The dead then also join the living, and pray for Israel, for the dead are also Israelites, and they love their brethren and pray for mercy for them.

Rabbi Yehudah Loew (1529–1609),
The Maharal of Prague,
Nethivoth Olam, Avodah 12.

This is one opinion. But in the Siddur, *Maaneh Lashon* (by Rabbi Yaakov ben Avraham Shlomo Darshan Shinan) there are prayers said on the graves of the dead, and it appears that we actually ask their souls to intercede for us.

Rabbi Yosef Teomim (1727–1792),
Pri Megadim, Eshel Avraham 581:16.

Attributes

It is written, "Who is a great nation who has God close to them, like our God, in all our callings to Him" (Deuteronomy 4:7). To Him, and not to His Attributes.

Bachya ad. loc.
also Sifrei ad loc. (not in our editions),
Quoted in Pardes Rimonim 32:2.

Emanations

Rabbi Shimshon of Kinon, one of the greatest rabbis in his generation, used to say, "In this respect, I pray just like a small child." His intent was to refute some Kabbalists who would sometimes pray to one of God's Emanations (*Sefiroth*) and sometimes to another, depending on the subject of their prayer.

They based this practice on the Talmudic teaching, "Let he who wants wisdom turn to the south, and he who wants riches turn to the north."[2] They claimed that this means that one's prayer should be directed toward the Attribute of the Right (south) or the Left (north). In the Amidah, they also had meditations, directing each blessing to a different Emanation. . . .

I was once in Saragossa, and the hoary sage, Don Yosef Ibn Shushan, whom I had earlier met in Valencia, also came there. He was a great Talmudic sage, well versed in philosophy, and was also a great Kabbalist, very stringent in observing all the commandments.

We became very good friends, and once I asked him, "How can you Kabbalists sometimes direct your prayers to one Emanation, and sometimes to another? Is there godliness in the Emanations, that one should pray to them?"

He replied, "Heaven forbid that there be any prayer other than to God. This is like a person who is involved in litigation and asks the king for justice. He asks the king to order the magistrate to judge him. He does not ask that the treasurer do so, for this would be an erroneous request.

Similarly, if one wanted the king to give him a gift, he would not ask him to issue an order to the magistrate; rather, he would want the order directed toward the treasurer. If one wants wine, he would seek an order to the winemaster; and if he wants bread, to the baker.

"The same is true of prayer, which must always be directed to the Cause of all causes. But then, one directs his thoughts so as to transmit His influence to the Emanation associated with that which he is seeking. Thus, when one prays for mercy for the righteous, he should keep in mind the Emanation of Mercy. Similarly, if one prays for the downfall of the wicked, he should have in mind the Emanation of Strength, which is the Attribute of Justice."

All this was told to me by that great Kabbalist, and it is all very good. But why go into all this? Is it not best just to pray to God in a simple manner, with devotion, trusting that He knows the best way to fulfill our request. It is thus written, "Commit your way to God, and trust in Him, and He will do it" (Psalms 37:5).

Rabbi Isaac ben Sheshet Perfet (1326–1408),
Teshuvoth Rivash 157.

Garments

Whoever serves any being other than God is not actually worshiping. Rather, he is commiting the sin of idolatry, substituting another for God.

One might then ask how the Kabbalists can direct their prayers to the Attributes, connecting them and unifying them. Is this not worshiping the Attributes? Regarding this, we must emphatically state that one who worships any Attribute is in absolute error. The *Sifrei* thus states, "We call Him—Him and not His Attributes."

Their intention is this. The Attributes are garments and vehicles for God. When we pray and unify the Attributes, our intent is to rectify them and ready them to be a vehicle for God. The Attributes can then bring themselves close to Him, and are rectified to receive His light and influence.

This is actually worship of God. He Himself does not derive any benefit from our worship; His entire will and desire is to do good to others. When those below are not prepared to accept His good, they cannot receive His good, since they lack preparation. His good is then not distributed to them. This is not because of any lack on the part of the Giver; the lack is on the part of the recipient.

Still, it is God's desire to benefit them. Therefore, when one prepares the Attributes to accept His good, this is called His service. God is not served through prayer, but through the fact that the Attributes bring themselves close to Him, prepared to receive the good that He bestows.

Prayer, Torah study, and religious observance all serve the purpose of uniting the Attributes, preparing and rectifying them to receive God's influence and good. Therefore, one who knows how to rectify the Attributes with the meditations associated with observance of the commandments, Torah study, and prayer, is actually worshiping God, since he directs his worship in the right direction....

Rabbi Moshe Cordovero (1522–1570),
Master Kabbalist,
Elimah Rabbati, Eyn Kol 1:2.

The Second Commandment

The second Commandment is, "You shall not have any other God before Me" (Exodus 20:3). This means that one should not even think that there is any other deity. . . .

Also included in this prohibition is choosing an Attribute, praying to it, and making requests from it. This is called "tearing up one's plantings," since one separates the branch from the tree.

None of these Attributes can act without being granted authority by the one Master, who rules over them all.

We have been taught, "Let he who wants wisdom turn ot the South, and he who wants riches to the North." This indicates that one should direct himself to the Attributes of North and South. But, heaven forbid, this does not mean that one should ask anything from the Attributes themselves.

When they said whoever wants wisdom should pray to the south . . . they didn't mean, God forbid, that one should make his request of that attribute.

Rather, one's thoughts and prayers should plumb to the depths of Thought, where there is simple will and desire. Only there does the absolute authority exist, to order the Attribute upon which his prayer depends, whether it be South, North, East or West. Influence and Blessing are increased, filling the Attribute with light, so that the request can be granted.

This is very much like making a request from the king, asking for the key to the storehouse where whatever one wishes is kept. Regarding this it is written, "I will set him on High because he knew My Name; he shall call Me, and I will answer him" (Psalms 91:14,15).

Understand this well, for many people have erred in this. This was the error that led to the sin of Adam. It was also the error of the generation that built the Tower of Babel, who said, "Let us make a name for ourselves" (Genesis 11:4), as well as that of Elisha ben Abuya.[3]

Rabbi David ben Zimra (1480–1574),
The Radbaz, Kabbalist and Legalist,
Metzudath David, #2.

Names and Decriptions

Shealtiel: Now I understand clearly that the mouth cannot speak of the Infinite Being (*Ain Sof*) or pray to His simple Essence, in any manner whatsoever. We must therefore say that the names and descriptions [of God] that are found in scripture and our prayers actually refer to the

Emanations. But if this is so, does it not come out that we are actually praying to the Emanations, and not to the Infinite Being Himself? This would be absolutely forbidden, as our sages say in the Sifrei, "We call Him—Him and not His Attributes."

Yehoyada: Heaven forbid that we pray to anything else! Even though the names and descriptions refer to the Emanations, we do not pray to the Emanations, but to the Power that acts in them. This Power is the Infinite Being, who is clothed in the Emanations. If one worships the Emanations, he is guilty of idolatry, as all the great Kabbalists write.

This is also logical. We believe that He illuminates all the world with His glory, and directs each thing with individual providence. Therefore, we should seek all our needs from Him and no other. . . . Everything comes from Him, and other than Him there is no power that can give anything or do good.

Rabbi Yosef Ergas (1685–1730),
Kabbalist Philosopher,
Shomer Emunim (HaKadmon) 2:64,65.

Body and Soul

If one prays to the Emanations, it is not considered prayer. . . . One must pray to the Infinite Being, even though no thought can grasp Him at all.

It is important to realize that the Emanations can only function through the power of the Infinite Being which influences them. He is in them like a soul is in the body. The body functions only through the power of the soul; it does what the mind directs. This is the power of the soul.

In a similar manner, the Emanations function only through the direction of their Soul, which is the Infinite Being. One should therefore direct his prayers to the power of the Infinite Being within the Sefiroth. [This is just like conversing with a person, where one actually directs the words to his soul, rather than to his body].

Rabbi Shalom Buzaglo (1695–1778),
Kisei Melekh, p. 94b #50.
Commentary on Tikkunei Zohar 22 (64b).

God's Prayer

Rabbi Yochanan said in the name of Rabbi Yose (ben Zimra). "How do we know that God prays? It is written, 'I will bring them to My holy mountain, and make them rejoice in the house of My prayer' (Isaiah 56:7). The scripture does not say 'their prayer,' but 'My prayer.' We thus see that God prays."

And what is His prayer?

Rav Zutra bar Tovia said in the name of Rav, "May it be My will that My mercy should overcome My anger and that My mercy dominate My attributes. May I act with My children with the Attribute of Mercy, and go beyond the requirements of law."

It is taught that Rabbi Yishmael ben Elisha said: Once I went in to burn incense in the innermost chamber [of the Holy of Holies]. There I saw Akatriel, Yah, YHVH Tzevaoth, and He was sitting on a high and exalted throne.

He said to me, "Yishmael My son, bless Me."

I said, "May it be Your will that Your mercy should overcome Your anger. May Your mercy dominate Your attributes so that You deal with Your children with the Attribute of Mercy, going beyond the requirements of law."

He nodded His head to me (Rashi: as if agreeing to my blessing and responding Amen).

From here we learn that the blessing of a commoner should not be taken lightly.

Talmud, Berakhoth 7a.

Rabbi Yochanan said: If it were not written, it would be impossible to say it. God wrapped Himself [in a Tallith], like a prayer leader, and showed Moses the order of worship. He said, "Whenever Israel sins and follows this order, I will forgive them."

Talmud, Rosh HaShanah 17b.

Interpretation

[Rav Hai] Gaon says that God taught Moses the concept of seeking mercy in a vision. It is therefore taught that God wrapped Himself with a

Tallith like a prayer leader standing before the ark, and taught Moses the Thirteen Attributes of Mercy. He thus told Moses, "I will make all My good pass before you, and I will call in God's name before you" (Exodus 33:19).

It is with regard to this episode that the Talmud asks, "How do we know that God prays?"

This is then explained in the Torah, as God said, "God, God, a merciful and gracious Lord, slow to anger and great in love and truth. . ." (Exodus 34:6). Moses later said, "You taught us to recite the Thirteen Attributes." It is thus written that he said, "And now, let God's power be great, as You have spoken, saying, 'The Lord, slow to anger and great in love. . .'" (Numbers 14:17,18)."

God's prayer is therefore, "May it be My will that My mercy overcome My anger." From this we also learn to pray., "May it be Your will that Your mercy overcome Your anger."

The Gaon's explanation would be excellent if it would agree with the wording of this Talmudical passage straightforwardly. In order to further clarify it, I will begin with a short introduction. . . .

God created three types of things. The first are the disembodied beings and spirits who praise Him with their constant works and perceptions. The second type are the lowly creatures, including all animals that do not speak.

God's praise emanates from these two types from their constant necessary actions. In the case of spiritual beings, this is mental, and in the case of lowly creatures, this is their natural functions.

After creating these two types, His Wisdom decreed to create an intermediate creature, combining the qualities of these two. This creature would be given absolute free will. Since man has free will, God constantly warns him and teaches him the way of life, as it is written, "Behold, I have set before you life and good, death and evil, and you shall choose life" (Deuteronomy 30:15,19). This teaches us that God desires that we be perfect.

In many cases, it appears as if God actually entreats us to draw close to Him, as if our righteousness or its absence could actually affect Him, heaven forbid. The prophet thus said in His name, "What unrighteousness have your fathers found in Me, that they have strayed from Me" (Jeremiah 2:5), and, "Return to Me, and I will return to you" (Malachi 3:7). In the Torah, God also says, "Who would give it that their hearts always be like this, to fear Me" (Deuteronomy 5:26).

It is in this sense that the Talmud says that God prays, "May it be My will that My mercy overcome My anger." It is God's standing decree that man be rewarded or punished for his deeds, and judged according to his actions. These deeds, however, are completely dependent on man's free will.

God therefore prays that man should rectify his deeds. The power of His mercy and His desire for their good deeds would then overcome His anger. This is very closely related to the teaching, "When Israel does God's will, they increase the strength of the Power on High, as it is written, 'And now, let God's power be great' (Numbers 14:17)."[4]

This is very much like the Midrashic interpretation of the verse, "God saw all that He had done, and behold, it was very good" (Genesis 1:31). Rabbi Chama said, "This is like a king who built a palace. He looks at it and enjoys it, saying, 'O palace, may you always be desirable just as you are now.'"[5]

*Rabbi Shlomo ben Avraham Adret (1235–1310),
Rashba on Eyn Yaakov, Berakhoth #27.*

This also clarifies the concept of what Rabbi Yishmael ben Elisha said when God asked him for a blessing. For this is the concept of all blessings. The Torah commands us, "You shall bless the Lord your God" (Deuteronomy 8:10). It is also written, "In him did God choose to serve Him and to bless in His Name" (Deuteronomy 10:8). This is the meaning of what we say [in the Kaddish], "May You bless Yourself, and may You exalt Yourself" (*tith-barekh ve-tith-romemp*).

Do not think that blessing is a concept of thanks. Rather it is a concept of increase and addition. A clear example of this is, "He will bless your bread" (Exodus 23:25). We thus find a blessing, "Blessed are You O God, teach me Your decrees" (Psalms 119:12).

It is written, "The prayer of the upright is His delight" (Proverbs 15:8). The prayers of the righteous overcome God's anger, and cause His mercy to be increased upon His creatures. This is the concept of Abraham's prayer when Sodom was overturned, as well as all other prayers.

Rabbi Yishmael said, "I saw Him sitting on a high and exalted throne." This is the same vision as that of the prophet, "I saw God sitting on a high and exalted throne" (Isaiah 6:1).

The nodding of the head alludes to the acceptance of the prayer. "Head" here is used in the same sense as, "His Head is the most fine gold" (Song of Songs 4:11). Both the sages and prophets speak in allegory.

Rabbi Shlomo ben Avraham Adret,
Teshuvoth Rashba 5:50.

Acceptance

It appears that the Talmud derives the form of the prayer from the verse from which it is derived. The verse states, "I will rejoice in the house of My prayer," and then concludes, "their offerings and sacrifices shall be desired on My altar" (Isaiah 56:7).

God's prayer is for this itself, namely that their offerings and sacrifices be accepted. This, however, is impossible unless God's mercy overcomes His anger, and He goes beyond the requirements of law.

Rabbi Yehoshua Falk (1680–1756),
P'nai Yehoshua, Berakhoth 7a.

We must understand how God can pray, "May it be My will. . ." Is God not omnipotent? What needs does He have that He must pray for them?

But the concept is this. It is written, "I have said that the world is built on love" (Psalms 89:3). This is the highest Love, with which the entire system of supernal universes was created. This had to come about through a constriction of the highest Will that desired love. This is called the "Will to Love."

We therefore say, "When His simple will decided."[6] This is because in essence, the Infinite Being is above Love. . . . The Will to Love therefore only comes about through constriction, and it can then be transmitted. Nevertheless, even Will comes from the Willer, which is the essence of the Infinite Being, and this is even higher than Will. . . .

The concept of Will itself therefore prays to the Willer. . . .

Rabbi Schneur Zalman of Liadi,
The Alter Rebbe (1745–1812),
Siddur, Birkath Nisuin (New York 1965, p. 272).

Chapter 16

BIBLICAL FOUNDATIONS

God's Advice

God said to [Abimelekh] in a dream, "Yes, I know that you did this in the innocence of your heart. . . . Now therefore, restore the man's wife, for he is a prophet, *and he will pray for you, and you will live."* . . . Abraham prayed to God, and God healed Abimelekh, his wife, and his servants. . . .

Genesis 20:6,7,17.

Unseen in Thunder

In distress, you called to Me,
    I rescued you;
Unseen, I answered you in thunder.

Psalms 81:8.

They Cried to God

Give thanks to God, for He is good,
    His love is infinite.
So say those redeemed by God,
        redeemed from the hand of the enemy
        gathered from every land,

from east and west, from north and south.
Some lost their way in the desert wilderness,
    they found no way to an inhabited city.
Hungry and thirsty, their spirit was faint.
Then, in their trouble, they cried to God,
    and he rescued them from their distress.
He led them by a straight way,
    bringing them to an inhabited city.
Let them give thanks to God for His mercy,
    His wonders to the sons of man.
For he satisfied the thirsting soul,
    filled the hungry soul with good.

Some sat in darkness, the shadow of death
    bound with misery and irons.
Because they rebelled against God's word,
    scorned the counsel of the Most High.
He humbled their heart with travail,
    they stumbled and there was none to help.
But in their trouble, they cried to God,
    and He rescued them from their distress.
He brought them out of darkness, from death's shadow,
    He broke their bonds asunder.
Let them give thanks to God for His mercy
    His wonders to the sons of man.
For He shattered the doors of bronze,
    He snapped the bars of iron.

Some were driven frantic by their sins,
    suffering from their wrongdoings.
They were repulsed by every food,
    they drew close to the gates of death.
But in their trouble, they cried to God,
    and He rescued them from their distress.
He sent His word and healed them,
    delivered them from their graves.
Let them thank God for His mercy,
    His wonders to the sons of man.
Let them offer a thanksgiving sacrifice,
    and recite His deeds with song.

Some go down to the sea in ships,
    doing work in the great waters.
They see the works of God,
    His wonders in the deep.
At His command the storm winds rise,
    they lift the waves aloft.
They mount to the heavens, they plunge to the depths,
    in despair their soul melts away.
They reel and stagger like a drunkard,
    their skill is all in vain.
Then in their trouble, they cried to God,
    and He rescued them from their distress.
He made the storm a calm,
    the waves become very still.
They rejoiced that all was quiet,
    as He led them to their port.
Let them thank God for His mercy,
    His wonders to the sons of man.
Let them exalt Him in the congregations,
    praise Him where the elders sit.

Psalms 107:1–32.

King Solomon's Prayer
At the Dedication of the Holy Temple

You shall hearken to the supplication of Your servant and Your people, who will pray toward this place. And You shall listen in the place of Your dwelling, in the heavens—You shall listen and forgive. . . .

Your people Israel may be smitten down before the enemy, when they sin against You. But if they turn to You, confess Your name, and pray and supplicate to You in this house, then in heaven You shall hear, and You shall forgive the sin of Your people Israel. . . .

The heavens may be shut up, and there may be no rain, when they sin against You. But if they pray toward this place, confess Your name, and turn from their sin when You afflict them, then in heaven You shall hear, and You shall forgive the sin of Your servants and of Your people Israel. . . . and You shall send rain upon the land. . . .

In the land, there may be famine or plague, blight, mildew, locust or weevil, their enemies may besiege them in the land of their cities, there may be some epidemic or sickness. Some prayer, some supplication may be made by any man, by any of Your people Israel—each one knowing the anguish of his own heart—and he shall spread his hands toward this Temple. And You shall hear from heaven, the place of Your abode, and You shall render to every man according to all his ways, as You know his heart—for You alone know the hearts of all humans. In order that they fear You all the days that they live in the land that You gave our fathers.

There may also be strangers, not from Your people Israel, who come from faraway lands for the sake of Your Name. For they hear of Your great Name, Your mighty hand and outstretched arm, and they come and pray toward this Temple. And You shall hearken from heaven, the place of Your abode, and You shall do all that the stranger calls You to do. So that all the peoples of the earth shall know Your Name and revere You, as do Your people Israel, and so that they make known that Your Name is called upon this Temple that I have built. . . .

Your eyes are open to the supplication of Your servant, and to the supplication of Your people Israel, to hearken to them whenever they cry to You. . . .

1 Kings 8:30–52.

For All Peoples

I will bring them to My holy mountain
    Make them joyous in My house of prayer;
Their burnt offerings and sacrifices
    Shall be accepted on My altar;
For My house shall be called
    A house of prayer for all peoples.

Isaiah 56:7.

The Crisis of Faith

O God, my God, why have You forsaken me?
Why are You far from saving me?
    From hearing my cry?
O my God, I call by day
    but You answer not,
    at night there is no respite.
But You are holy,
    enthroned in the praise of Israel.

In You our fathers trusted—
> they trusted and You saved them.
To You they cried and were delivered,
> In You they trusted, and they were not ashamed.

Psalms 22:2–6.

To You, O God, I call,
> O my Rock, be not deaf to my cry.
For if You answer me with silence,
> I shall be like those who go down to the grave.
Hear the voice of my supplication when I cry to You,
> when I lift my hands to Your holy sanctuary.

Psalms 28:1,2.

To You, O God, I called,
> I pleaded to God,
What profit is there in my blood
> if I descend to the grave?
Does dust then praise You?
> Does it declare Your truth?
Hear, O God, and be gracious to me,
> O God, be my Help.

Psalms 30:9–11.

From the Ends of the Earth

Hear my cry, O God,
> Listen to my prayer.
From the ends of the earth I call You
> with a fainting heart.
Lift me up on a high rock
> for You are my shelter
> a tower of strength in the face of the enemy.

Psalms 61:2–4.

Turn to Me

Turn to me, O God, and answer,
> for I am poor and needy.

Keep my soul, for I am pious.
Save Your servant, O my God,
    the one who trusts in You.
Be gracious to me, O God,
    for to You I cry all the day.
Fill Your servant's heart with joy,
    for to You, O God, I lift my soul.
For You, O God, are good and ready to pardon
    You have ample mercy for all who call You.
Listen to my prayer, O God,
    pay attention to the sound of my plea.
In my time of trouble I call You
    for You will answer me.

Psalms 86:1–7.

Save my Soul

I love God, for He has heard
    my voice and my plea;
Because He listened to me
    on the day I called.
The cords of death had bound me
    The grave had grasped me
    I was in trouble and sorrow.
But I called in the name of God,
    "O God, save my soul!"
God is gracious and righteous,
    our God has compassion.
God preserves the simple—
    I was brought low, but He saved me.

Psalms 116:1–6.

Let my Tongue Sing

Let my cry approach You, O God,
    Give me understanding according to Your word.
Let my supplication come before You
    deliver me according to Your word.

Let my lips utter praise
> because You teach me Your decrees.
Let my tongue sing of Your word,
> for all Your commandments are just.
Let Your hand be ready to help me
> for I have chosen Your precepts.

Psalms 119:169-173.

Out of the Depths

Out of the depths I call You,
> O God, hear my voice.
> Listen to the sound of my plea.
If You keep account of sin,
> O God, who could stand?
But with You there is pardon
> that You may be feared.
I yearn, O God,
> O how my soul yearns
> I hope for His word.
My soul is to God
> like the watchers of the dawn
> watching for the dawn.

Psalms 130:1-6.

You are my Refuge

With my voice I cry to God
> With my voice I plea to God.
I pour out my thoughts before Him
> I declare my trouble before Him.
When my spirit faints within me—
> You know my path
>> The way where I walk,
>>> Where they have hidden a snare for me.
Look to my right and see,
> for there is none who knows me.
I have no way to flee,
> no man cares for my soul.

I have cried to You, O God.
I have said, "You are my refuge,
    my portion in the land of the living."
Pay attention to my cry
    for I have been brought very low.
Deliver me from my persecutors
    for they are too strong for me.
Bring my soul out of prison
    that I may thank Your name.
The righteous shall crowd around me
    for You will give me bounty.

Psalm 142.

God is Near

God is near to all who call Him,
    to all who call Him in truth.
He will fulfill the desire of those who fear Him,
    He will hear their cry and save them.

Psalms 145:18,19.

Seek Earnestly

If you would earnestly seek God
And plead before the Almighty;
If you were pure and upright,
He would surely awaken to you
And see your just intent fulfilled.

Job 8:5.

From the Dungeon

I called upon Your name, O God,
    from the lowest dungeon,
You have heard my voice,
    hide not Your ear from my sigh
        from my cry.

You drew near on the day I called,
  You said, "Do not fear."

Lamentations 3:55–57.

The Cry from Egypt

And it came to pass in the course of those many days that the king of Egypt died, and the children of Israel sighed because of their bondage. And they called out, and their cry, stemming from the bondage, rose up to God. And God heard their groan, and He remembered His covenant with Abraham, Isaac and Jacob.

Exodus 2:23,24.

Moses' Intercession

God said to Moses, "I have seen this people, and behold, they are a stiff-necked people. Now therefore let Me alone, that My wrath may be ignited against them, and that I may consume them...."

But Moses beseeched the Lord his God, and he said, "O God, why does Your anger rage against Your people, whom You brought out of Egypt with great power and with a mighty hand? Why should the Egyptians say, 'With evil He brought them forth, to slay them in the mountains, to consume them from the face of the earth?' Turn from Your burning wrath, and repent this evil against Your people. Remember Abraham, Isaac and Israel, Your servants, to whom You swore by Your own self, saying, 'I will multiply your offspring like the stars of heaven, and all the land of which I have spoken, I will give to your offspring, that they inherit it forever.'"

And God repented the evil that He said He would do to His people.

Exodus 32:9–14.

Hannah's Prayer
Before the Birth of Samuel

She was bitter to the soul, and she prayed to God and wept bitterly. She made a vow and said, "O Lord of Hosts, if You will indeed look upon the affliction of Your servant and remember me, and not forget

Your servant, but give Your servant a child. Then I will give him to God all the days of his life, and no razor shall pass over his head."

She prayed to God for a long time, while Eli watched her lips. Now Hannah had spoken in her heart, only her lips moved, but her voice could not be heard. Eli thought that she was drunk, and he said to her, "How long will you continue to be drunk? Put away your wine!" But Hannah answered and said, "No, my lord, I am a woman of sorrowful spirit. I have drunk neither wine nor liquor, but I have poured out my soul before God."

1 Samuel 1:10–15.

Elijah's Call

It was the time of the afternoon offering, and Elijah the prophet approached and said, "O God, Lord of Abraham, Isaac, and Israel, let it be known this day that You are the God of Israel, that I am Your servant, and that I have done all these things according to Your word. Hear me, O God, hear me, that this people may know that You, O Lord, are God, for You will make their heart return.

1 Kings 18:36,37.

Seek God and Find Him

Thus says God: . . . You shall call Me and pray to Me, and I will hearken to you. You shall seek Me and find Me, when you shall search for Me with all your heart.

Jeremiah 29:10–13.

תושלב"ע

NOTES

Chapter 1.

1. *Pesachim* 112a.
2. *Tikunei Zohar* 17a.

Chapter 2.

1. Quoted in full on page *5* 227–8.
2. Paraphrasing Psalm 55:23.
3. Rosh HaShanah 18a. See page *264* 201.
4. See page *55* 36.
5. See page *140* 114.
6. *Avoth* 3:15.
7. *Berakhoth* 31b.
8. *Taanith* 16a.
9. *Zohar* 1:21a.
10. *Zohar* 2:42b.
11. See page *75* 52–53.
12. Quoted in *Lekhem Mishnah, Tefillah* 1:1.
13. Rashi, *Berakhoth* 5b.
14. *Zohar* 1:24a.
15. *Zohar* 3:141b.
16. *Tikunei Zohar* 18 (32b).

Chapter 3.

1. *Berakhoth* 34a. See page *84* 58.
2. *Berakhoth* 32b.
3. *Berakhoth* 32b.
4. See *Avoth* 5:3,4.
5. *Berakhoth* 9:5.
6. *Berakhoth* 9:5.
7. *Berakhoth* 4b.

Chapter 4.

1. *Avodah Zarah* 3b.

Chapter 5.

1. See Isaiah 18:5. *Cf.* Rashi on Exodus 15:2, Isaiah 25:5. Also see Radak, *Sefer Sherashim, Zamar.*
2. *Sefer Yetzirah* 4:4.
3. Quoted in Chaim Yosef David Uzulai (Chida), *Avodath HaKodesh, Moreh BeEtzba* 35.
4. Quoted in *Eliahu Rabbah* 132:3, *Beer Hetiv* 132:3.
5. See page *274f* 211 p.
6. Sotah 49a.
7. Quoted in Teshuvoth Rivash 115. A similar story is found in *Tana DeBei Eliahu Zuttah* 17. See *Shulchan Arukh, Yoreh Deah* 376:4 in *Hagah.*
8. *Edduyoth* 2:10.
9. See page *80* 58.
10. *Sanhedrin* 106b.
11. *Berakhoth* 1:4.
12. However, in his commentary on *Menachoth* 4.1, Maimonides writes that these things were so well known that there was no need to codify them.
13. See Rabenu Chananel, *Eruvin* 40b, *Magen Avraham* 68:0.
14. *Shekalim* 6:1,2.

Chapter 6.

1. *Avoth* 5:1.
2. See page *67* 46.
3. *Pesachim* 88a.
4. *Yoma* 8:9.
5. *Bava Kama* 82a.

Chapter 7.

1. See page *76* 53.

Chapter 8.

1. *Shabbath* 104a.
2. *Berakhoth* 6b.
3. See page *153* 110.
4. *Shabbath* 104a.
5. *Berakhoth* 12b.
6. One of the greatest first century Kabbalists, and reputed author of the *Bahir.*

Chapter 9.

1. Deuteronomy 10:17, Nehemiah 9:32.
2. *Berakhoth* 31b. See Chapter 2, note 7.
3. *Megillah* 18a. See page *181* 132.
4. *Tosefta Bava Kama* 9:11.

Chapter 11.

1. *Sotah* 48b.
2. *Berakhoth* 33b.
3. *Tikkunei Zohar* 6(22a).
4. *Avoth* 1:3.
5. *Shabbath* 55a. Cf. *Yoma* 86a.
6. *Sanhedrin* 6:5.
7. *VaYikra Rabbah* 2:3.

Chapter 12.

1. *Chullin* 86a.
2. *Berakhoth* 5b.
3. *Shavuoth* 39a.
4. *Berakhoth* 5b.
5. *Berakhoth* 33b.

Chapter 13.

1. *Berakhoth* 6b.
2. *Taanith* 16a.
3. *Berakhoth* 63a, according to reading in *Eyn Yaakov* 9:139.

Chapter 14.

1. *Kiddushin* 36a.
2. *Keritoth* 6b.
3. See Exodus 30:34.

Chapter 15.

1. *Berakhoth* 18a.
2. *Bava Bathra* 25b.
3. See *Chagigah* 15a.
4. *Eikhah Rabbah* 1:33.
5. *Bereshith Rabbah* 9:4.
6. See *Etz Chaim, Shaar HaKelalim* 1.

Index

Biblical Verses

Genesis		15:1	116
1:12	5	15:11	136
1:31	223	18:10	52
2:5	5	20:3	219
2:7	36	20:7	135
9:26	51	20:15	146
11:4	219	20:21	96
12:8	14	20:23	62
14:20	51	22:22	203
15:1	59	23:20, 21	208
15:13	47	23:25	28, 29
16:5	178	23:25–27	32
18:32	94, 95	30:34	204
19:27	46, 95	32:9–14	233
20:6	225	32:13	32, 139
20:7	12, 225	32:14	139
20:17	12, 169, 225	33:19	222
21:1, 2	169	34:6	222
21:17	174	38:23	54
22:12	59		
24:27	51	Leviticus	
24:63	14, 46, 97	6:2	47
25:21	31	6:18	73
27:4	179	16:17	171
27:22	15	19:18	137
28:11	14, 46	22:32	93
28:12	59, 86	26:21	18
30:8	13	26:27, 28	18, 107
30:21	154		
30:33	188	Numbers	
32:12	157	5:22	79
33:7	15	6:22–27	39
42:3–5	94	6:27	59
48:22	14	10:9	18, 107
		12:13	129, 172
Exodus		13:22	215
2:23	6, 14, 33	14:17	222, 223
2:24	33	14:18	222
2:25	6	14:27	93
8:8	61	16:21	93
14:10	6, 14	20:14–16	15
14:15	151	20:18	15
14:31	116	21:2	156
15	57		

239

Deuteronomy

3:23–25	20
3:23	41, 106, 189
3:24	41
3:25	41
3:26	189, 198
3:27	107
4:7	91, 216
4:29	30
5:26	222
6:4–9	40
6:4	7, 55
6:5	48
6:13	28
8:10	223
9:14	31
9:18	182
9:25	129
9:26	129
10:8	223
10:10	129
10:17	132
11:13	27, 35, 110
12:23	36
13:5	28
13:18	137
14:1	204
15:10	31
16:22	148
18:5	64
19:16	188
20:19	146
21:6–8	39
22:7	31
26:12–15	40
27:26	79, 80
28:8	154
28:47	141
30:15, 19	222
33:7	178

Joshua

7:6	14
8:18	14

Judges

6:7	14

1 Samuel

1:10–15	233–234
1:12	130
1:13	45, 60, 110
1:15	35
7:9	14
10:5	142
12:23	170
17:45	15
25:32	52

2 Samuel

7:10	96
15:32	96
21:1	31

1 Kings

8:28	41, 98
8:30–52	227–228
8:30	28
8:38	148, 207
8:39	197
8:41	19, 33, 197
18:28	60
18:36	139, 183, 234
18:37	49, 139, 234
18:38	183

2 Kings

20:5	31, 143

Isaiah

1:15	130, 188, 189
6:1	233
6:3	7, 61, 95, 212
29:12	128
29:13	111, 128
38:2	63
40:6	163
41:14	14
45:7	68
45:23	149
46:6, 7	8
49:8	90
50:2	98
51:16	37
52:6	193
53:12	175
56:7	221, 224, 228
57:19	191
58:7, 9	183
63:9	170
65:24	183, 194, 196, 202
66:22	37

Jeremiah			2:11	120
2:5	222		4:2	194
5:3	18		4:5	99
5:25	107		5:2	167
10:24	11		5:2–4	65
12:2	19		5:4	34, 49
12:8	143		6:7	106
12:14	90		6:10	208
17:13	99		10:17	110, 190
28:6	80		16:8	115
29:10–13	234		17:1	183
31:3	68		17:15	64
31:6	14		19:15	69, 111
31:19	167		20	54
33:3	8		20:2	69
			20:6	171
Ezekiel			20:8, 9	15
1:7	62		22:6	228–229
11:16	99		22:25	187
33:11	34		24:4, 5	188
36:20	166		27:14	42, 130
38:23	25		28:1, 2	229
			29	54–55
Hosea			29:2	64
14:2	33		29:3	55
14:3	64		30:9–11	229
			32:6	157
Joel			33:1	7
3:5	207		34:5	13
			34:19	174
Amos			35:10	54, 56, 136, 145
3:6	157, 159		35:13	170, 176
4:12	63		37:5	217
5:4	13		39:13	144
			41:4	129
Jonah			44:7	15
2:12	182		50:15	193, 202
			51:17	162
Micah			51:19	190
3:3, 4	189		55:17	43
7:18	208		55:18	43, 45
			55:19	90
Zechariah			55:23	8
7:13	187, 189		56:9	144
8:10	159		57:2	161
			60:13	151
Malachi			61:2–4	229
2:7	63		63:5	148
3:7	222		65:2	7, 132
			65:3	7, 9, 117
Psalms			68:18	57
2	54			

68:20	158	148:1–3	7
68:27	89	150	66
69:14	89, 91, 183	150:6	66
69:31, 32	33		
78:35, 36	189	Proverbs	
78:37	90	3:9	143
78:38	90	11:4	178
79:8	32	13:12	42, 130, 196
80:9	139	14:28	89
81:8	225	15:8	223
82:1	93, 98	15:29	183
86:1–7	229–230	16:14	174
88:10	148	20:27	146
88:14	65	21:13	188, 189
90:1	187	23:25	173
91:5	202	28:9	188
91:14	219		
91:15	163, 193, 213	Job	
92	55	8:5	232
92:3	69	14:19	198
96:1, 2	46	16:17	187
98:1	141	19:26	27, 113
100:2	120, 144	21:7, 14	22
102:1	62, 187	33:23	127, 210
103:1	35	33:24	210
104:21	157	36:5	90
104:33	141	36:32	173
106:2	132	36:33	172, 173
106:30	11, 46, 61, 95	37:20	132
106:48	79	37:23	132, 211
107:1–32	225–227	42:10	169
116:1	7		
116:1–6	230	Song of Songs	
119	66	2:1	194
119:10	116	2:14	6
119:12	52, 223	4:11	224
119:169–173	231		
130:1	62, 116	Ruth	
130:1–6	231	4:2	94
136:25	66		
141:2	27, 34, 49	Lamentations	
142	231–232	3:8	144
143:1	163	3:41	90
145	66, 73	3:44	67
145:1	136	3:55–57	232–233
145:16	66, 152, 158		
145:18	19, 195, 202, 232	Ecclesiastes	
145:19	198, 212, 232	5:1	131
145:21	136	10:11	172
146:1	35	10:20	37
148	66		

Esther		28b	55, 115
4:1	9	29b	137
		30a	137
Daniel		31a	60
2:18	152	31b	25, 133
6:11	27, 44, 45, 97, 149	32a	41
6:21	28	32b	9, 33, 48, 130, 144,
9:3	163		196, 198
9:18	20	33a	52, 135
10:3	182	33b	132, 161, 176
10:12	195	34a	42, 58, 72, 129
		34b	97, 112, 185, 191
Ezra		47b	98
8:23	152	53b	82
9:5	149	54b	130
		55a	196
Nehemiah		60a	154
5:13	79	61a	131
8:6	79	63a	198
9:5	52		
13:24	53	Shabbath	
		10a	63, 188
1 Chronicles		12a	137
16:10	122	12b	126, 137
29:10	52	104a	114, 119
		118b	66
2 Chronicles		127a	99
6:13	149		
14:10	15	Pesachim	
33:12, 13	203	88a	97
		112a	6
Talmud Bavli			
Berakhoth		Rosh HaShanah	
3a	76	16b	177
4b	48, 66, 69, 162	17b	221
5b	63, 170, 175	18a	201
6a	98		
6b	49, 95, 98, 116, 182	Yoma	
7b	90, 96	29a	181
8a	90, 157	52a	207
10a	175, 198		
10b	62	Megillah	
11a	68	17b	53
11b	68	18a	53, 133, 135
12a	69	23b	93
12b	120, 170	29a	99
14b	66	31b	73
15a	66		
18a	215	Taanith	
24b	60	2a	27
26b	46	8a	90, 173

8b	152, 195	Shavuoth	
16a	26, 194, 214	36a	80
23b	175, 215		
24a	155, 184	Avodah Zorah	
24b	184	3b	57
25a	166, 172, 185	7b, 8a	160
25b	144, 186		
		Harayoth	
Chagigah		13a	171
15a	219		
		Menachoth	
Yevamoth		110a	77
64a	5, 202		
		Chullin	
Kethuvot		60b	5
7a	94	89a	169
		91b	7
Sotah			
14a	175	Arakhin	
32b	60	11a	141
33a	125		
34b	215	Kerithot	
48b	151	6b	204
49a	77		
		Talmud Yerushalmi	
Kiddushin		Berachoth	
36a	204	1:1	62, 69
		1:5	68
Bava Kama		4:1	45, 110
82a	100	4:3	55
92a	169	4:4	96, 101, 110
92b	29	5:1	91
93a	177	9:1	8, 132, 207
Bava Metzia		Eruvin	
42a	154	3:9	85
Bava Bathra		Megillah	
10a	64	4:4	94
25b	217		
116a	174	Taanith	
		2:1	201
Sanhedrin		3:6	153
17b	99	4:3	152
43b	190		
44a	11	Mishnah	
44b	153, 210	Berakhoth	
63a	208	1:3	41
106b	84	1:4	68, 84
		4:1	44
Makkoth		4:3	52
11a	171	4:4	110

4:5	61	Rosh HaShanah	
5:1	121	16b	196
5:5	191		
9:3	154	Sotah	
9:4	154	34b	215
9:5	48		

Shekalim
6:1, 2   86

Yoma
8:9   99

Megillah
4:3   93

Taanith
3:8   173

Sotah
7:1   125

Sanhedrin
6:5   166

Avoth
1:3   164
2:5   109
3:6   93
3:15   24
5:15   24

Tosefta
Berakhoth
3:1   44
3:6   110
3:7   145
3:8   45
3:9   41, 45
3:21   121

Baba Kama
9:111   137

Bava Metzia
11:12   100

Tosefoth
Berakhoth
3a   77
11a, b   68
34b   97

Midrash
Midrash Aggadath Bereshith
80:1   82

Midrash Pesiktai Rabbatai
20 (p95b)   178

Midrash Rabbi Akiba ben Yosef Yud
            95

Midrash Bereshith Rabbah
9:4   223
45:5   178
59:13   94
52:13   13
53:14   174
71:2   201

Midrash Shemoth Rabbah
21:1   15
21:3   194
21:4   187, 210
21:5   6
22:3   116, 188
32:4   208
38:4   9, 14, 33
44:1   139

Midrash BaMidbar Rabbah
14:17   190

Midrash VaYikra Rabbah
2:3   167
5:8   152
9:9   59
10:5   191

Midrash Devarim Rabbah
2:1   166
2:6   9, 107, 194
2:7   91
2:10   183
7:4   190
10:1   189
11:10   211

Midrash Eikhah Rabbah
1:33   223
3:8   91

Midrash Koheleth Rabbah
1:34   188
9:12   181

Midrash Esther Rabbah
9:5   145

Midrash, as quoted in Menorath HaMaor
3:3:1:13   103

Midrash Tehillim
4:3   8
4:5   202
5:6   167
6:10   208
7:18   177
20:1   163
33:1   7
39:3   33
55:6   8
57:1   161
61:2   130
65:2   7, 117
66:1   9
90:6   130
91:8   193
96:1   46
104:2   136
104:17   157
106:2   136
108:1   163, 190
116:1   7
143:1   163

Midrash Tanchuma
VaYerah 1   58, 202
Beshelach 9   15
Ki Thavo 1   34
BeChukothai 2   187
Haazinu 4   181

Midrash Tanchuma B
Toldoth 4 (134)   192
Tzav 5 (9a)   34

Zohar
1:21a   26
1:24a   36
1:89a (Sithrei Torah)   126
1:94b   171
1:105a (Midrash Ne elam) 176
1:167b   210
1:169a   157
1:225a   215
1:234b (Tosefta)   91
1:243b   117
1:249b   143
2:12b   144
2:15a   181, 186
2:42b   26
2:62a   158
2:163a, b   116
2:129b   78
2:165a   144
2:178a   82
2:213b   36
2:244b (Hekhaloth)   129
2:259b   131
3:218b   146
3:228a (Raya Mehemna) 192

Zohar Chadosh
Yithro 34a   95

Tikunei Zohar
6 (22a)   163
17a   10
18 (32b)   37
18 (35b)   94
22 (65b)   57

Bahir
138   148

Bachya, also Sifrei,
quoted in *Pardes Rimonim*
32:2   216

Sefer Yetzirah
4:4   70

Mekhilta to Exodus
14:15   129
15:25   131

Mekhilta of Rabbi Yishmael
Exodus 14:15   151

Mekhilta of Rabbi Shimon Bar Yochai
Mishpatim p. 211   203

Sifrei
Vezoth HaBrachah 343   59

Index of Sources

Othioth de Rabbi Akiba Daleth, 188
Aaron HaKohen, Rabbi, *Orath Chaim*, 78
Aaron HaLevi of Barcelona, Rabbi, *Sefer HaChinuch*, 31
Abele of Gombin, Rabbi Avraham, *Magen Avraham*, 138, 153, 158, 171
Aboav, Rabbi Shmuel, *Teshuvoth D'var Shmuel*, 128
Aboav, Rabbi Yitzchak, *Menorath HaMaor*, 47, 153
Adret, Rabbi Shlomo ben Abraham (the Rashba), *Rashba on Eyn Yaakov, Berakhoth*, 54, 63, 223; *Rashba on Berakhoth*, 84; *Teshuvoth Rashba*, 138, 143, 224
Albo, Rabbi Yosef, *Sefer HaIkarim*, 20, 23, 33, 155, 195, 203
Aldabi, Rabbi Meir, *Shevilei Emunah*, 26
Al-Fasi, Rabbi Yitzhak (the Rif), *Code Berakhoth*, 67
Arama, Rabbi Yitzhak, *Akedath Yitzhak*, 20, 112
Asher ben Yechiel, Rabbi, *Teshuvoth Ha-Rosh*, 83, 127; *Rosh, Berakhoth*, 135
Ashkenazi, Rabbi Yehudah, *Ba'er Hetev, Orach Chaim*, 88
Ashkenazi, Rabbi Yitzhak Luria, *Likutei Torah, Taamei HaMitzvoth on Leviticus*, 138
Azkani, Rabbi Elazar, *Sefer Charedim, Tshuva 3*, 104
Azulai, Rabbi Chaim Yosef David (the Chida), *Midbar Kedemoth, Tav*, 4, 50; *Avodath HaKodesh, Tziporen Shamir*, 51, 105

Baal Shem Tov, Rabbi Israel, *Kether Shem Tov*, 113, 182; *Tzava'ath HaRivash*, 114, 117, 121
Bachya ben Asher, *Rabbi, Commentary on Genesis*, 202
Bachya ibn Pakudah, Rabbi, *Chovoth HaLevavoth*, 18, 111
Boaz, Rabbi Yehoshua, *Shiltei Giborim, on Mordechai, Berakhoth* 4:5, 145
Buzaglo, Rabbi Shalom, *Kisei Melekh*, 220

Cardova, Rabbi Moshe, *Pardes Rimonim*, 148; *Elimah Rabbati, Eyn Kol*, 218
Caro, Rabbi Yosef, *Beth Yosef, Orach Chaim*, 68; *Maggid Mesharim*, 88; *Shulkhan Arukh, Orach Chaim*, 153, 195
Chabib, Rabbi Yaakov, *HaKothev in Eyn Yaakov*, 212
Chabiba, Rabbi Yosef, *Nimukei Yosef*, 174
Chagiz, Rabbi Yaakov, *Halakhoth Ketanoth*, 149
Chaim of Volozhin, Rabbi, *Nefesh HaChaim*, 36, 37, 84, 110, 116, 129, 166
Chasdei Crecas, *Or HaShem*, 19, 179, 185

David ben Shmuel HaLevi, Rabbi (Taz), *Turei Zahav, Orach Chaim*, 160
Dov Baer, Maggid of Mesritch, *Maggid Devarav LeYaakov*, 27, 87, 119, 123, 164, 165; *Likutei Yekarim*, 115, 147

Edels, Rabbi Shmuel Eliezer, *The Maharsha, Commentary on Talmud, Sota*, 61
Efraim of Sudylkov, Rabbi Moshe Chaim, *Degel Macheneh Efraim*, 16
Egras, Rabbi Yosef, *Shomer Emunim*, 220
Eilenberg, Rabbi Yisacher Baer, *Beer Sheva*, 148
Eliahu, Rabbi, The Gaon of Vilna, *Gloss on Shulkhan Arukh, Orach Chaim*, 136
Elimelech of Lizensk, Rabbi, *Noam Elimelekh*, 193

Gabbai, Rabbi Meir ibn, *Avodath HaKodesh*, 57
Gerondi, Rabbi Yonah, *Commentary on Rif*, 127, 135
Gikatilla, Rabbi Yosef, *Shaarei Orah*, 67

Hai HaGaon, Rabbi, *Responsum*, 75
Heller, Rabbi Yom Tov Lipman, *Maadanei Yom Tov*, 127
Hirsch, Rabbi Shimshon Raphael, *Commentary on Genesis*, 12
Horowitz, Rabbi Isaiah, *Shnei Luchoth HaBrith*, 101, 147, 157

Isaac of Corbeil, Rabbi, *Sefer Mitzvath Katan*, 30, 197
Isserles, Rabbi Moshe, *Mapah on Shulkhan Arukh, Yoreh Deah*, 79; *Darkei Moshe, Orach Chaim*, 81; *Mapah on Orakh Chaim*, 167; *Darkei Moshe, Yoreh Deah*, 174

Jolles, Rabbi Yaakov Zvi, *Kehillath Yaakov*, 182

Kelonemos Kalman of Cracow, Rabbi, *Maor VaShamesh*, 10

Kimchi, Rabbi David (Radak), *Sefer HaShorashim*, 11, 80; *Radak on Psalms*, 81; *Radak on Isaiah*, 195

KolBo, anonymous, 75

Leow, Rabbi Yehudah, The Maharal of Prague, *Netivoth Olam*, 35, 48, 161, 175, 197, 214, 216

Levi Yitzhak of Berditchov, Rabbi, *Kedushath Levi*, 6, 162

Luria, Rabbi David (Radal), *Commentary*, 13

Luria, Rabbi Yitzhak, The Ari, *Shaar HaPesukim*, 195

Luzzatto, Rabbi Moshe Chaim, *Derekh HaShem*, 22, 72, 74

Maimonides, Rabbi Moshe ben Maimon (Rambam), *Yad Chazakah, Tefillah*, 28, 41, 47, 54, 58, 64, 67, 73, 149; *Sefer HaMitzvoth*, 28; *Moreh Nevukhim*, 18, 112, 134, 142; *Yad Chazakah, Keriath Sh'ma*, 83; *Thirteen Principles of Faith*, 208; *Commentary on Mishneh, Sanhedrin*, 209

Margolioth of Brody, Rabbi Efraim Zalman, *Yad Efraim on Magen Avraham*, 128

Mat, Rabbi Moshe, *Mateh Moshe*, 76

Menashe Azaria de Fano, Rabbi, *Asarah Maamaroth*, 128

Menashe ben Israel, Rabbi, *Nishmath Chaim*, 147

Mizrachi, Rabbi Eliahu, *Commentary*, 175

Moellin, Rabbi Yaakov, *Sefer Maharil*, 156, 172, 216

Moshe of Coucy, Rabbi, *Sefer Mitzvoth Gadol*, 149

Moshe ibn Makhir of Safed, Rabbi, *Seder HaYom*, 76

Moshe of Trani, Rabbi, *Beth Elokim, Tefillah*, 43, 61, 62, 151, 159, 170, 210; *Kiryath Sefer*, 29; *Beth Elokim, Yesodoth*, 100

Nachman of Breslov, Rabbi, *Sichoth HaRan*, 16, 102, 105, 106, 118, 120, 153, 159, 162, 199, 204; *Likutei Moharan*, 197; *Likutei Moharan B*, 103, 106, 131; *Shivchei Moharan, Avodath HaShem*, 120

Nachmanides, Rabbi Moshe ben Nachman, Ramban, *Commentary on Genesis*, 13; *Commentary on Sefer HaMitzvoth*, 29; *HaEmunah VeHaBitachon*, 194

Orechoth Tzadikim, Simcha, anonymous

Perfet, Rabbi Isaac ben Sheshet, *Teshuvot Rivash*, 122, 217

Pinchas of Koretz, Rabbi, *Midrash Pinchas*, 176

Rashi, Rabbi Shlomo Yitzhaki, *Commentary*, 80, 97, 125, 135, 137, 142, 151, 174, 185, 192, 207, 210

Saadia (ben Yosef) Gaon, *Emunoth VeDeoth*, 189

Shmuel ben David HaLevi, Rabbi, *Nachalath Shiv'ah*, 156

Shneur Zalman of Liadi, Rabbi, The Alter Rebbe, *Likutei Torah*, 213; *Siddur, Shaar HaChanukah*, 214; *Siddur, Birkath Nisuin*, 224

Shternhortz of Nemerov, Rabbi Nathan, *Likutei Etsoth*, 158, 205; *Alim LeTerufah*, 167

Sofer, Rabbi Moshe, *Teshuvoth Chatham Sofer, Orach Chaim*, 87

Tanya Rabbati, Rosh HaShanah, anonymous

Teomim, Rabbi Yosef, *Pri Megadim, Eshel Avraham*, 216

Ucedah, Rabbi Shmuel, *Midrash Shmuel*, 109

Vital, Rabbi Chaim, *Pri Etz Chaim*, 85; *Shaar Ruach HaKodesh*, 176

Volf of Gorodna, Rabbi Zev, *Commentary (Moharzav)*, 13

Yaakov ben Asher, Rabbi, *Tur, Orach Chaim*, 64, 73, 83, 115; *Baal HaTurim*, 146

Yaakov Yosef of Polonoye, Rabbi, *Toledoth Yaakov Yosef*, 10, 119, 121, 164, 198;

Ben Porat Yosef, 113, 213; Kethoneth Passim, 122
Yehudah HaChassid, Sefer Chasidim, 82, 112, 122, 127, 136, 137, 138, 142, 155, 156, 157, 159, 160, 161, 170, 178, 203, 215
Yehudah HaLevi, Rabbi, Kuzari, 71, 93, 146
Yisroel of Koznitz, Rabbi, Avodath Yisroel, 11
Yitzhak Isaac of Komarno, Rabbi, Chumash, Heichal HaBrachah Otzar HaChaim, 113
Zechariah of Jaroslaw, Rabbi, Darkei Tzedek, 122
ben Zimra, Rabbi David, The Radbaz, Metzudoth David, 219
Zundle of Biolystok, Rabbi Chanoch, Etz Yosef, 56

Index of Names

Aaron 39
Abahu, Rabbi 46, 110, 132
Abaye 136
Abba, son of Rabbi Chiya, Rabbi 96
Chiya ben Abba, Rabbi 97
Abba Benyamin 98
Abba Chilkia 175
Abba Shaul 110
Abba Yudin of Sidon 203
Abba ben Yirmeya, Rabbi 69
Abigail 52
Abimelekh 169, 225
Abon, Rabbi 132
Abraham 12, 13, 46, 47, 51, 59, 73, 95, 97, 139, 169, 170, 176, 178, 225, 233, 234
Acha, Rabbi 91
Acha, son of Rabbi Chanina 90
Adam 5, 50, 165
Akiba, Rabbi 145, 184, 186
Alshekh, Rabbi Moshe 176
Ami, Rabbi 69, 90, 172
Amnon, Rabbi 87
Amram, Rabbi 87
Anan, Rabbi 126
Antoria, Rabbi Yuden 55
Ari 85, 86, 87, 119
Asa 15
Asaph 32
Ashi, Rabbi 5
Avigdor, Rabbi 211
Avina, Rabbi 66
Azaria Rabbi 207

Baal Shem Tov, Rabbi Israel 113, 114, 122, 147, 198, 212
Bar Kapara 143

Benjamin 94
Benjamin ben Avraham, Rabbi 77
Berachiah, Rabbi 130, 178
Beruriah, 175

Caleb 93, 215
Caro, Rabbi Yosef 88
Chabiba, Rabbi Yosef 174
Chaggai, Rabbi 152
Chalafta of Kfar Chananya 93
Chana bar Bizna, Rabbi 115
Chama ben Chanina, Rabbi 12, 130, 187, 198
Chanina, Rabbi 54, 58, 80, 129, 132, 157
Chanina ben Dosa, Rabbi 172, 185, 191, 192, 193
Chanina bar Pappa, Rabbi 189
Chelbo, Rabbi 49, 95, 130, 171
Chisda, Rav 172
Chiya, Rabbi 130, 169, 178, 193
Chiya bar Abba, Rabbi 52, 65, 77, 93, 97, 129, 210
Chiya bar Adda 143
Chiya bar Ashi, Rabbi 160
Chiya the Great, Rabbi 178
Chiya bar Va, Rabbi 54
Choni the Circle Drawer 173, 175

Daniel 27, 28, 44, 45, 182
David 15, 31, 45, 52, 58, 67, 91, 96, 106, 116, 122, 136, 151, 167, 176, 177, 194, 202, 208
Dima, Rav 133
Dina 154

Edom 14

Eleazar, Rabbi 9, 11, 33, 64, 132, 144, 153, 166, 198, 201
Elazar ben Pedat, Rabbi 194
Eli 60, 234
Eliezer 51
Eliezer, Rabbi 110, 115, 129, 144, 154, 184, 186
Eliezer ben Yaakov, Rabbi 62, 99
Eliezer, son of Yose of Galilee, Rabbi 28
Elijah 49, 76, 139, 171, 182, 234
Elisha ben Abuya 219
Ephraim 167
Esau 15, 157, 179
Evo, Rabbi 121
Ezekiel 86
Ezra 53, 79, 82

Gabriel 216, 207
Gamaliel, Rabban 52, 53, 55, 58, 83, 191
Gamliel, Rabbi 203
Goliath 15

Hai HaGaon, Rav 221
Hanna 31, 35, 45, 324
Hezekiah, King 31, 32, 33, 63
Hezekiel, Rabbi 116, 117
Hillel, son of Rabbi Shmuel bar Nachmani, Rabbi 55
Humnuna, Rav 60, 188
Huna, Rav 49, 60, 95, 131, 132
Huna, son of Rabbi Yitzhak, Rav, 171

Ibn Ezra, Abraham 26
Ibn Shushan, Dof Yosef 217
Ikhu 172
Illfai (Rabbi) 184
Isaac 14, 15, 32, 46, 59, 97, 139, 179, 233, 234
Isaiah, son of Amoz, the Prophet 31

Jacob 14, 15, 46, 47, 59, 139, 233, 234
Jethro 51
Job 22, 169, 170, 187
Jonah 31, 182
Joseph 14, 94, 126
Joshua 14, 75, 93
Judah 15

Kahana, Rav 63

Lakish, Rabbi 90, 134, 210

Lazer, Rabbi 201
Leah 154
Levi 166
Levi, Rabbi 54, 62, 130, 188, 189

Maimonides 102
Mani, son of Rabbi Yonah, Rabbi 215
Mani of Shaab, Rabbi 59
Meir, Rabbi 81, 130, 131, 175, 201, 210
Meir of Rothenberg, Rabbi 87
Melchizedek, 51
Menassah, son of Hezekiel 203
Michael 207
Miriam 172
Mordecai 9
Moses 9, 15, 20, 34, 39, 41, 51, 53, 59, 61, 100, 106, 107, 116, 129, 130, 132, 133, 139, 151, 166, 211, 221, 222

Nachman, Rav 184
Nachman bar Pappa, Rabbi 5
Nachman bar Yitzhak, Rabbi 49, 157
Nachman of Media 160
Nachmanides 104
Nathan, Rabbi 90, 157
Nathan, Rav 89
Nebuchadnezzar 53
Nehorai, Rabbi 82
Nehuniah ben Hakanah, Rabbi 122
Nissim, Rabenu 173

Oholiab, son of Achisamach 54
Oshaya, Rabbi 68

Pedat, Rav 68
Pharaoh 6
Pinchas 11, 61, 95
Pinchas, Rabbi 8, 54, 210
Pinchas ben Chama, Rabbi 174
Pinchas ben Yair, Rabbi 193

Rabba 184
Rabba bar Chanina 170
Rabba bar Mani 169
Rabba, son of Rav Shela 157
Rabbi 184
Rabbin, son of Rav Adda 98
Rachel 154
Rashi 87, 215
Rav 63, 69, 126, 131, 132, 154, 160, 170, 184, 221

Rava 171, 188
Rava, son of Chanina the Elder 69
Rava, son of Rav Huna 63
Rebecca 31

Safra, Rav, 112
Sandalfon 210
Sarah 169, 178
Sennacherib 31, 33
Shem 51
Shimon, Rabbi 109, 146, 152
Shimon bar Abba, Rabbi 188
Shimon the Cotton Broker 53, 55
Shimon bar Chalafta, Rabbi 130
Shimon the Great, Rabbi 87
Shimon ben Shetach 173
Shimon bar Yochai, Rabbi 29, 60, 89, 95
Shimshon of Kinon, Rabbi 122, 216
Shkiel, Rabbi Shmuel bar Abraham 104
Shmuel 68
Shmuel the Little 55, 186
Shmuel bar Nachman, Rabbi 132, 152
Shmuel bar Nachmani, Rabbi 45, 54, 130, 190
Simlai, Rabbi 41
Simon, Rabbi 54, 62, 94
Solomon 19, 33, 41, 197, 227

Tanchum, Rabbi 55
Tanchum bar Chanina 96
Terah 176

Yaakov, Rabbi 68, 172
Yaakov of Kfar Neburaya, Rabbi 132

Yechiel, Rabbi 83
Yehoshua ben Levi 6, 46, 54, 55, 63, 68, 76, 98, 160, 171, 187, 190, 191
Yehoshua the Priest, Rabbi 187
Yehoshua of Sikhin, Rabbi 59
Yehudah, Rabbi 44, 58, 63, 68, 125, 126, 127, 130, 145, 181, 184, 188, 191
Yehudah, son of Rabbi Shmuel bar Shelath, Rabbi 160
Yehudah bar Simon, Rabbi 8, 9
Yermiya, Rabbi 188, 210
Yishmael, Rabbi 154, 179
Yishmael ben Elisha, Rabbi 221, 223
Yitzhak, Rabbi 5, 34, 54, 73, 98, 99, 154, 177, 193, 196, 201, 202
Yochanan, Rabbi 9, 49, 53, 54, 60, 65, 69, 91, 93, 95, 97, 98, 125, 129, 130, 132, 134, 157, 162, 166, 188, 198, 210, 221
Yochanan bar Zakkai, Rabbi 75, 185
Yonathan, Rabbi 132
Yose, Rabbi 66, 82, 85, 117, 137, 158, 207
Yose bar Avin, Rabbi 68
Yose, son of Rabbi Bun, Rabbi 94
Yose, son of Rabbi Chanina, Rabbi 45, 46, 62, 79, 90, 110
Yose (ben Zimra) Rabbi 221
Yose of Yukrat, Rabbi 155
Yosef, Rabbi 55
Yudin, Rabbi 152, 163, 207

Zalman, Rabbi 156
Zeira, Rabbi 7, 69, 188, 195
Zutra bar Tovia, Rabbi 221

Subject Index

Abraham, Shield of 13, 59
Acceptance 224
Acco 104
Afternoon Service
  Careful to recite 49
  Continue drawing sustenance 48, 49
  Elija answered 49
  First prayer
  Isaac, ordained by 46, 47
  Subjugate financial resources 49
Ain Sof 219
Akraziel, proclaimer of God 211

Alenu 75, 76
Amen
  Blessing greater than 82
  Confirmation 80
  El Melekh Ne'eman 80
  Gematria, relating to 82
  Ignorant, merit by 81, 82
  Implications, three 79, 80
  Truth, *Emeth* 80
Ami-Imi 37
Amidah, the
  Alter wording, not 83

Beginning of 162
Concentrating and 112
Eighteen thousand universes 57
Eighteen times a week 57
Ezra and his legislature 53
Maimonides history 53
Parallels commandments regarding tabernacle, 54, 56
    Times God's name mentioned 54, 56
    Times patriarchs mentioned 54, 56
    Vertebrae in spine 54, 55
    Verses in song of Red Sea 57
Petition in middle blessing 58
Reasons for 52
Represents God's name 55
Return us 161
Sabbath, Eighteen, why no 58
    Seven 54, 55, 58
Shmuel the Little composed 55
Simon the Cotton Broker's accomplishment 53, 54
Worldly needs 160
Ancestor's weapon 13
Angels
    Help in prayer 210-214
    Prohibition of praying to 209, 214
    Sing 9
Aramaic 77, 125-127, 212
Ashkenazim 85
Atonement 171
Attachment
    To God 113
    To Spiritual 114
Attributes
    Like garments 218
    Praying to 218, 219
Attribute of Wisdom 123
Avodah 34

Babel, Tower of 219
Balel 12
Barren,
    Conceive 31
    Forefathers, reasons why 5
Best request 10
Beth Kenesseth 100
Body and Soul 220
Bow, as petition 15
Blessing, nineteenth 55, 58
Bless God 222, 223
Blessings,
    Additional 134, 135

David to Abigail 52
Eliezer 51
Melchizedek to Abraham 51
Rest on hidden things 154
Of *Sh'ma*, see *Sh'ma*, Blessings of

Calling in truth 19
Cantor 142
Catalonia 85
Charity 31
    Before prayer 64
Child, dandled 167
Circle drawer 173
Clapping hands 164
Coccyx 55
Codification 41, 102
Commandment to Pray 30, 31
    Reward for 31
        Barren conceive 31
        Death, saves from 31
        Famine 31
        Heals sick 31
        Trouble and exile 20, 33
        War 31
    Second 218, 219
Community 136, 137
Concentration 190
Confession after tithing 40
Congregation
    Acceptance 89, 90
    Bad neighbor 90
    Empty handed, never returns 91
    Heart in hands 90
    Iron walls 91
    Sinner 91
    Ten men 83-95
Conversing with God 225-227
Creation, two categories 71, 72
Creation, Universe of 123
Cried to God 225-227
Crisis of Faith 228-229
Crucial Initiation 21
Customs, diverging from 85
Cry
    Sign of faith 16
    Beneficial sign 16, 61
Cry from Egypt 233
Cry of faith 16
Cuthites 152

Daily service,
    Three 43-48

Fixed number 48, 149
Ordained by partriarchs 45
Dead, intermediaries in prayer 214–216
Deaf man 16
Devotion,
    Meaning of 30
    Praying with 30
Divine providence 19
Divine truth 12
Division of day and night 48
Drowning, motion 147
Dungeon, from the 232, 233

Eating, prohibited before morning service 237
Eden, garden of, 192
Eighteen blessings, see *Amidah*
Elevation 122
El Melekh Ne'eman 80
Elija's call 234
Emanations 216, 219, 220
Emeth Emen-eth 80
Emotions 142
Ends of the earth, From 229
Evening service
    Careful to recite 49
    Longer than afternoon service 49
    No set time 45
    Ordained by Jacob 46, 47
    Rabbi Yochanan and, 59
Evil urge 48
Exile 53
    Three 46
    Alluded to in our prayers 46, 47
Existence,
    Renewal each day of, 71
    Potential 192

Faith,
    Cry, a sign of 16
    Reinforcing 18
    Tree of, 20
Famine 31
Fasting 104
Food of the universe 36
Formation, Universe of, 123
Four universes 74, 75
Free mercy 203
Free samples 113
Free will 161, 162

Golbanaum 204

Garden of Eden 192
Garden of Rabbi Nachman bar Pappa 5
Gate of tears 143–145
God
    Above all praise 136
    Accepting His good 6
    Attachment to 113
    Change His mind 24–26
    Conquering 162
    Desires prayer 34
    Includes souls 176
    Knowing His essence 10
    is Near 232
    Prayer of 221–224
    Reproaching 166
    Seeking Him 13
    Sustenance, receiving 21, 74
        As pertaining to blessings of Sh'ma 74
God's advice 225
God's answer 195–198
God's child 204
Godly influence, Universe of 75
Golden calf 31
Good deeds, 184, 185
Good points 205
Good urge 48

Habit, during prayer 109
Hands, uplifted 148, 149
Handwriting secrets 147
Halakhic literature 1
Havdallah 184
Heart
    Depth of 116
    Desire of 171
    Purify 116, 117
    Stone, of 198
Heathens, difference between, and Jews 146
Heaven, yoke of 65
Hebrew 101, 126–129
Heretics 55, 58, 83
Highest places 182
Hith-palel, Hithpael 11, 12
Holy God 59
House of Hillel 41
House of Shammai 40
Human status, defined by prayer 23
Humility 121

Idolatry 77

Idols 8
Ikhu's beam 172
Inheritance 15
Intercession of Moses 233
Israel
    Beloved before God 7
    Like worm 14
Italy 85

Joy,
    and Reverence 120–121
    and Song 142
Judgment 11
Justice 177, 178

Kabbalah 2
Kaddish 76–79
Kapudkeia 117
Karbonath 75
Kavannah 110
Kiddush 184
Knot 13, 70, 71
Kohanim 87

Language of man 25
Language of prayer 77, 101, 102, 125–127, 211, 212
Length of prayer 48, 114, 129–131, 151
Levites 87
    Duty of 142
Let my tongue sing 230–231
Level of Nothingness 123
Libra 178
Life of Worlds 57
Lights 114, 115
Little sanctuary 99
Love, 192
    Will to 224

Main purification 10
Mamzer 67
Man,
    Involved with physical world 21
    Like tree 146, 147
Manna, each day 29
Master of the Voices 37
Master of the Wing 37
Meditation 115
    In field 106
    Practiced by saints 104
    Special room 106

On word 116
Mezuzoth 40
Mikveh 26, 99
Mincha see afternoon service
Ministering angels 7
Miracles, don't ask for 155
Miser 188
Mishneh 1
Morning service
    Abraham ordained 46, 47
    Four sections 73, 74
    God's sustenance renewed 48
    Length, reason for 48
    Rabbi Nachman bar Yitzhak 48
    Subjugate body 49
    Until noon 44
Morning sleep 48
Mother bird, sending away 31
Motions, during prayer 145–147
Murder, unsolved 39
Musaf 47
Musician 16

Nearness, Universe of 123
Nefesh 35
Noblemen and servants 185, 186
Nothingness, Level of 123

Out of the depths 231

Palel 22
Parables,
    Deaf man 15
    Gifts to poor man and prince 121
    Gold and silver bars 134
    Magistrate and treasurer 217
    Mortal patron 207
    Optical illusion 212, 213
    Princes and robbers 6
    Store 113
    Wise man's petition 10
Parallels 44, 57
Partners in creation 37
Passion 113
Pesukei DeZimra 75
Patriarchs 139
Peace 59
Personal prayer 163
Petition 8, 208
    As bow 15
    Change decree 24

Conversing with God 105
Is prayer 41, 58, 59
As remedy 21
With speech 24
Plural form 138
Portion in the World to Come 66
Powerful supplications 203
Praise
   Accepted, reasons why not 189
   Before petition 41, 42, 58, 59
   Before prayer 41, 42
   Extravagant 132–136
   Fluency 191
   Reasons for 42
   For sick 192
   Song is 41
   Spontaneous 132–136
   Verses of 66, 67, 74
Prayer,
   Answer, anticipating 42
   Answered late 182, 183
   Answered, not 181
   Answered, partially 182
   Birds 112
   Brevity 129–131
   Childlike 167
   Clothing, fine 63, 64
   Commandment, see Commandment to pray
   Concentration 110, 112, 147
   Dead and 214–216
   Dead, for 178, 179
   Devotion, with 30
   Difficulty regarding 43
   Discouraged 118
   Divine providence, for 19, 164, 165
   Elevate creation 122
   Elevation 213, 214
   Enthusiasm 118, 119
   Fast 114
   Food, for 158
   Generalities, in 156, 157
   Goal, main 42, 43
   God, of 221–224
   Habitual 109
   Hanna's 233, 234
   Heart and mind 111, 112
   Heart, advice of 27
   Hebrew 101, 126–129, 212
   Human status, defined 23
   Impure 187, 188
   Inability 117
   Injuries and 117
   Joy 121
   Kneeling 149
   Language 101, 102, 125–127, 211, 212
   Length of 48, 114, 129–131, 151
   Levels, of 163
   Life, for 177
   Mercy, seeks 125
   Motions 145–147
   Necessities, for 151
   Needs, all 158, 159
   Neighbours, for 169–171
   Never give up 198, 199
   Only to God, 208, 209
   Oneself, for 117, 118
   Ordained, why 26
   Order of 72, 73
   Passion 113
   Personal 103, 163
   Petition 41
   Pillar of Universe 25
   Poor 187
   Powerful 201, 203
   Prolonging 129–131
   Purpose of 43
   Repent, sinner 175, 176
   Riding a donkey, while 61
   Righteous, a rake 202
   Robbery 187, 188
   Sacrifice 47, 64, 65
      Greater than 33
   Service 35
   Set times for 44–46
   Sick, for 137, 156, 172, 174
   Silence 60, 61
   Small things first 152
   Song 46, 141, 142
   Special place, see Special place for prayer
   Spontaneous 61–63, 148, 149
   Standing 61–63, 148, 149
   Suffering, removal of 166
   Sword, as 15
   Tears 143–145
   Testing 118
   Times for 45, 46
   Troubles 106, 107, 153
   Two things at once 152, 153
   Universal remedy 25
   Untrodden path 103

Vain 153, 154
Whisper of 172, 173
Priestly blessing 39
Prisoner 175
Prophecy 115
Providence Confirming 19
    Divine 19
Pruning shears, 67
Psalms, daily recital of

Rake 202
Read 114, 115
Readiness to receive goodness 23
Rectifications 84
Regal 63
Repentance 191
Reproaching God 166
Reptile 26
Request numerous times 43
Rosh HaShanah 165

Sacrifice 33–36
    Purpose of 36
    Spirit of 190
Sacrificial readings 73, 74
Sacrificial system 28
Sagittarius 178
Saints 121, 209, 210
Saint's prayer 17
Sandalfon 210
Scorpio 178
Seek God and find Him 234
Sefardim 85
Self improvement 161, 162
Self judgment 12
Self mortification 104
Selichoth 211
Service of the heart 27, 109
Service, lead with pleasant voice 143
Service, brings rectifications 84
Sex, motion of 147
Shacharith see morning service
Shealtiel 219, 220
Shekhina 148
Shem HaMeforash 193
Shinan-She-ainan 57
Sh'ma 40
Sh'ma, blessings of 68–74
Showing off 142
Sick 137, 156, 159, 172, 174
Silence, during prayers 60, 61

Sing before God 7
Snail 213
Song, Open gates 141
    Praise, is 41
Soul 114
    Animals 36
    Blood 213
    Difference between man and animal 62
    Expense of 48
    God includes 176
    Called prayer 35
    Purified 25
    Purification of 10
    Subjugate to God 49
Speaking, forbidden 67
Special place for prayer 95–99
    Field 106
    History 100
    Obligation 100
    Room 102, 106
Speech, expression of soul 36
Spoken word,
    Gives human status 24
    Needed for prayer 24
Standing for prayer 61, 148, 149
Suffering, removal of 166
Sweet meats 113
Sword and bow 15
Synagogue 89–93

Tachanun 73
Tallith 106
Talmud 1
Ten men 93–95
Thirteen attributes 222
Thirteenth gate 86
Thought alone not enough 24
Thought, Universe of 165
Three daily services 46
Three exiles 46
Three songs 46
Throne 75
Thunder, unseen in 225
Tikkun Chatzoth 49
Time for prayer, time for Torah 188
Tranquility, need of 105
Transmission of life force 26
Tree, like man 146, 147
Tref 192
Troubles
    Not a result of chance 18

Prayer, and 20, 106, 107
Twelve gates 85
Twelve tribes 85, 86
Two cases 201
Two things 210
Two urges 48
Tzaddik HaDor 173

Universal remedy 31, 33
Universe of
   Creation 31, 33
   Formation 123
   Godly influence 75
   Nearness 123
   Thought 165
Unseen in thunder 225
Urges, two 48

Waters of Insolence 147
Weapons, ancestors' 14, 15
Whisper of prayer 172, 173
Who brings dead to life 59
Wicked, why not punished 22
Wise man's request 10
Worm, Israel likened to 14

Yehoyada 220
Yoke of heaven 65
Yom Kippur service 160
You 10
You are my refuge 231
Yud 95

Zemiroth 67